Praise for *Sams Teach Yourself 3ds Max® in 24 Hours*

"*Sams Teach Yourself 3ds Max in 24 Hours* by Stewart Jones is the perfect book to start an artist who has never used 3ds Max and is new to 3D. Stewart has put in enough detail and challenges to give readers a solid grounding in techniques while leaving room to explore on your own. Stewart writes with humor, making something that could be dry interesting and fun to read. I enjoyed going through the book and even picked up a few tips along the way that I didn't know in Max. I would recommend the book without hesitation to students and artists looking for a great start to quickly feel accomplished instead of frustrated with all aspects of 3D production in 3ds Max 2014."

—**Brad Clark**, Cofounder, Rigging Dojo.com

"*Sams Teach Yourself 3ds Max in 24 Hours*—'challenge accepted!' If you are looking for a textbook to guide you through the intricacies of Autodesk 3ds Max, this is the 24 for you. Blending a perfect balance of technical and demonstration, Stewart's witty, stylish, and pointed approach to introducing 3D modeling, animation, and the 3D modeling production environment is well worth staying up all day and night to read."

—**Dr. Tim J. Harrington**, Teaching and Learning Applications Analyst

"*Sams Teach Yourself 3ds Max in 24 Hours* is a great way to learn the basics of working in 3D on a computer. This is a fantastic book for anyone who wants to start in this field."

—**Gregory Scott Johnson**, Professor of Game Development, SCAD

"For anyone looking to get a solid foot into the 3D industry, *Sams Teach Yourself 3ds Max in 24 Hours* is the perfect solution to get you started. Stewart Jones puts his years of experience into 24 simple and concise 'hours' that make learning the basics fun and then build into more advanced steps as you work your way through. *Sams Teach Yourself 3ds Max in 24 Hours* is the perfect guide to putting that first foot forward and opening the door to the exciting world of 3D."

—**Matthew Johnson**, Principal 3D Artist

"*Sams Teach Yourself Teach Yourself 3ds Max in 24 Hours* not only gets the reader started with 3ds Max, it gives a comprehensive survey of all aspects of 3D. Through clear and succinct tutorials, readers will learn to model, rig, skin, animate, create particles, utilize dynamic, fur, and even experience a little scripting. *Sams Teach Yourself 3ds Max in 24 Hours* has everything needed to get the successful digital artist proficient in 3ds Max in a short 24 hours. You'll keep this on your shelf as a go-to resource guide for 3ds Max."

—**Tina O'Hailey**, Dean of Digital Media, SCAD

Stewart Jones

Sams **Teach Yourself**

3ds Max®

in 24 Hours

SAMS 800 East 96th Street, Indianapolis, Indiana, 46240 USA

Sams Teach Yourself 3ds Max® in 24 Hours

3ds Max® is a registered trademark or trademark of Autodesk, Inc., in the USA and other countries. This book is independent of Autodesk, Inc., and is not authorized by, endorsed by, sponsored by, affiliated with, or otherwise approved by Autodesk, Inc.

ISBN-13: 978-0-672-33699-7

ISBN-10: 0-672-33699-5

Library of Congress Control Number: 2013916424

Printed in the United States of America

First Printing December 2013

Trademarks

All terms mentioned in this book that are known to be trademarks or service marks have been appropriately capitalized. Sams Publishing cannot attest to the accuracy of this information. Use of a term in this book should not be regarded as affecting the validity of any trademark or service mark.

Warning and Disclaimer

Special Sales

For information about buying this title in bulk quantities, or for special sales opportunities (which may include electronic versions; custom cover designs; and content particular to your business, training goals, marketing focus, or branding interests), please contact our corporate sales department at corpsales@pearsoned.com or (800) 382-3419.

For government sales inquiries, please contact governmentsales@pearsoned.com.

For questions about sales outside the U.S., please contact international@pearsoned.com.

Editor-in-Chief
Mark Taub

Executive Editor
Laura Lewin

Development Editor
Songlin Qiu

Managing Editor
Kristy Hart

Senior Project Editor
Betsy Gratner

Copy Editor
Kitty Wilson

Indexer
WordWise Publishing Services

Proofreader
Williams Woods Publishing

Technical Editors
Brad Clark
Tim Harrington
Greg Johnson
Matthew Johnson

Publishing Coordinator
Olivia Basegio

Media Producer
Dan Scherf

Cover Designer
Mark Shirar

Compositor
Nonie Ratcliff

Contents at a Glance

Table of Contents

About the Author

Stewart Jones started his visual journey in graphic and multimedia design. He has since moved into the computer graphics industry, where his focus has been on animation and visual effects. Now a company director and freelance VFX/CG/animation consultant for the film, TV, and games industries, he has previously served in multiple roles in media and entertainment, including mentor and course author, animator, technical animator, character technical director, and computer graphics supervisor. Stewart also wrote *Digital Creature Rigging*.

Dedication

For the person who is always there for you. You know who that is.

Acknowledgments

This book would not have been possible without the guidance and support of some amazing people. I hope they all know how thankful I am for their help, and I'd like to take a little time here to mention a few of them as they totally deserve the recognition for their awesomeness!

Kirsty, I love you. You're amazing. Thank you for always making everything better and my life so fantastic; without you, I'd be a wreck—or even more of a wreck than I currently am!

Thanks to my parents, Carol and Keith. Your love and support mean everything to me; I can't thank you enough for always being there for me.

Susan and Nana, thank you for all your support and being there to listen to my random chats. Oh, and of course thank you so much for that first "super-awesome" computer you bought me that allowed me to start my journey into 3D.

Nathan, although your face did not appear in this book (like it did in my last one), thank you for being the one who introduced me to 3ds Max way back in the day. I know that an older version of this series of books helped you start out on your own 3D journey, and I hope my version will do the same for others. Thanks for being a great friend!

A big thank you to everyone in the CG industry, as well as all the friends I've made at so many places throughout the world. Your drive, determination, and incredible talents keep pushing me forward. Keep up the great work, everyone; I'm sure I'll see you around!

Thank you to my technical editors: Brad, Greg, Tim, and Matt. The feedback, notes, comments, critiques, and thoughts you shared with me made this book so much better than it would have been without you.

We Want to Hear from You!

As the reader of this book, *you* are our most important critic and commentator. We value your opinion and want to know what we're doing right, what we could do better, what areas you'd like to see us publish in, and any other words of wisdom you're willing to pass our way.

We welcome your comments. You can email or write to let us know what you did or didn't like about this book—as well as what we can do to make our books better.

Please note that we cannot help you with technical problems related to the topic of this book.

When you write, please be sure to include this book's title and author as well as your name and email address. We will carefully review your comments and share them with the author and editors who worked on the book.

Email: errata@informit.com

Mail: Sams Publishing
          ATTN: Reader Feedback
          330 Hudson Street
          7th Floor
          New York, New York, 10013

Reader Services

Visit our website and register this book at informit.com/register for convenient access to any updates, downloads, or errata that might be available for this book.

Preface

Welcome! Please sit down, make yourself comfortable, and relax. Before you get started on your 24-hour-long journey into the world of 3D and Autodesk 3ds Max, let's take a bit of time to get to know each other.

I'll start. My name is Stewart, and most people call me Stu. I've been doing this kind of thing for a while now.... Well, not typing creepy messages like this one, but you know—3D stuff. Like a lot of other folks, I started out my journey watching cartoons as a kid, and through a series of twists and turns, I ended up in this creatively technically artistic (that's a new term I just created right there) field of 3D and the "entertainment industry."

All right, so I've introduced myself. Who are you? This is probably much easier for you to just tell me, but as there is no one else here, I'm going to take a wild guess, and hopefully I'm somewhere in the right area with it. Right, hang on while I channel my psychic abilities.[1]

You're human. Yes, most definitely. I see someone who is taking the first steps into the world of 3D. I also notice that you want to learn more about Autodesk 3ds Max and what it has to offer as a leading 3D software application. Yes, you are eager to start your adventure, and you're a little bit sick of me rambling on. And you're starting to think that I might be actually a bit crazy. Or maybe you have picked up the wrong book completely!

Am I right? I am, aren't I?

I knew it! Are you impressed?

Of course you're not! That was, obviously, a completely wild guess, and I may have hit a home run, or I could be way off target, but only you and I know which it is! Well, that guy behind you does as well. Just kidding! Or am I?

Enough with this babble! I do know that you're here to expand your mind and learn new and wondrous techniques that will set you on the path to 3D excellence. Thank you for choosing to take the first steps of your journey with me. Let's have some fun.

---

[1] I have no actual psychic abilities, just so you know!

Introduction

What You'll Learn in This Hour:

▶ What this book is about and what topics are covered

▶ How this book is structured

▶ What Autodesk 3ds Max actually is

▶ Where to get Autodesk 3ds Max

▶ How to access the extra content

Captain's Log, Stardate....Hang on a second! I'm way off track here. Let me start again.

Hello! Welcome to the first hour of a 24-hour crash-course into the basics of Autodesk 3ds Max. (That sounds much better.)

I still remember my first steps into the 3D world, and without getting into too many details and being too sentimental, one thing that stands out the most is that this stuff is difficult. For starters, you're jumping into something that's completely new, and we know that anything new or unknown can be scary and confusing. Actually, it's pretty much the same as getting dropped into a new city in a new country for the very first time: You have no idea where anything is, street signs don't mean a thing to you, and, possibly, you have no idea what the language is, so you can't even ask for help or directions. I guess the new-city-in-a-new-country scenario is probably a little more scary than trying to learn 3D and a new application, but you get what I'm trying to say, right?!

Now. Autodesk 3ds Max, like most big cities, has a lot of people who know about it. Many of those people understand plenty of aspects of 3ds Max, and some of them have been super helpful and have written guides and tutorials that are freely available. You shouldn't disregard those valuable resources; lots of them are fantastic for learning specific elements of 3ds Max and enhancing your skills in other areas. However, this book that you're reading right now has everything you need to get started. It covers many topics that will give you a solid foundation in 3ds Max and allow you to get a good taste of many of the different facets that this 3D application has to offer.

What This Book Covers

So, what's this book all about, and how does it work for you? This book is a 24-hour guide to the workings of 3ds Max. Each hour of this book covers a specific topic and acts as a stand-alone guide. All 24 hours are written as stand-alone lessons, so you can jump in at any point you like and learn just what you need to. For maximum awesome-learning effect, I recommend starting here, with Hour 1, and working your way through this book numerically. Here's what you'll learn in each of the 24 lessons:

VIDEO 1.1
_____

Introduction to *Sams Teach Yourself 3ds Max in 24 Hours*

Hello! If you head on over to this video, you can get an introduction to the book and to me (Stewart "Stu" Jones), as well as some general guidance for this incredible journey you are about to undertake.
_____

▶ **Hour 1: Introduction**—This is where you are right now. This hour provides an introduction to this book and everything you need to know to follow along.

▶ **Hour 2: Exploring the Interface**—In this first hands-on 3ds Max hour, you'll explore the interface and figure out where to find things.

▶ **Hour 3: Navigating the Viewports**—The third hour introduces you to viewport navigation and how you can view objects in 3D.

▶ **Hour 4: Primitives and Transforms**—Primitive shapes form the basis of a lot of 3D scenes, and in this hour you'll learn how to create them and move them around.

▶ **Hour 5: 3ds Max Modifiers**—You can easily change primitives with the multitude of modifiers available in 3ds Max. This lesson looks at a few of the most common modifiers.

▶ **Hour 6: Sub-Object Exploration**—Objects often have sub-objects that you can edit and tweak. This hour covers some of the basics for doing this.

▶ **Hour 7: 3D Modeling**—3D modeling is an artistic task with some technical challenges. In this hour you'll look at modeling both hard-surface and organic objects.

▶ **Hour 8: Materials and Textures**—This hour takes a look at the techniques you can use to add color and textures to your creations.

▶ **Hour 9: Computer Animation**—Animating objects can be fun and challenging. This hour takes you through the basics of the animation toolset.

▶ **Hour 10: Illuminating Scenes Using Lights**—You can't see anything without lighting it. In this hour you'll learn about creating lights for your scenes.

▶ **Hour 11: Adding and Editing 3D Cameras**—This hour takes a look at real-world cameras and how they relate to the cameras in 3ds Max. Oh, and you'll also create some!

▶ **Hour 12: Rendering for Production**—Unlike in a live-action movie, when you're using 3ds Max, shouting "ACTION!" won't actually do anything. However, to show your 3D stuff, you need to render it for production, which is the subject of this hour.

▶ **Hour 13: Combining Techniques to Create a Showcase**—In this hour you'll use all the skills you've learned so far to display your creations.

▶ **Hour 14: Rigging Objects for Easier Animation**—Rigs are often needed to make character and object animation easier. In this hour you'll learn about the various built-in rigging techniques and some custom rigs, too.

▶ **Hour 15: Influencing Geometry Using Skinning Techniques**—Controlling geometry with your rigs sometimes requires you to "skin" objects to the rigs you create. You'll learn how to do that in this hour.

▶ **Hour 16: Character Animation**—Character animation is different from other kinds of animation. This hour takes a brief look at the principles of character animation.

▶ **Hour 17: Dynamic Simulations**—Sometimes animation is easiest if it's done automatically! This hour covers the built-in dynamic system inside 3ds Max.

▶ **Hour 18: Particles and Effects**—It's time to add some visual effects to your creations. In this hour you'll learn the basics of particles and effects so that you can start adding various effects to your scenes and start blowing stuff up!

▶ **Hour 19: Cloth, Hair, and Fur Creation**—You can add even more believability to scenes with the cloth, hair, and fur techniques covered in this hour.

▶ **Hour 20: Mental Ray Rendering**—In this hour you'll expand your rendering knowledge by dipping your toes into mental ray rendering for a more professional finish to your renders.

▶ **Hour 21: 3ds Max Project Management Techniques**—This hour covers working with multiple scenes in a production environment for a sample real-world project.

▶ **Hour 22: Combining Advanced Techniques to Create a Showcase**—In this hour you need to call on all the skills you've learned so far to create a professional final showcase.

▶ **Hour 23: Scripting in 3ds Max Using MAXScript**—This hour covers some basic scripting to get you started with automating tasks. This is a good way to avoid some of the rather boring challenges in 3D.

▶ **Hour 24: Conclusion**—You're finished with the learning? Well, not really! The final hour of this book wraps up what the other lessons cover and guides you past the basics you've just mastered.

Make no mistake: Learning 3ds Max in 24 hours is kind of a big task, and I honestly don't recommend reading and working through this book all in one sitting. Instead, maybe read through an hour, try out some awesome "Try It Yourself" sections, fail or succeed, try again and make it better, and then take a break and come back to it later. Remember that resting is just as important as training, so be sure to do both in good measure!

This Book's Structure

Learning something new—in this case 3D and Autodesk 3ds Max—can be difficult. Written texts and tutorials can be a little boring and dry to read through. This book is as fun and entertaining as possible, while gradually explaining everything you need to know to get started with Autodesk 3ds Max. This book uses a few special conventions to help you learn easily and painlessly. Read on!

About the Images in This Book

Let's talk about images. Figure 1.1 shows an example of the images you'll see in this book.

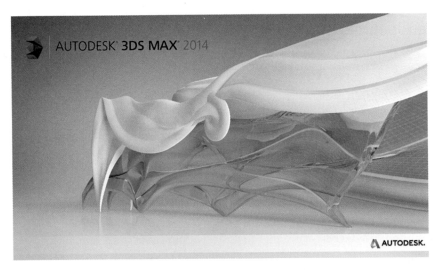

FIGURE 1.1
This is an image. Well, you're actually reading the figure caption, which relates to the image displayed.

There are a lot of images throughout this book, and you now know what they look like.

About the Sidebar Elements Used in This Book

This book provides a lot of tips and tricks that are both interesting and useful. They look something like this:

TIP
___

Did You Know?

Sidebars that look like this one include tips and tricks to help you out.
___

Notes like this one provide general information·

NOTE
___

By the Way

These kinds of sidebars contain general information that you may find interesting.
___

Of course, there are times when the information is just not enough, and you need to be warned about something that could totally destroy all that hard work we've been doing. This book includes Caution sidebars for this very reason:

CAUTION
___

Watch Out

If you're not careful, you could make a big mistake, risk losing work, and get so angry that you flip the desk over. These sidebars help you avoid such situations.
___

About the Try It Yourself Sections

You know this book is chock full of text, sidebars, and images, but there's even more! This book also includes step-by-step instructions on how to create objects, effects, animations, and so on. These "Try It Yourself" sections give you quick, direct access to the techniques and methods to use. In short, they allow you to just jump right in and create things in 3ds Max.

▼ TRY IT YOURSELF

Trying It Yourself

Here's an example that shows how the "Try It Yourself" feature works:

1. Place a bookmark at this page.

2. Flick through the book and find another "Try It Yourself."

3. Take a quick look at it. Smile, knowing that you just followed along with your first "Try It Yourself."

4. Come back to this page and continue reading. Nice going!

The End-of-Hour Elements in This Book

Now that you know what the main text of each hour looks like, you're ready to hear about the special elements at the end of each hour. These sections let you test what you've learned in that lesson. First up is a "Q&A" section that lists common questions and their answers. The next element is the "Workshop," where you have to go outside into a wooden hut and create furniture. Just kidding! The "Workshop" section includes quiz questions and their answers; then come the exercises that help you practice your new skills. Here's an example of how these sections look:

Q&A

Q. What is this?

A. This is a question and answers (Q&A) area, which is found at the end of each hour.

Q. Why have you put questions here?

A. This is a demonstration of what this Q&A section will look like, silly!

Workshop

This is where a brief workshop explanation usually appears.

Quiz

This is an example of a "Quiz" section.

1. What is the purpose of the "Quiz" section?

2. Why is there a workshop here?

Answers

1. The purpose of the "Quiz" section is to quiz you on the hour (although this one in particular is just an example).

2. It's here just as an example, so you know what to expect.

Exercise

This section usually includes a practical exercise where you can try out the techniques you would have just learned throughout the hour.

What Is Autodesk 3ds Max?

Autodesk 3ds Max is a three-dimensional (3D) computer graphics application for creating 3D models, animations, and images. It is frequently used to create film visual effects (VFX), pre-visualizations, TV commercials, architectural visualizations, and video games.

Getting Autodesk 3ds Max

The craziest thing just occurred to me! If you're looking into 3D for the very first time, you may not even have access to Autodesk 3ds Max. Luckily, the folks over at Autodesk give everyone a free 30-day trial of their software (at the time of writing this at least). How do you get hold of it? Simply head over to the Autodesk website, at www.Autodesk.com, and take a look around. After a bit of searching, you should come across the 3ds Max product trial. (I've deliberately not provided a link to a specific page on the Autodesk website because company websites change so fast that a specific link could end up leading you to a page that doesn't exist anymore.)

Once you've downloaded the 3ds Max product trial, go ahead and install it, following the installation steps provided with the software. From there, you should be ready to get going.

Extra Stuff

Before you actually dive into 3D and 3ds Max, I want to let you know what else is included with this book to help you out along the way.

Website

This book comes with its very own companion website, www.informit.com/title/9780672336997, which you can access as long as you have an Internet connection and a web browser.

On the website you can find more information about this book, links to helpful resources, the tutorial videos (which require registering your book from the website), and a little more information about me. Be sure to check it out and send your friends that way, too.

DVD

The companion DVD contains a number of useful files that are used for the examples throughout this book. There is also a list of helpful links to other resources, as well as all the tutorial videos that supplement the text in this book.

Tutorial Videos

You'll find tutorial videos on both the companion website (www.informit.com/title/ 9780672336997) and the DVD for this book. Both locations contain all the training videos you need to understand and follow along with the book. Note that to access the videos on the website, you need to register your book first. To do so, click the "Register Your Product" link from the website, log in or create a new account, and then enter the ISBN, 9780672336997, when prompted. Answer the challenge questions as proof of purchase. Then click the "Access Bonus Content" link in the "Registered Products" section of your account page, which will take you to the page where your downloadable content is available.

Disclaimer and Disclosure

This book will serve you well for your first foray into 3D and 3ds Max. It is comprehensive without being completely dry and boring.

As you will see as you begin to use it, 3ds Max is huge, and this book couldn't possibly cover everything that it has to offer. There are so many nuances and facets to working with 3ds Max that talking about them all would require a much bigger book—and would probably be pretty boring.

You don't need to know everything about 3ds Max in order to take advantage of it. This book provides enough information to get you on your way toward being successful in this field. You'll learn a lot of tips and tricks that make working in 3ds Max better, faster, and more amazing. I believe that I have enough knowledge and superpowers on the subject to give you some great information that will help you on your way to 3D world domination.

Keep in mind that 3D is evolving constantly. The tips, tricks, tools, and techniques people are using today may be changed and rewritten tomorrow. However, the foundations of 3D have stayed the same for so long, and this book provides the kind of solid advice you'll carry with you on your 3D journey for a long time. When you finish this book, you will have a greater understanding of many areas of 3ds Max, and you will be able to use the application to a reasonable level.

Summary

You're off on your journey into 3D! Although you haven't yet dove into the application itself, this hour has introduced you to what you'll find in this book and its companion materials.

Q&A

Q. Are there any specific requirements for following along with this book?

A. You need a copy of Autodesk 3ds Max 2014 and a computer to run it. That's pretty much it!

Q. Where can I get access to my free trial of Autodesk 3ds Max?

A. Go to the Autodesk website: www.Autodesk.com.

Workshop

We haven't jumped into any 3D yet, so this workshop section is simple!

Quiz

1. What do the "Try It Yourself" sections in this book include?

2. Which version of Autodesk 3ds Max does this book use?

Answers

1. The "Try It Yourself" sections are step-by-step guides to the specific techniques covered throughout an hour.

2. This book uses Autodesk 3ds Max 2014.

Exercise

1. Download the free trial of 3ds Max (if you don't already have access to it).

2. Install Autodesk 3ds Max (if you don't already have it installed).

HOUR 2
Exploring the Interface

What You'll Learn in This Hour:

▶ An introduction to the 3ds Max interface

▶ How to work with the various toolbars

▶ An introduction to the viewports

▶ Getting to grips with the *Command Panel*

▶ What quad menus are and how to access them

The Autodesk 3ds Max interface is an evil demon, and if you do anything wrong, you will literally destroy your computer, and possibly the entire universe. Okay, you got me; I totally made all that up! Really, though, using the 3ds Max interface for the first time—or even first few times—can be daunting, and let's face it, it's not exactly welcoming, is it? I mean, there are image icons everywhere, text buttons and drop-down menus galore, and crazy grids all over the place. It is confusing and a little overwhelming. This hour will help you make sense of it all, though.

Turning the pages of this book seems really simple, and so will using the 3ds Max user interface (UI) after you spend some time working with it. Consider this: If you couldn't turn the pages of this book, you wouldn't be able to learn more from it. Likewise, if you can't work with the interface of 3ds Max, you can't operate the features of the software. I know it's pretty mind-blowing information right there!

This hour focuses on some of the main elements of the 3ds Max UI. The following hours cover further elements, when you need them.

The Interface Elements

▼ TRY IT YOURSELF

Getting Going: Try It Out!

Before you start to take a detailed look at the main elements that the user interface has to offer, you should at least "kick the tires" just a little. Bookmark this page and take a bit of time to click around things in the 3ds Max application. This way, you can get more accustomed to this new software. If you are starting 3ds Max for the very first time, you should see a welcome screen that links to six Essential Skills Movies that are a big help. Check them out!

The 3ds Max interface may seem a little bit scary, at least at first, but with some practice, you should start to get a feel for everything and be ready to roll through the rest of this hour. Catch you back here in a bit, soldier!

Welcome back! How did you find being let loose in the 3ds Max interface? Did you find it interesting or boring? Was it complex or simple? Or was it a bit of everything? Whatever you feel about your experience so far, I hope that you've found your way around just a little. Now you're ready to start digging in and analyzing the interface.

By default, the 3ds Max UI groups together similar elements into five main sections (see Figure 2.1):

▶ **Title bar and main menu**—Figure 2.2 shows the first section of the interface, which contains the title bar and main menu.

▶ **Main toolbar and *Modeling* ribbon**—3ds Max has several toolbars that can float independently or be docked to places in the interface. The main toolbar is visible and docked under the title bar and main menu by default, and the *Modeling* ribbon sits just underneath that, as shown in Figure 2.3.

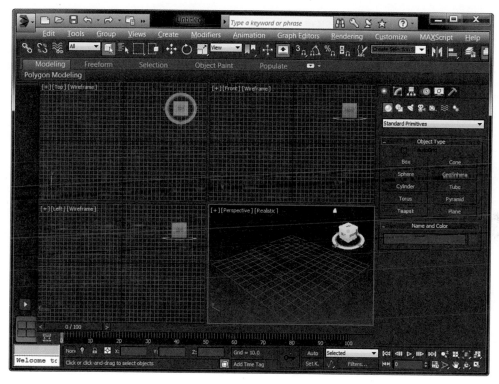

FIGURE 2.1
The default 3ds Max interface has five main sections.

FIGURE 2.2
The title bar and main menu are at the very top of the 3ds Max UI.

FIGURE 2.3
The main toolbar and *Modeling* ribbon are at the top of the UI, just under the title bar and main menu.

▶ **Viewports and the Viewport Layout tab**—The *Top*, *Front*, *Left*, and *Perspective* viewports allow you to view and visualize your 3D scenes. The *Viewport Layout* tab allows you to store various viewport layouts that you often use. These sections are highlighted in Figure 2.4.

FIGURE 2.4
The viewports are the most prominent element of the UI.

▶ **Command Panel**—The *Command Panel* is located to the right of the viewports (see Figure 2.5). This important area of the UI gives you direct access to many attributes, parameters, and settings. You'll learn more about these in the upcoming hours.

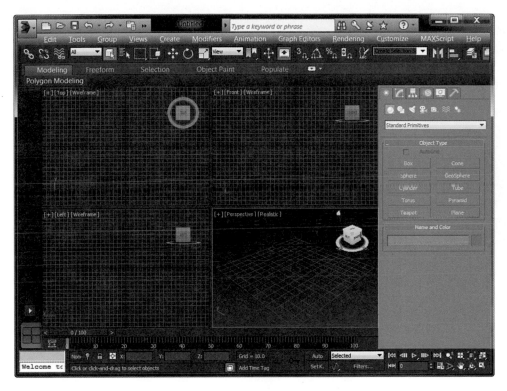

FIGURE 2.5
The *Command Panel* contains tabbed icons that open the various panels.

▶ **Lower toolbar**—The lower toolbar contains animation and miscellaneous interface controls for quick access (see Figure 2.6).

FIGURE 2.6
At the bottom of the UI lives the lower toolbar, which contains animation and miscellaneous controls.

These five main sections give you access to pretty much all the tools and functions that 3ds Max has to offer.

TIP

Customizing the 3ds Max Interface

You can customize the 3ds Max interface in a variety of ways. For example, you can move toolbars and the *Command Panel* around, you can create new toolbars and buttons, and you can even add your own custom scripted commands into toolbar buttons.

The following sections dig a little deeper into each of these interface elements to give you a better idea about their usefulness.

The Title Bar and Main Menu

The top of the 3ds Max UI is the perfect place to start deconstructing the UI elements. Of course the usual minimize, maximize, and close buttons appear in the top-right corner of the application, and I'm sure you already know what they do.

This area of the UI also contains a few nonstandard elements:

- ▶ *Application* button and text-based main menu
- ▶ *Quick Access* toolbar
- ▶ *InfoCenter* toolbar

These three sections are highlighted in Figure 2.7.

FIGURE 2.7
These are the three elements of the title bar and main menu of the 3ds Max interface.

The *Application* button is like a fancy version of the *File* menu found in many other applications. It has some 3ds Max–specific elements, but the usual *New*, *Open*, *Save*, *Save As*, and other options are all found here. The rest of the text-based main menu is pretty self-explanatory; when you click one of the options, a drop-down menu appears. Drop-down menus have plenty of options for you to check out, and if a keyboard shortcut is available for an option, it is displayed on the right side of the menu option for quick reference (for example, *Alt+1* for the *Parameter Editor* option).

Figure 2.8 shows the *Animation* drop-down menu as an example.

The *Quick Access* toolbar includes some of the most common commands that are found within the *Application* button menu, and it gives you an easy and quick way to get to those options. In addition, there is a handy workspace switcher that allows you to switch between various workspace layouts.

The *InfoCenter* toolbar gives you direct access to information about 3ds Max and other products available from Autodesk. It also includes a place where you can quickly type in help queries if you get stuck or need additional information at any time while using 3ds Max.

FIGURE 2.8
The *Animation* drop-down menu includes additional levels of options, indicated by the small arrow on the right side. Note that any keyboard shortcuts are also displayed on the right-hand side of the menu options.

The Main Toolbar

By default, the main toolbar is docked under the title bar and main menu, but you can make any docked toolbar into a floating toolbar. This is super simple: You simply click and drag the two vertical lines on the left of the toolbar away from the edge of the interface. You can then resize the toolbar and dock it to another place. I'm sure you'll agree that this is awfully neat!

The main toolbar is pretty awesome because it contains buttons and drop-down menus for controlling many 3ds Max functions that you will need to access constantly. It can, however, be a little confusing to use at first because its many icons are not self-explanatory. Luckily, if you hover your mouse cursor over any of the icon buttons (including any found in other toolbars, dialog boxes, and the *Command Panel*), a handy tooltip appears, telling you the name of the button.

One final thing to note about the main toolbar is that any buttons with a small triangle next to them have what is called a *flyout* menu. A flyout menu displays different icons, which in turn have different options/operations for the various tools. You simply click and hold on one of these buttons and drag to the new option that you desire!

Figure 2.9 highlights a flyout menu example and a tooltip example.

FIGURE 2.9
Tooltips help you understand what each icon does. Flyout menus bundle together multiple related tools into one button.

Am I forgetting something? Oh, yeah! Shoved under the menu you've just been looking at is the *Modeling* ribbon. This ribbon-style interface includes a collection of pretty amazing modeling tools called the *Graphite Modeling* tools. I have to come clean here and let you know that I really dislike this section of the 3ds Max interface. Sure, it contains brilliant tools, but with all the contextual menus, it's a bit of a mess. The contextual menus show options that are available for selected objects only. This often means that options are hidden when you are trying to find them, and you need to know when they appear. For instance, most of the *Graphite Modeling* options are available only when an *Editable Poly* object is selected. (You'll learn more about *Editable Poly* objects in the upcoming hours.)

So now you know! I don't like this ribbon menu one bit, but as I've already said, the tools included here are pretty great, so you shouldn't completely disregard it. Figure 2.10 shows an expanded view of the *Modeling* ribbon.

FIGURE 2.10
The ribbon-style menu gives you access to the *Graphite Modeling* tools. These tools really are fantastic, but in my opinion, the ribbon-style contextual interface is hard to use.

Viewports

Those big things that take up most of the 3ds Max interface are called *viewports*. They act as portals or gateways to where you can view objects within a 3D scene. Just as you can customize other facets of the interface, you can configure each of the viewports differently so that they are unique.

The viewports are where you're probably going to spend most of your 3ds Max days, so you better shake hands, hug, and make friends with each other quickly! Here you'll take a quick look at the most basic operations of viewports, and you'll pick up more as you start creating some 3D imagery from Hour 4, "Primitives and Transforms," onward.

Figure 2.11 shows the default four-viewport layout.

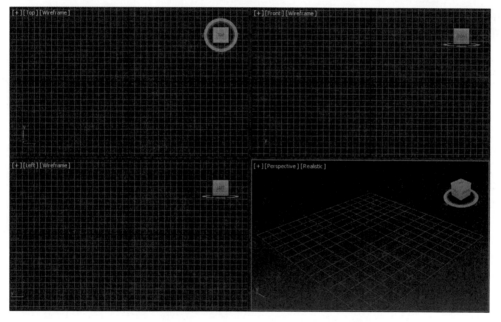

FIGURE 2.11
Four viewports are shown by default and they take up the most screen space of the 3ds Max user interface.

In the top left of each viewport, you can see a little plus (+) icon that gives you access to some options for that specific viewport. Next to the plus icon is the name of the viewport; clicking it allows you to change to a different view. Finally, you can choose the visual style and appearance of the viewport by clicking the text next to the viewport name.

At the top right of the viewport is the *ViewCube*, which gives you a visual and interactive way to quickly move along the various views that are available. Go on: Try it out! I've found that using the *ViewCube* is a great way to get used to navigating the views, although once you get more familiar with everything, it's likely that you won't use it too often—at least I don't.

Check out the *ViewCube* in Figure 2.12.

FIGURE 2.12
Using the *ViewCube* is an interactive and visual way to navigate between different views. You use the *Home* icon to jump back to the default view.

TRY IT YOURSELF ▼

Working with the ViewCube

Try clicking a *ViewCube* in a variety of places. Notice how clicking the various points of the *ViewCube* changes the view of that specific viewport. Pretty neat, huh?!

Command Panel

If the viewports will be your BFF in 3D, the 3ds Max *Command Panel* will be your second best friend in 3D ever. The *Command Panel* is located to the right of the viewports and is where you can find, access, and edit things like parameters, settings, and controls. Oh, like the other toolbars, you can customize the *Command Panel* in both size and docking or undocking location.

▼ TRY IT YOURSELF

Resizing the Command Panel

We don't have to be happy with just one size of the *Command Panel*. We can change it to suit our needs in just two steps.

1. Move your mouse over the left side of the *Command Panel* until the cursor changes to a double arrow. Click and drag to resize the *Command Panel*.

2. Notice the six icon tabs at the top of the *Command Panel* and the blank space on the right. Click and drag that empty area to undock the *Command Panel* and dock it to a location of your choice.

Figure 2.13 shows an example of the *Command Panel* resized.

FIGURE 2.13
You can resize the *Command Panel*, and you can undock and dock it as well.

The *Command Panel* includes six icon tabs that open different panels, each with its own options:

 ▶ **Create**—The *Create* tab contains controls for creating various objects.

 ▶ **Modify**—After an object is created, you can assign modifiers to it from this tab.

 ▶ **Hierarchy**—This tab contains controls for managing hierarchical links and related options.

 ▶ **Motion**—If you're working with animation, you can get to controllers and trajectories from this tab.

 ▶ **Display**—Need to change how things are displayed in the viewports? This is the tab you need to click.

 ▶ **Utilities**—This tab contains miscellaneous utility programs.

Although each tab is different, the general interface for each is the same. Controls, buttons, and other parameters are stored in sections that 3ds Max calls *rollouts*. In the simplest terms, a rollout is a box that groups together similar commands and makes viewing all the tools easier and a little more logical. You can even open and close rollouts, and you can click and drag them to reposition them into an arrangement that better suits your needs. Figure 2.14 shows what a rollout looks like in 3ds Max.

The Lower Toolbar

The bottom section of the 3ds Max interface contains the lower toolbar. Unlike other parts of the UI, you can't move or edit this section, which sits as a static collection of various sets of controls that you often need to access. Figure 2.15 shows the lower toolbar, which has the following components:

 ▶ **Time slider and track bar**—Located under the viewports, the *Time* slider lets you *scrub* (that is, slide the time slider left and right) the frames of your animation. Alternatively, you can use the left and right arrows to move to the previous frame or the next frame. The track bar sits directly underneath the *Time* slider, and it works in conjunction with it. The track bar displays color-coded animation keys that you can select, move, and delete as needed. The small button on the left of the track bar opens the *Mini Curve Editor*, which gives you quick access to animation function curves; you'll learn more about this in Hour 9, "Computer Animation."

FIGURE 2.14
Rollouts are organizational boxes that group together similar buttons, tools, parameters, and commands.

FIGURE 2.15
The lower toolbar includes a selection of various controls and tools.

▶ *MAXScript Mini-Listener*—Divided into two parts—one pink and one white—the *MAXScript Mini-Listener* gives a single-line view of the contents of the full version of the *MAXScript Listener* window. *MAXScript* is the built-in scripting language of 3ds Max, and you will learn some basic scripting with it in Hour 23, "Scripting in 3ds Max Using MAXScript."

▶ **Prompt line and status bar controls**—If you have no idea what to do next, it's a good idea to take a look at the prompt line and status bar for valuable information and some pointers on what 3ds Max is expecting from you. There are also buttons, options, and information for *Selection Lock Toggle*, *Transform Type-In*, *Grid Size*, and *Adaptive Degradation*. It's worth checking out the help files for more information on these tools.

▶ **Animation keying controls**—These controls allow you to create animation keys for currently selected objects. There are also filters for creating keys as well as for turning on *Auto-Key* and changing the key tangents. You'll learn about animation in Hour 9, so if some of these words sound completely bizarre, take a breath, move on, and know that it will all make sense at some point!

▶ **Animation playback controls**—These controls look like the controls you would find on an audio or visual playback device, and they do what you would expect them to do—except that they relate to the animations you have in your current scene.

▶ **Viewport navigation controls**—You use these controls to manipulate the viewports and do things in the current viewport such as zoom, pan, and rotate.

Quad Menus

When you right-click in a viewport (or on an object in a scene), you get a quad menu. You might not always get four menus (as the name suggests), but you will see at least one section of a quad menu.

Quad menus are contextual, meaning that they change depending on what you have selected or what keyboard buttons you have pressed down at the same time. You don't need to worry about these for now. You will start using them in the following hours and will get used to them quickly.

TRY IT YOURSELF ▼

Accessing a Quad Menu

Right-click in one of the viewports to open up the quad menu. Go on: I dare you to try it!

By right-clicking in one of the viewports you can open up a quad menu, as shown in Figure 2.16.

FIGURE 2.16
You open a quad menu by clicking the right mouse button.

VIDEO 2.1

Exploring the Autodesk 3ds Max Interface

This video discusses the 3ds Max default interface and its elements. It will really help you understand this rather complicated application.

Summary

Wow! In a very short time, you've learned a lot about the 3ds Max UI and its workings. Of course, you haven't seen every single option, setting, and quirk of the interface, but you now have enough knowledge to really start trying things out in 3D.

There's still plenty to learn and discover in the 3ds Max interface, so onward, 3D warrior!

Q&A

Q. How many elements does the main interface include?

A. There are five elements to the main 3ds Max interface; these include the title bar and main menu, the main toolbar and *Modeling* ribbon, the viewports and the viewport layout tab, the *Command Panel*, and finally the lower toolbar.

Q. Can I customize the interface?

A. Yes, you can customize it—well, at least most of it. You can move and resize the toolbars and the *Command Panel*, you can create new toolbars and buttons, and you can even add your own custom scripted commands into the toolbar buttons.

Workshop

Getting to grips with the interface of any program or system can take a little time. The solution to learning the 3ds Max interface is simple: The more time you spend with it, the more accustomed to it you will become. Having said that, this workshop section should get you thinking about what you have learned in this hour and start you off on your interface customization journey to make your working days a little quicker, stronger, and better!

Quiz

1. Where will you spend most of your time while using 3ds Max?

2. Where can you get access to object parameters?

3. What are the three separate elements that create the title bar and main menu?

Answers

1. The viewports are where you will spend most of your time while using 3ds Max. The user interface is a close second!

2. The *Command Panel* gives you access to object parameters. You can also find a number of other tools and features here, too.

3. The three separate elements are the *Application* button and text-based main menu, the *Quick Access* toolbar, and the *InfoCenter* toolbar.

Exercise

Spend some time right now getting familiar with the default 3ds Max interface. It's a complicated beast, and because you are going to be spending a lot of time with it, you need a good understanding of its basic usage.

After exploring the default interface and once you feel confident enough, you can start thinking about the various customizations that are available. Why not resize the *Command Panel*? Or even move that main toolbar to another location? Using the tips, tools, and techniques discussed in this hour, go ahead and create your own customized interface that feels most comfortable for you right now.

HOUR 3
Navigating the Viewports

What You'll Learn in This Hour:

▶ An introduction to 3D space

▶ How to use the *ViewCube* and *SteeringWheels*

▶ How to use viewport navigation controls

▶ Handy shortcuts for viewport manipulations

▶ Configuring viewports

I know what you're thinking! "Umm, didn't we just cover viewports in the last hour?"

You're totally right! We did begin to look at them! The thing is that you spend so much time working in the viewports that you really need to get some solid time with them, here at the beginning, to make sure you are totally comfortable with navigating and customizing the viewports to your best advantage.

The viewports have a kazillion settings and controls that provide a kazillion-trillion ways to view your 3D scene. Not being able to manipulate the views, settings, and controls comfortably is frustrating, to say the least. I hope I've made my point with my fake numbering system!

3D Space

Everything you create in 3ds Max is located in a three-dimensional (3D) world. In fact, take your head out of this book and check around you. Yep, you and I are living in a three-dimensional world. So the concept of 3D isn't new to you at all. You're used to it, and it feels natural. In fact, two-dimensional (2D) space can be more confusing for some of us; I mean, just think of those people who find it difficult to read a map. (You know who you are!) Figure 3.1 shows an example of both 3D and 2D space.

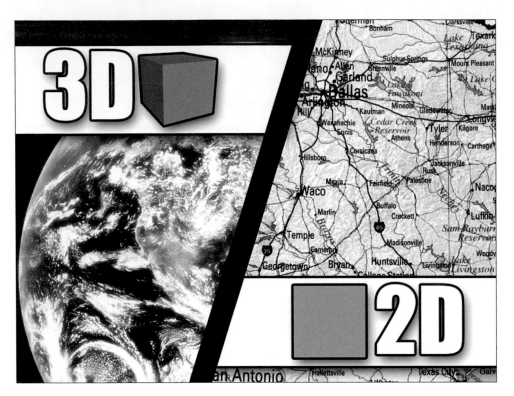

FIGURE 3.1
Three-dimensional (3D) space around us and two-dimensional (2D) space on a map can be hard to reconcile with one another.

Now think about this: The computer screen you're looking at displays only a 2D image, just like TV screens. (Okay, I know that we can have 3D screens on our laptops and TVs, but it's not true 3D, so let's just forget about that stuff!) The point I'm trying to make is that you are going to create 3D objects on a 2D screen, and you're going to do this by using multiple views.

For instance, look at the room around you. It's in 3D. This view in 3ds Max is called the *Perspective* viewport. It allows you to visualize a 3D scene easily, and you can navigate around the 3D objects just like you can by walking around in the real world! 3ds Max also includes 2D views that allow you to view your 3D scenes from different angles. Just like a 2D map shows a top-down view of the world, the *Top* viewport in 3ds Max does the same thing. Of course, 3ds Max has more options than that, and you can look at your 3D scenes from the *Perspective*, *Top*, *Bottom*, *Front*, *Back*, *Left*, *Right*, and even *Camera* views. Figure 3.2 shows the differences between *Perspective* and *Orthographic* viewports.

Using both the 3D and 2D views within 3ds Max, we can work and create 3D images that are only limited by our skills and imagination.

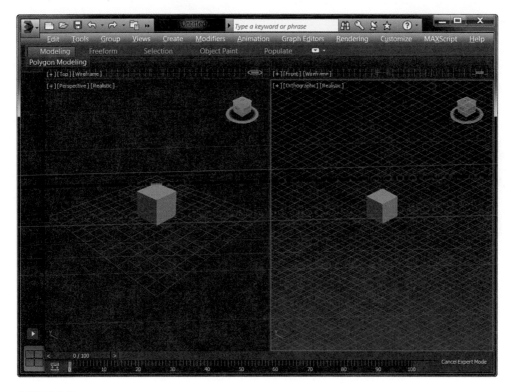

FIGURE 3.2
Perspective (left viewport) and *Orthographic* (right viewport) viewports help you visualize your 3D scenes. You can clearly see the differences in their displays.

The ViewCube

The 3D *ViewCube* represents the current orientation of the viewport and gives you an interactive way to quickly move among the various views available. The labels on each side of the *ViewCube* allow you to quickly understand exactly which view and orientation you are currently in. By clicking a label, you can move to that orientation.

In addition, you can click and drag the *ViewCube* to edit your view orientation manually. To do this, you simply click and hold the left mouse button and drag your mouse. You can even click around the sides of the *ViewCube* to get specific orientations if you need to.

As with many other objects in 3ds Max, you can right-click the *ViewCube* to bring up a contextual menu of options.

SteeringWheels

The *SteeringWheels* give you additional options for manipulating the camera and the current view. By default, the *SteeringWheels* are turned off, but you can easily turn them on (enable them) from within the main menu or by pressing the plus (+) icon in any viewport to bring up that viewport's options.

▼ TRY IT YOURSELF

Toggling On the SteeringWheels

Why not turn on the *SteeringWheels* yourself and take them for a spin? Follow these steps:

1. Access and enable the *SteeringWheels* either from the main menu (from the main menu, choose *Views, SteeringWheels, Toggle SteeringWheels*) or from the viewport options (in the viewport, choose *+, SteeringWheels, Toggle SteeringWheels*).

2. For quicker access, use the keyboard shortcut *Shift+W* that is shown on the right side of the *Toggle SteeringWheels* menu option.

Once they are enabled, the *SteeringWheels* appear in the viewport and follow your mouse cursor. Sections of the *SteeringWheels* are highlighted as you mouse over them. You can access those sections by simply clicking and dragging. Figure 3.3 shows the standard *SteeringWheels*.

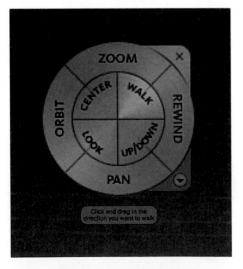

FIGURE 3.3
When the *SteeringWheels* are enabled, you find them in the viewports.

Get Out of My Way!

It's worth noting that the *SteeringWheels* gizmo has the super-annoying habit of getting in the way of your scene while you're working. So if you enjoy using this gizmo, it's a good idea to remember that keyboard shortcut *Shift+W*, which you use to toggle *SteeringWheels* both on and off.

Viewport Navigation Controls

You can find the main viewport navigation controls in the bottom-right corner of the 3ds Max interface. All of them have tooltips and are very well documented within the 3ds Max help files. It's definitely worth reading through the help files to get a good understanding of each of the tools available. Figure 3.4 shows a close-up version of the tools and where to find them.

FIGURE 3.4
The viewport navigation controls are available in the bottom-right corner of the UI.

Now, personally, I prefer to navigate the 3ds Max viewports by using keyboard and mouse short-cuts. Using these shortcuts instead of the interface buttons can really speed up your workflow and make you way more confident working within 3D space. Table 3.1 lists some of the neatest shortcut combinations for your reference.

TABLE 3.1   Viewport Navigation Keyboard Shortcuts

Shortcut	Description
Alt+W	Maximize/minimize viewport toggle
MMB (middle-mouse-button)	Pan
Alt+MMB	Orbit
MMB wheel	Zoom
Ctrl+Alt+MMB	Zoom
P	Perspective
F	Front
L	Left
B	Bottom

Viewport Configuration

You can configure each viewport individually. Keep in mind that viewports enable you to see the 3D scenes you are working on in a number of different ways. The upper-left corner of each view-port gives you access to the current viewport's configuration settings.

From left to right, you have options for general configuration, viewport view, and viewport visuals.

The general configuration menu allows you to choose a number of general settings. From config-uring the viewport layout, to turning the grid on and off, this is an incredibly handy menu.

Viewport view settings allow you to change the current viewport's view! These settings aren't as accessible as the *ViewCube*, but they do offer many more options.

Finally, the viewport visuals settings allow you to change how the viewports display your 3D scenes. For instance, you can add a background image to the viewport, or you can turn off light-ing if there is any in the scene.

NOTE

Additional Configuration Options

There are many more configuration settings available. You access them by choosing the bottom option in the general configuration settings (under the + icon) or the viewport visuals settings. It's worth your time to test the options available in this section to understand what is possible with the viewport configurations.

Figure 3.5 shows the location of the general configuration (+ icon), viewport view, and viewport settings options, which give you access to additional viewport configuration options.

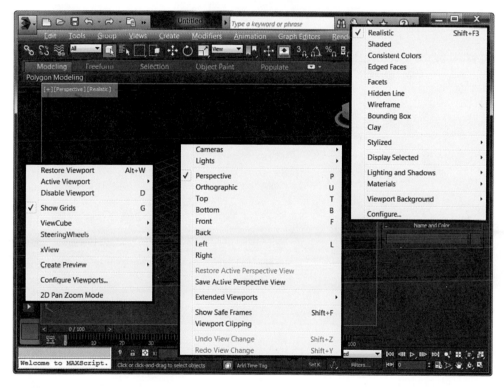

FIGURE 3.5
Found in each viewport, these three main sets of options give you direct access to a number of tools and commands for working within the current viewport.

The Viewport Layout Tab

On the left side of the viewports you see the *Viewport Layout* tab. This handy tab allows you to store various viewport layouts that can be accessed quickly and easily at a later point. You can use the arrow icon to create additional layouts, which are then stored on the tab to allow you to switch between your favorites rapidly by clicking on them. Right-clicking a favorite gives you the opportunity to rename the layouts, delete them, or save the current tab as the preset for when 3ds Max starts.

Figure 3.6 shows a customized *Viewport Layout* tab and the various options available while you're working with it.

FIGURE 3.6
The *Viewport Layout* tab is an area where you can save your favorite viewport layouts and access them all easily.

VIDEO 3.1

Viewport Configuration

This video takes a quick look at a few of the viewport configuration options and how they directly affect what you see in the viewports. It also shows you some hands-on work with the *Viewport Layout* tab.

Summary

In this hour, you have taken a deeper look into the 3ds Max viewports as well as their configuration options and settings. With this additional knowledge, you should be much more comfortable navigating the viewports, where you are going to be spending most of your time in 3ds Max!

Q&A

Q. What is 3D space?

A. 3D space is all around us; it is the world we live in. The 3D space within 3ds Max is displayed via multiple views on 2D screens.

Q. What viewport gizmos are available in 3ds Max?

A. Two viewport gizmos are available in 3ds Max: the *ViewCube* and the *SteeringWheels*.

Q. I have changed my viewport configuration, and it's just how I like it. Can I save it for later?

A. You sure can. Take a look at the *Viewport Layout* tab, where you can save multiple layouts for quick access while you work.

Workshop

As you now know, the viewports are the windows into the 3D world of 3ds Max. They are the place where you can see and manipulate all the objects in your scenes. A number of tools and options that are available in the viewports will allow you to enhance your workflows. You need to become very comfortable working with the viewports; in fact, it should be your number-one priority in 3ds Max right now. This workshop section covers a few specific tools and some configuration settings that you might still be getting used to.

Quiz

1. What does the *ViewCube* do?
2. What does the *SteeringWheel* gizmo do?
3. Where can you toggle the *ViewCube and SteeringWheels* on and off?

Answers

1. It allows you to quickly manipulate the orientation of your current viewport.

2. It gives you onscreen control of various view manipulation options.

3. You can toggle the *ViewCube* and *SteeringWheels* on and off either in the main menu or by pressing the plus (+) icon in any viewport to bring up that viewport's options.

Exercise

Experiment with the *ViewCube and SteeringWheel* gizmos and see which one you prefer. You might find that you prefer to use the keyboard shortcuts instead of those gizmos. In that case, review the content of Table 3.1 in this hour.

Once you're comfortable with the gizmos and viewport navigation, make sure to learn and discover more viewport configuration options in the *Configure Viewports* menu.

HOUR 4
Primitives and Transforms

What You'll Learn in This Hour:

▶ How to create primitive objects
▶ How to use different primitive types
▶ Naming and coloring objects
▶ Object manipulation in 3D space
▶ Placing and editing objects in 3D

You're here because you want to build some pretty awesome stuff in 3D, but so far you haven't actually built anything at all. Sure, you've played around with the viewports and taken a look over the main interface, but you still haven't created a single 3D object. You're still a few hours away from creating really awesome stuff in 3D, but now it's about time you start to actually create some objects.

During this hour you're going to lay the foundation of 3D element creation in 3ds Max. You're going to be using what 3ds Max calls *primitive* objects. With only a few exceptions, primitives are the starting point for pretty much any and every modeling job that you will come across. In this hour you are going to use the primitives in their default shapes and learn how to manipulate and move them around in 3D space, using the various viewports and some basic tools that are going to become the standard instruments you use for most object manipulations.

Primitive Creation

Remember that *Command Panel* thing that you looked over just briefly in Hour 2, "Exploring the Interface"? That is where you find the *Create* tab/panel, which you can use to start the creation process. Figure 4.1 highlights the *Create* tab as well as the *Category* and *Subcategory* sections.

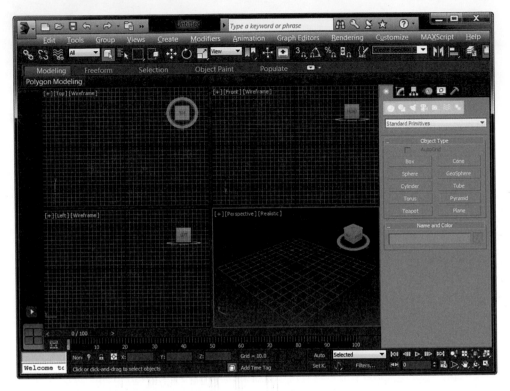

FIGURE 4.1
The *Create* tab includes both categories and subcategories so that you have access to many different creation options.

You use the *Create* tab to create objects for your scenes. Notice in Figure 4.1 that you have *Categories* (highlighted in green) and *Subcategories* (highlighted in red). These lead you into a huge variety of creation options. This is truly the best way to start creating objects in 3ds Max.

NOTE

The Create Tab and Create Menu

Although in this case you're working directly with the *Create* tab in the *Command Panel*, you can do the same things with the *Create* menu, found on the main menu! Check it out for an alternative way to start your creations.

To create an object, you simply find the button for the object you would like to create, click it, and click or click and drag in one of the viewports.

Creating a Sphere

Follow these steps to create a sphere object within your 3D scene:

1. Open the *Create* tab of the *Command Panel*. Make sure you're in the default *Geometry* category (the sphere icon) and the default *Standard Primitives* subcategory.

2. Click the *Sphere* button.

3. Click and drag in a viewport to create the sphere. You should have something similar to Figure 4.2.

FIGURE 4.2
It's a sphere! This could be the best sphere that has ever been created.

Whoa! Take a deep breath. You just created your first-ever *primitive object*, in totally amazing three-dimensional awesomeness.

I know, I'm being pretty dramatic. It's not the most exciting thing ever, but you did just create a 3D sphere. You may have noticed that some extra rollouts appeared as you clicked the *Sphere* text button. Actually, if the *Sphere* text button is still highlighted, you should still see those additional rollouts.

NOTE

Remember Rollouts?

As discussed in Hour 2, rollouts group similar elements together, in a kind of a "box" structure so that you can find and access them easier.

Rollouts appear when you are in the process of creating an object. They allow you to change and edit various *attributes* of the object that you are going to create before you create it.

▼ TRY IT YOURSELF

Editing an Object's Parameters

In the following steps, you'll create a sphere, but this time you will edit its parameters to change its appearance.

1. Reset 3ds Max to its default start-up layout by clicking the *Application* button and then clicking the *Reset* option.

2. On the *Create* tab of the *Command Panel*, click the *Sphere* button, just like you did in the previous Try It Yourself section.

3. Create the sphere by clicking and dragging in the viewport.

4. Edit the *Radius* parameter under the *Parameters* rollout to change the sphere's size. Edit the *Hemisphere* parameter, too, to see what happens (see Figure 4.3).

5. When you've finished experimenting, right-click in the viewport to exit the "creation mode."

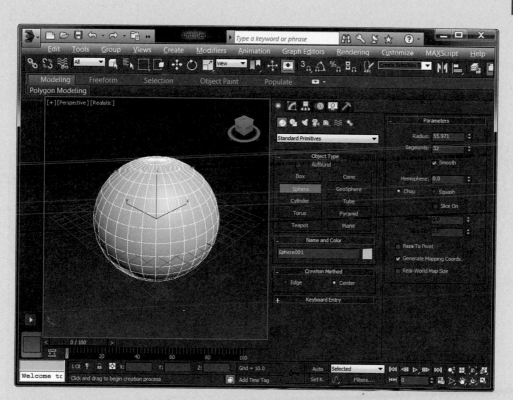

FIGURE 4.3
You can change the options for the newly created sphere in the additional rollouts that have appeared in the *Command Panel*.

CAUTION

Never-Ending Creation

It is important that you exit creation mode by right-clicking in the viewport. If you don't end this mode, your next mouse click will create another object, and you will continue to do so until you manually exit the creation mode.

TIP

How Do You Know You're in Creation Mode?

A highlighted button visually shows you that 3ds Max is still in its creation mode.

Names and Colors

Every single object in a scene will have a name and a color assigned to it. By default, 3ds Max automatically assigns a unique name (the type of object and a number) and a random color to a newly created object.

The default names and randomly assigned colors are totally fine for small scenes and quick tests, but once you start building bigger scenes with greater complexity, those default names will make it pretty difficult to find specific elements that you are looking for. I mean, if you have 150 spheres, and they are named Sphere01 to Sphere150, it's going to be kind of ridiculous to find a specific sphere. The good news is that you can change an object's name and color at any time by modifying the *Name* and *Color* fields in the *Name and Color* rollout of the *Command Panel*, highlighted in Figure 4.4.

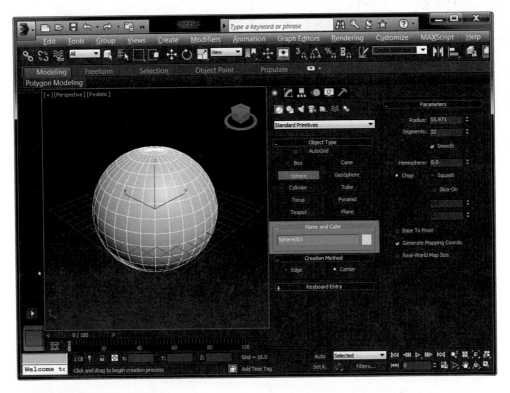

FIGURE 4.4
The *Name and Color* rollout allows you to change the name and color of an object in your scene.

TIP

Different Objects, Same Name = Not Good

When assigning names to objects within 3ds Max, it is possible to give the same name to two or more objects. Doing so is not a good idea—after all, having more than one object with the same name can be confusing; I highly recommend using a unique name for each object. In fact, I demand it!

VIDEO 4.1

Creating and Editing Objects

Check out this video to get a better understanding of how you can create and edit objects in 3ds Max.

Types of Primitives

You may have noticed that you are currently working with standard primitives (because you have *Standard Primitives* selected in the subcategory drop-down menu). In addition to the sphere you've created already, 3ds Max provides a number of other standard primitives as a starting point for geometric modeling. Figure 4.5 shows all the different types of standard primitives 3ds Max has to offer.

Each of these standard primitives has its own creation methods as well as its own specific parameters, attributes, and options.

 TRY IT YOURSELF ▼

Creating a Box Instead of a Sphere

Although creating objects is very simple, the creation methods vary slightly depending on which object you are creating. Here are the steps for creating a box:

1. In the *Create* tab of the *Command Panel*, click the *Box* button.
2. Click and drag in the viewport to create the base of the box.
3. Let go and move your mouse cursor up to build the height of the box.
4. Click once more in the viewport to end the box creation.
5. Adjust the *Length*, *Width*, and *Height* options in the *Parameters* rollout if you want to.
6. Right-click to exit the creation mode.

Try this same method to experiment with creating other standard primitives.

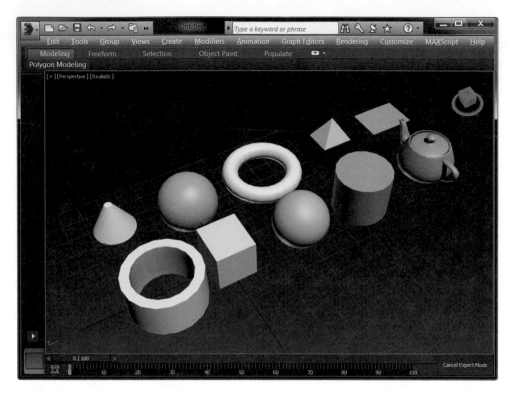

FIGURE 4.5
The 3ds Max standard primitives: box, sphere, cylinder, torus, teapot, cone, geosphere, tube, pyramid, and plane.

Now that you know a little about the standard primitives, you're ready to take a look at what 3ds Max calls *extended primitives*. You might not use these primitives as much as you use the standard primitives, but they are handy to have around.

To use extended primitives, you select *Extended Primitives* from the *Geometry* subcategory on the *Create* tab of the *Command Panel*. Once again, these extended primitives have their own creation methods and their own sets of parameters, so you should take some time to try them out.

Creating Extended Primitives

Although you probably won't use the extended primitives as much as the standard primitives, it's still a good idea to take a look at them and see how they could help out. Follow these steps to begin experimenting:

1. Reset 3ds Max (*Application* button, *Reset*).

2. In the *Create* tab, under the *Geometry* category, switch from *Standard Primitives* to *Extended Primitives*.

3. Click the *Gengon* button.

4. Click and drag in the viewport to create the base of the gengon.

5. Slide your mouse up and click when you are happy with the height.

6. Now slide your mouse to the left to create additional sides for the gengon. Click once again when you are happy with the look of it.

7. Check out the rollouts and parameters available for this primitive. Try editing them to see what they do.

8. Right-click to exit the creation mode.

Try creating some (or all) of the other available extended primitives.

Figure 4.6 shows all the extended primitives that 3ds Max makes available.

VIDEO 4.2

Standard and Extended Primitives Creation Methods

This video quickly runs through all the standard and extended primitives that you can create in 3ds Max and how their creation methods vary ever so slightly from one another.

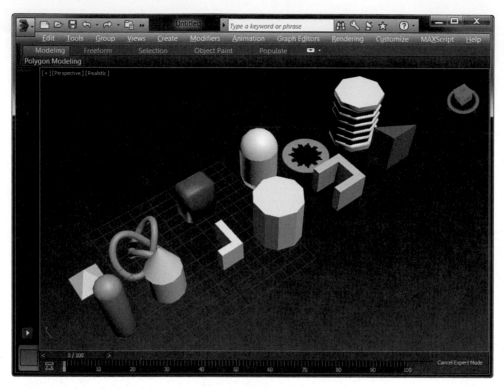

FIGURE 4.6
The 3ds Max extended primitives; hedra, chamferbox, oiltank, spindle, gengon, ringwave, prism, torus knot, chamfercyl, capsule, l-ext, c-ext, and hose.

More Than Primitives

Standard primitives and extended primitives often provide starting points for more detailed modeling projects. The *Create* tab in the *Command Panel* gives you direct access to them, but I'm sure you've already noticed that there are plenty of other categories and subcategories that haven't been discussed in this hour. Check out Figure 4.7 to see how many subcategories there are in just the *Geometry* category of the *Create* tab.

The thing is, you now already know how to create various objects, and I guess that you have been cheekily clicking away at anything and everything. So, using time in this hour to talk about each and every button, parameter, option, and setting would be kind of dull, and really, the best way to learn is to just do it. So get clicking around and see what amazing things you can create from the *Create* tab. Be sure to jump into the various categories—*Geometry*, *Shapes*, *Lights*, *Cameras*, *Helpers*, *Space Warps*, *Systems*—as well as all the many subcategories (way too many to list here). If you're having difficulty navigating your scene due to all of the exciting things you're creating, simply reset 3ds Max (*Application* button, *Reset*) and start again.

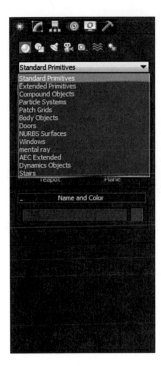

FIGURE 4.7
What the heck do all these categories and subcategories actually do?

You will learn more about the creation of specific objects in later hours. For now, you should experiment and have some fun.

Object Manipulation in 3D Space

In Hour 3, "Navigating the Viewports," you took a quick look at what 3D space is, and hopefully you're starting to understand it a little more as you create various objects. You now know how to create objects as well as view them from different angles by navigating the viewports. It's probably a good time to learn how to manipulate objects so that you can select, move, rotate, and scale them into different positions within a 3D scene.

Before you jump right in, you need to know about the coordinate system that 3ds Max uses. It is called the *Cartesian coordinate system*, and it uses numbers, or coordinates, to determine the position of a point in the 3D space/scene.

In fact, you use three numbers (coordinates) to describe the horizontal (left and right), vertical (up and down), and depth (forward and backward) positions for a point. This stuff is definitely easiest to understand when you see it, and Figure 4.8 should help you understand 2D coordinates (*X* and *Y*) and translate that information into 3D by adding a third coordinate (*X*, *Y*, and *Z*).

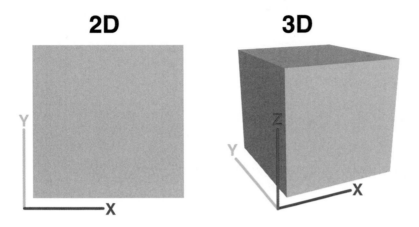

FIGURE 4.8
2D coordinates (*X* and *Y*) correspond to the horizontal and vertical positions of a point. 3D coordinates (X, Y, and Z) correspond to the horizontal, vertical, and depth position of a point. Note that the vertical axis in 3ds Max changes from *Y* to *Z*.

The *X*, *Y*, and *Z* coordinates are known as the *axis* and are often written as [*X,Y,Z*], where you replace the letters with corresponding numbers. You calculate each axis from the "center of the 3D world"—in other words, the very middle of a 3ds Max scene, where the grid intersects in the middle. That central point relates to the coordinates [0,0,0]. What this means is that if you were to create a sphere positioned at the 3D scene's center and then moved it 10 units horizontally, you would have positional coordinates of [10,0,0], as shown in Figure 4.9.

The units that you use to describe each axis can be changed, and they often relate to real-world measurements, such as centimeters, feet, inches, and meters. Setting up the unit in 3ds Max is extremely important. You do this in the *Customize* menu, as you'll see in the following Try It Yourself.

FIGURE 4.9
A sphere positioned at [0,0,0], and a sphere moved horizontally to [10,0,0].

TRY IT YOURSELF ▼

Changing the Units Setup

Setting up the units in a 3D scene is incredibly important. Throughout this book, you are working with *generic units*, but if you are working in production, you may need to change to specific units. Here's how you do it:

1. From the main menu, click the *Customize* menu.

2. In the *Customize* menu click the *Units Setup* option. The *Units Setup* dialog appears, as shown in Figure 4.10.

3. In the *Display Unit Scale* section of the dialog, select the *Metric* radio button and then the *Centimeters* drop-down menu. Then click *OK*.

4. Create a sphere and notice that the *Radius* parameter now displays in centimeters.

5. Head back to the *Units Setup* dialog and switch back to the *Generic Units* radio button, as shown in Figure 4.10, so you're ready to follow along with the book again.

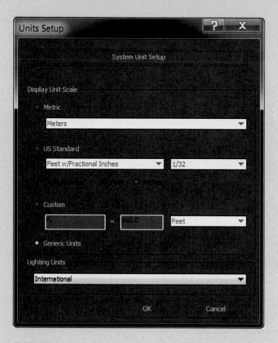

FIGURE 4.10
Changing the units setup can cause problems if you work in a production environment. It's best to change it to what you need and then leave it alone.

You use the coordinate system to plot not only positions for objects but also their orientation and scale (as well as some other more complicated stuff that you don't need to worry about right now). These X, Y, and Z positions are similar to the measurements for a carpenter's piece of wood. Figure 4.11 shows a great example of using such measurements in the real world.

You can find the *Select*, *Move*, *Rotate*, and *Scale* commands on the main toolbar at the top of the default 3ds Max interface layout. You use these commands to manipulate the objects you've created in the viewports. Figure 4.12 shows the icons for the *Select*, *Move*, *Rotate*, and *Scale* commands on the main toolbar.

Each of these commands brings up a different manipulation gizmo that you can manipulate to edit the currently selected object.

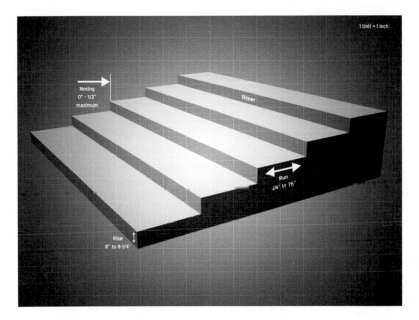

FIGURE 4.11
3ds Max measurements are the same as real-world measurements, but they're inside the computer.

FIGURE 4.12
Select, *Move*, *Rotate*, and *Scale* commands on the main toolbar.

TRY IT YOURSELF ▼

Selecting, Moving, Rotating, and Scaling

Follow these steps to use the *Select*, *Move*, *Rotate*, and *Scale* tools to manipulate a sphere:

1. Create a sphere.

2. Create another sphere. Exit the creation mode by right-clicking.

3. Click the *Select* button and then click a sphere in the viewport.

4. Click the *Scale* button and then click and drag one of the axes to scale it.

5. Click the *Rotate* button and then rotate the sphere.

6. Finally, click the *Move* button and then move the sphere.

7. Select the other sphere and manipulate it. Take note of the different gizmos that are shown when switching between the *Select*, *Move*, *Rotate*, and *Scale* tools.

TIP

Selecting Multiple Objects at One Time

You can select multiple objects by clicking and dragging in an empty area of the viewport. A dotted box should appear, and anything within that area will be selected. Alternatively, you can hold down the *Ctrl* key and click objects to select them.

You will use these commands more than any others in 3ds Max, so it's worth spending some time getting super comfortable with them. Oh, and be sure to check out the various methods for scaling and try the *Scale* tools flyout menu (indicated by the small arrow in the bottom-right corner of the *Scale* command button).

The lower toolbar includes the *X*, *Y*, and *Z* coordinate information for the tool you currently have enabled (see Figure 4.13). You can manually enter values into the *X*, *Y*, and *Z* fields to place an object in an exact location (such as to the center of the world).

FIGURE 4.13
Check the lower toolbar for coordinate information, which changes and updates depending on the tool you are using.

You've just encountered a lot of information. You should practice with these tools because you are going to be using them a lot in the upcoming hours. And, if you're like me and enjoy using quick-access keyboard shortcuts, take a look at Table 4.1, which shows how you access these tools from the keyboard rather than onscreen.

TABLE 4.1   Keyboard Shortcuts for Select, Move, Rotate, and Scale

Keyboard Shortcut	Description
Q	Select
W	Move
E	Rotate
R	Scale

TRY IT YOURSELF ▼

Creating a Primitive Snowman

You're going to use standard primitives with the *Select*, *Move*, *Rotate*, and *Scale* tools to create a snowman. Make sure you have a brand-new scene (reset if you need to) and follow these steps:

1. Create a sphere with a radius of 25.0.

2. Exit the creation mode and move your sphere to the center of the world ([0,0,0]).

3. Create another sphere with a radius of 20.0 and move it so that it is on top of the bigger sphere. (The second sphere should intersect the first one.)

4. Create another sphere with a radius of 15.0 and position it above the other two spheres.

5. Now that you have the body for the snowman you need a head! Once again, create a sphere, place it where you want the head to be, and change the radius to an appropriate size.

6. With the body and head in place, this snowman needs a mouth, some eyes, a nose, some buttons, and if you're feeling adventurous, even a hat! Use any standard primitives and the techniques you've been using to complete this character. Figure 4.14 shows my finished primitive snowman, and you can take a closer look at him as well as edit or update him by opening the file *SAMS_Hour4_Snowman.max*.

FIGURE 4.14
A finished snowman model that uses only standard primitives.

TIP

Whoops! Something Went Wrong!

Don't worry if you make a mistake. Like most other programs, 3ds Max has an *Undo* command. You can use the main menu to access it (*Edit*, *Undo*), or you can use the *Undo* icon found on the *Quick Access* toolbar next to the *Application* button. You can even use the keyboard shortcut *Ctrl+Z*.

VIDEO 4.3

Creating a Snowman

Follow along with this video as I create a snowman in 3ds Max. As I work through this creation, I discuss the various tools you can use to manipulate objects in 3D space.

Summary

In this hour you've learned about the creation of primitive objects, including both standard primitives and extended primitives. You have also had a chance to explore the vast number of other objects that 3ds Max lets you create directly from the *Create* tab of the *Command Panel*. Finally, you have learned how to manipulate your created objects in the viewports by using the *Select*, *Move*, *Rotate*, and *Scale* commands.

Armed with all this information, you should be able to confidently fly around in 3D space, creating and manipulating objects and being awesome at this 3D stuff.

Q&A

Q. How do I start to create an object in 3ds Max?

A. The *Create* tab on the *Command Panel* gives you access to all the objects you can create in 3ds Max. Alternatively, you can use the *Create* menu on the main menu for text-based access to the same creation modes.

Q. Why is it important to use unique names for the objects you create?

A. Naming your objects is important for scene clarity. Being able to quickly identify elements of a complex scene can help you understand what each element is. Duplicate names will cause confusion.

Workshop

You can use standard and extended primitives as the basis of many 3D projects. This workshop should challenge your understanding of them, as well as some of the methods used to manipulate and create them.

Quiz

1. What two kinds of primitives are covered in this hour?

2. How do you exit creation mode when you have finished creating an object?

3. What letters represent the three axes found in 3D space?

Answers

1. Standard primitives and extended primitives are covered during this hour, and this gives us access to a total of 23 primitive objects.

2. We can exit creation mode by using the right-click button in the viewport.

3. There are three axes found in 3D space: *X (Horizontal), Y (Depth)*, and *Z (Height)*. These axes can be switched depending on what is needed, but this quickly becomes an advanced topic and something which we should not be thinking about right now!

Exercise

Now that you've created a snowman, try creating your own character, using standard primitives and extended primitives. How about creating a bear or a pig? Experimenting like this will help you understand how to use both standard and extended primitives, as well as give you some really great practice using the *Select*, *Move*, *Rotate*, and *Scale* tools.

3ds Max Modifiers

▶ Using the *Modify* tab

▶ Checking out the *Modifier List* drop-down menu

▶ Working with the modifier stack

▶ Deforming objects with modifiers

▶ World space versus local/object space

Do you see the second tab in the *Command Panel*? It's the *Modify* tab, and it's where you can access a whole bunch of modifiers.

3ds Max modifiers allow you to modify objects. (I know, totally crazy. Who could work that one out without help?) You can use modifiers to make a number of modifications, including reshaping an object, changing an object's materials (such as color and texture—which you'll learn more about in Hour 8, "Materials and Textures"), and deforming an object's surface. There are many different modifiers available straight out of the 3ds Max box, and this hour introduces you to the concept of using modifiers and their basic operations. You're also going to spend a little more time learning about 3D space and its application in world space as well as local/object space—you know, just for fun!

The Modify Tab

When you click the *Modify* tab on the *Command Panel*, you should see something that looks like Figure 5.1.

I know, this thing doesn't exactly scream "fun!" straight off the bat, but it livens up once you start selecting objects within your viewports. Actually, if you switch on over to the *Create* tab, create a sphere, and then hop back to the *Modify* tab, you will see that you have access to the parameters of the sphere (see Figure 5.2). This means you can edit the sphere's parameters even after you've exited the creation mode.

FIGURE 5.1
The *Modify* tab in its default form is not exactly the most exciting thing in the interface—at least not yet!

FIGURE 5.2
Parameters appear in the *Modify* tab when you select objects in the viewport, so you can edit them even after you've exited the creation mode.

Also notice that as you select objects in a scene, the *Modify* tab gives you access to the *Name and Color* settings as well. This is super handy for being able to arbitrarily create objects and refine them at a later point.

Under the *Name and Color* rollout settings area, notice the drop-down menu labeled *Modifier List*. This menu gives you access to the various modifiers that are available for the currently selected object, or objects, within the scene you are working on. That's right: This drop-down list is contextual, meaning that it changes ever so slightly depending on what you currently have selected.

NOTE

Finding Object Parameters

As you create an object, you get direct access to its parameters. If you exit the creation mode, those parameters disappear out of the *Create* tab and reappear in the *Modify* tab!

Each modifier has its own settings and parameters, which affect the object(s) that they are being applied to. As you apply modifiers, they are added to the *modifier stack*, which is found directly under the *Modifier List* drop-down menu in the *Modify* tab. The currently selected modifier is highlighted, and its corresponding parameters are shown. By editing the parameters for each modifier, you change the appearance of the object that the modifier is applied to. Figure 5.3 shows an example of how an object is affected when you edit the parameters of a modifier.

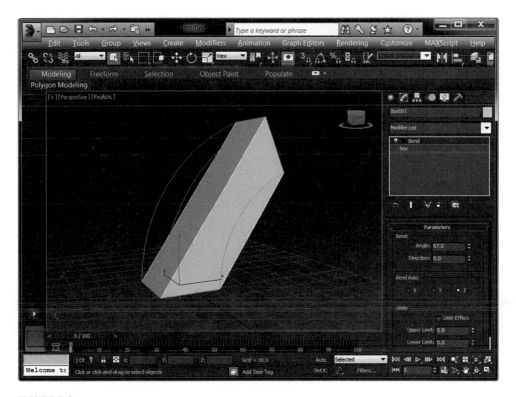

FIGURE 5.3
A box with a *Bend* modifier applied to it.

NOTE

Base Objects

The first (bottom) entry in the modifier stack is not actually a modifier at all; it is the base object that you initially created. Clicking it gives you access to the original parameters you had access to when you first created the object. When you click the base object, you may see a warning pop up on your screen. This warning pops up as you travel down the modifier stack and is simply a note that tells you that changing certain parameters lower in the modifier stack can drastically change a modifier you have already created—and that could lead to some undesirable effects. This warning also tells you which *modifier(s)* is affected, and it asks you if you want to continue (*Yes*), decline (*No*), or try it out first (*Hold/Yes*).

An object can have multiple modifiers applied to it, and this gives you endless possibilities of modifications. You can also select multiple objects and apply the same modifiers to all of them at the same time.

TIP

Modifiers from the Main Menu

You can add modifiers to objects by using the *Modifiers* menu, found at the top of the screen in the main menu.

▼ TRY IT YOURSELF

Adding Modifiers to an Object

Adding a modifier to an object is incredibly simple. Just follow these steps:

1. Create an object.

2. With the object selected, select the *Modify* tab and apply the *Bend* modifier from the *Modifier List* drop-down menu.

3. Adjust the *Angle* parameter to see how the *Bend* modifier affects your object.

VIDEO 5.1

Understanding Modifiers and the Modifier Stack

This video takes an in-depth look at the *Modify* tab as well as how to add modifiers to an object and manipulate an object using the modifier's parameters.

The Buttons Under the Modifier Stack

See the five buttons that are sitting under the modifier stack (see Figure 5.4)? These buttons affect the current modifier stack and can really help out when you're working with various objects and modifiers. The following sections discuss these buttons.

FIGURE 5.4
The modifier stack buttons are found just under the modifier stack.

The Pin Stack Button

There will be times when you want to keep an object's modifiers visible while you're selecting other objects in a scene. The *Pin Stack* button allows you to do this by "pinning" the current modifier stack to the interface so that you still have access to it while you're clicking around and selecting other objects.

The Show End Result (On/Off Toggle) Button

As you move up and down the modifier stack, you will notice that not all the results are visible (unless you are at the very top of the modifier stack list). If you want to see the results of the entire modifier stack when you're editing a modifier lower in the list, you can click the *Show End Result* button to turn it on. You click the button again to turn it off.

The Make Unique Button

If you have applied a modifier to multiple objects in a scene, those objects will share the same modifier. This is often beneficial because one change on the modifier affects all the objects that have that specific modifier. However, at times you will want to ensure that an object has its own parameters. You can do this by clicking the *Make Unique* button.

The Remove Modifier Button

You use the *Remove Modifier* button to delete a modifier from the stack. Deleting a modifier does not delete the object; it simply restores the object to its previous state—before the modifier was applied to it.

The Configure Modifier Sets Button

You click the *Configure Modifier Sets* button when you want some options for editing the layout of the *Modify* tab—and to include some quick-access buttons for modifiers you use a lot. When you click the *Configure Modifier Sets* button, you get a pop-up menu that allows you to set various options related to the *Modify* tab.

Figure 5.5 shows what an edited *Modify* tab looks like with some quick-access buttons added to it.

TIP
___

Modifier Stack Greatness

If you right-click a modifier, you get access to even more options, and from there you can copy a modifier and paste a modifier onto another object. You can even reorder the modifier stack by clicking and dragging modifiers in the stack. There are also options for collapsing modifiers, which removes all the modifiers and directly applies those changes to the base object itself. You will be experimenting with this in the upcoming hours, and it could be fun to give it a little try right now!

FIGURE 5.5
I have edited my *Modify* tab to include some quick-access buttons for modifiers that I use regularly.

World Space Versus Local/Object Space

Alas, it's time to talk more about 3D space. I know this stuff is a little dry, but it's kind of important for folks working in 3D. 3D positions and transformations exist within coordinate systems called *spaces*.

So, take a look at the *Modifier List* drop-down menu. By default it is split into three sections:

▶ *Selection Modifiers*

▶ *World-Space Modifiers*

▶ *Object-Space Modifiers*

Selection modifiers allow you to modify the selection of objects. This is straightforward and easy to understand. World-space modifiers do their fancy calculations from world-space coordinates, whereas object-space modifiers do their fancy calculations from the object's local-space coordinates.

What does all this mean? Well, in general terms, *world space* is the coordinate system for the entire scene; its origin is at the center of the scene, and the grids in the viewports show the world-space axis. *Local space* is the coordinate system that is associated with an object. (Note that the terms *object space* and *local space* are used interchangeably.)

When you first create an object, the local space of that object is the same as the world space. After you manipulate the object—for example, rotate it—the local space of that object changes and updates with the rotation, so that it is no longer the same as the world space of the scene. Figure 5.6 shows these changes, and the following "Try It Yourself" section lets you try out local-space manipulation of an object.

NOTE

Space Switching When Working with Objects

Just next to the *Scale* button on the main toolbar is where you can find the *Reference Coordinate System* flyout menu. This menu allows you to change the coordinate system you are currently using while working with objects in your scene. Try rotating an object and then switching from *View* to *Local* to see how the different coordinate systems affect how you can interact with an object.

TRY IT YOURSELF

Switching Spaces

You can interact with objects in a number of different spaces (coordinate systems). Follow these steps to learn how to switch between them:

1. In a new scene, create a box.

2. Rotate the box arbitrarily.

3. Use the *Move* tool and make sure *Reference Coordinate System* (on the main toolbar) is set to *View*. Notice that the axis of the gizmo replicates the axis of the world.

4. Change *Reference Coordinate System* to *Local*, and you see that the axis of the gizmo changes to local space. Do you think this might be a better space for rotating objects?

Repeat these steps using the *Rotate* tool to see what happens when you rotate in view and local spaces.

When it comes to modifiers, world-space modifiers remain with the world position, orientation, and scale. Local-space modifiers remain with the local position, orientation, and scale of the object. It's definitely easier to understand this stuff by looking at an image, so check out Figure 5.6.

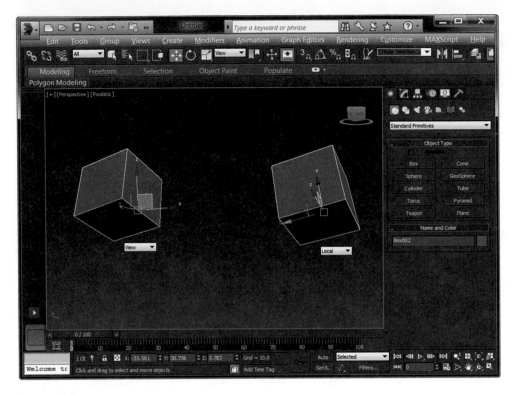

FIGURE 5.6
World-space and local/object-space coordinate systems can seem confusing at first, but you'll quickly get the idea. The box on the left shows world-space coordinates, and the box on the right shows local/object-space.

You will be working with both world-space and local-space modifiers in the upcoming hours, and you will also learn how pivot points affect the position from which you manipulate objects.

NOTE

World-Space Modifiers

World-space modifiers sit on top of the modifier stack at all times. This means that they are always evaluated last, after all object-space modifiers.

Summary

In this hour, you've taken a good look at the *Modify* tab and the modifier stack. You've dug a little deeper into 3D space, as well as tested the differences between the world-space and local/object-space coordinate systems. Some of these concepts are difficult to grasp at first, but with some practice and perseverance, you will know them like a good friend. The following hours take a much more practical, hands-on approach to 3D learning.

Q&A

Q. What are 3ds Max modifiers, and why should you care about them?

A. The 3ds Max modifiers allow you to directly modify an object, based on the set of pre-determined parameters that a specific modifier has. You can use the built-in modifiers to enhance, manipulate, edit, and change your created objects into other shapes that would be incredibly difficult to make without them.

Q. Where can you get access to the modifiers?

A. You can find the modifiers and the modifier stack in the *Modify* tab of the *Command Panel*.

Workshop

Using modifiers is a simple and easy way to manipulate objects in a variety of different ways. To use modifiers successfully, you need to know which modifier is needed for each circumstance. In addition, you need to have a good understanding of world and local/object space in order to work with some modifiers at an advanced level. This workshop should challenge your thinking when it comes to modifiers and their effects, as well as push your creativity for using modifiers in your work.

Quiz

1. Which element of the interface helps you visualize the world space of a scene?

2. How can you check the local/object space of an object?

3. Is it possible to look at an object's modifier stack while selecting other objects in a scene?

4. What is the base object?

Answers

1. The grid in a viewport gives you a visual reference for the world space of a scene.

2. By changing *Reference Coordinate System* to *Local*, you can check the local/object space of a selected object.

3. Yes, you can look at an object's modifier stack while selecting other objects in a scene by using the *Pin Stack* button found on the *Modify* tab.

4. The base object is the initial object that you created. You can find and edit its parameters and options at the bottom of that object's modifier stack.

Exercise

It's time to go crazy and really start experimenting with various modifiers. So get yourself a brand-new scene and create some standard primitives. Be ready to add some modifiers to them.

Try using the *Bend* and *Twist* modifiers first. See how they affect the objects you are applying them to and then adjust the base object's parameters to see how this affects the manipulations on the modifiers. When you're comfortable with these two modifiers and editing the base objects, go wild and test the *Melt* modifier and even the *Ripple* modifier; you can get some pretty awesome results using these two modifiers!

When you're feeling super confident about modifiers and their uses, test a few others on your own. When that excitement wears off, customize your *Modify* tab by using the *Configure Modifier Sets* button.

HOUR 6
Sub-Object Exploration

What You'll Learn in This Hour:

▶ What sub-objects are and how to use them

▶ Basic modeling concepts

▶ How to use editable polys

▶ How to use normals

No more Mr. Nice-Guy! You are officially in detention! The first five hours of this book have been easy, but from here on out, you're going to toughen up. No more prodding and poking at concepts and theories! You're going to jump head-first into three-dimensional craziness.

At this point, you're pretty confident handling objects in 3D space, navigating the viewports, finding your way around the user interface (UI), and using modifiers to deform objects in a variety of different ways. Armed with all this knowledge, you are ready to start working on 3D images. To start this hour, you're going to transform basic objects into not-so-basic objects.

In this hour, you'll take a look at the elements, called *sub-objects*, that make up an object's shape. From there you are going to grab hold of those sub-object elements and edit them to make new shapes. Are you ready? Are you excited? I am!

An Introduction to the Three Sub-Objects

When you create a sphere or any other standard primitive object, 3ds Max happily presents you with a geometric object. Every geometric object is made up of three sub-objects: vertex (the plural is vertices), edge, and face.

VIDEO 6.1

An Introduction to Sub-Object Levels

Watch this video to come to grips with sub-object levels in 3ds Max.

You can more easily visualize these sub-objects by turning on *Edged Faces* by pressing the F4 key on your keyboard. Figure 6.1 shows an object with *Edged Faces* turned on.

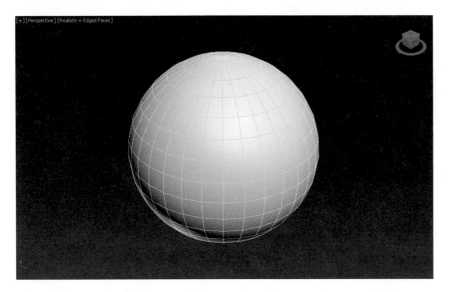

FIGURE 6.1
When you enable *Edged Faces* in the viewport, you can see the various sub-objects of an object.

The lines running along the surface of the object in Figure 6.1 are called *edges*. Where each edge crosses another is the point that creates a *vertex*, and the bit in the middle of the edges is called a *face*. These three sub-objects form the basis of geometric objects.

TIP

Turning on Edged Faces

You turn on *Edged Faces* by using the viewport display modes or by simply pressing *F4* to toggle *Edged Faces* on and off.

You can edit all these sub-objects, but first you need to make your object editable. As with most other things in 3ds Max, there are a number of ways to make objects editable; this hour focuses on using *editable polys*.

Working with Sub-Objects

To gain access to sub-objects, you can convert an object into an editable poly, which is a way for us to make polygonal objects "editable" within 3ds Max.

TRY IT YOURSELF ▼

Converting an Object to an Editable Poly

Follow these steps to convert a standard primitive to an editable poly object.

1. Create a sphere or another standard primitive of your choosing.

2. Right-click the object.

3. In the quad menu that has appeared, choose *Convert To*, *Convert to Editable Poly*.

By turning your object into an editable poly, you replace the base object with an editable poly. This means you have lost direct access to your sphere parameters, which have been replaced by a crazy number of new rollouts with plenty of new options for you to play with.

Because you lose access to the base object parameters, you should make sure that your base object has the correct settings before you convert it to an editable poly object.

NOTE

Keep Your Base Object

If you would like to keep your base object with all its parameters, you can do so by simply adding an *Editable Poly* modifier from the *Modifier List* drop-down menu as an alternative to right-clicking and converting.

The *Editable Poly* modifier has a little plus (+) button placed next to it in the *Modifier List* drop-down menu. This tells you that you have access to some additional elements of the modifier. Click it to take a look! As you can see, you get *five* additional options from the drop-down menu that has appeared, as shown in Figure 6.2:

▶ *Vertex*—This option gives you access to the vertex (point) sub-object level.

▶ *Edge*—This option turns on the edge (line) selection sub-object.

▶ *Border*—This option allows you to select a sequence of edges that are placed around any holes within an object.

▶ *Polygon*—This option gives you access to the polygon (face) sub-object mode.

▶ *Element*—When you have multiple objects within a single editable poly, you can use *Element* to select just one element of the geometry.

You can also find these drop-down menu options under the first section of the *Selection* rollout in the *Modify* tab. Figure 6.2 shows an expanded plus (+) button and the five buttons shown in the *Selection* rollout.

FIGURE 6.2
You can gain access to sub-objects from the modifier stack or the *Selection* rollout of an editable poly.

Vertex, Edge, and Polygon Sub-Object Levels

The sub-object modes *Vertex*, *Edge*, and *Polygon* are the most used and applicable sub-object levels, and once you figure out how to use them, you'll find the other two, *Border* and *Element*, easy to use as well.

You can access each sub-object level by pressing the corresponding sub-object button or by using the plus (+) button and the drop-down menu that appears. As you navigate through each of the sub-objects, various rollouts become available, and you can select a specific sub-object in the viewport.

You can directly edit the appearance of an object by using these sub-object modes with the *Select, Move, Rotate,* and *Scale* tools. In just a few moments, you can transform the look of an object.

VIDEO 6.2

Editing a Sphere by Using Sub-Objects

This video show how to grab hold of a sphere and create a character by using only sub-object selections.

 TRY IT YOURSELF ▼

Editing Geometry by Using Sub-Objects

Technically, by editing the sub-objects of a geometric object, you will take your first steps into polygon modeling. Here's what you do:

1. Create a standard primitive, such as a sphere.

2. Right-click and select *Convert to Editable Poly*.

3. Turn on *Edged Faces* in the viewport so you can visualize the sub-objects easier.

4. In the *Modify* tab, use the *Selection* rollout in conjunction with the five sub-object selection buttons to select the various elements on your object to gain a better understanding of sub-object modes.

5. Use the *Select, Move, Rotate,* and *Scale* tools to modify the appearance of your object.

6. Click the highlighted sub-object button to return to the default object select mode, so that you are no longer in sub-object mode.

Working with sub-objects is the basis for bigger modeling projects, and this pulling and pushing of sub-objects is often where you'll spend a lot of your time in 3ds Max. Figure 6.3 shows an example of what you can do by modifying sub-objects of a sphere.

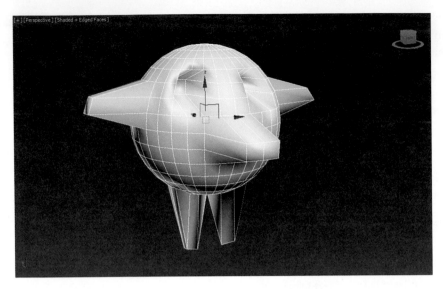

FIGURE 6.3
By using various sub-object modes to edit the appearance of a sphere, I've managed to create some sort
of basic character.

TIP

Selecting Multiple Sub-Objects

To make things easier when selecting sub-objects, you can click and drag around an area of the
object you want to affect. For more precision, you can hold down the *Ctrl* key to add to your current
selection; you can press the *Alt* key to remove currently selected sub-objects from the current selection. This works at the object level, too, so it's a handy thing to note down and remember.

CAUTION

Duplicating Selections

It's important to remember that unlike most other applications, 3ds Max requires you to use the *Ctrl*
key when you need to select multiple objects. Other applications generally have you use the *Shift*
key to add objects to a selection. If you use the *Shift* key in 3ds Max, however, you will actually create duplicates of the selected object or sub-object. This can be very handy, but you need to watch
out for this as you may accidentally duplicate stuff when you don't mean to!

Editable Poly Sub-Object Rollouts

When you click the various sub-object levels, you see additional options and rollouts. Well,
all these extra tools and commands can really enhance your modeling workflow, and they

introduce additional techniques that are extremely powerful. Of course, going through each and every option that is on offer at the sub-object level would be incredibly time-consuming, but this hour takes a look at some of the tools that will have the most impact on your creations, and it briefly summaries others that are available so that you have some point of reference.

Shrink, Grow, Ring, and Loop

In the *Selection* rollout, underneath the five sub-object selection buttons, you'll find the *Shrink*, *Grow*, *Ring*, and *Loop* buttons, as shown in Figure 6.4.

FIGURE 6.4
Just under the five sub-object selection modes, you can access the *Shrink, Grow, Ring, and Loop* buttons.

These buttons apply to the selection of sub-objects that you currently have and can help you refine the selection to be more specific to your needs:

▶ **Shrink**—Clicking this button deselects the outermost sub-objects that are currently selected. If there are no outermost sub-objects available, the remaining sub-objects are deselected.

▶ **Grow**—Clicking this button expands the current selection in all available directions. A selection can continue growing until all elements of the sub-object mode are selected.

▶ **Ring**—This button is available only with *Edge* sub-object selection mode. This tool selects all parallel edges with reference to the currently selected edges. The *Ring Shift* spinner next to this option allows you to move the current *Ring* selection in either direction.

▶ **Loop**—This button is available only with *Edge* sub-object selection mode. Looping expands an aligned edge selection as far as possible. The *Loop Shift* spinner next to this button moves the currently looped selection in either direction.

Figure 6.5 shows some examples that used the *Shrink, Grow, Ring,* and *Loop* tools.

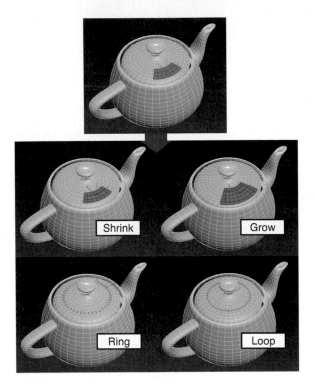

FIGURE 6.5
Shrink, Grow, Ring, and *Loop* tool examples.

Soft Selection

By enabling the *Soft Selection* tool, you can directly affect a sub-object selection and its surrounding sub-objects with less effect.

VIDEO 6.3

Using the Soft Selection Tool

This video shows how to use the *Soft Selection* tool to edit sub-objects.

Think of a table cloth. If you pinch and lift the center of it, the rest of the cloth is affected by the pinch and lift, but to a lesser extent than the exact pinch spot. The *Soft Selection* tool works in kind of the same way.

Figure 6.6 shows an example of the *Soft Selection* tool being used.

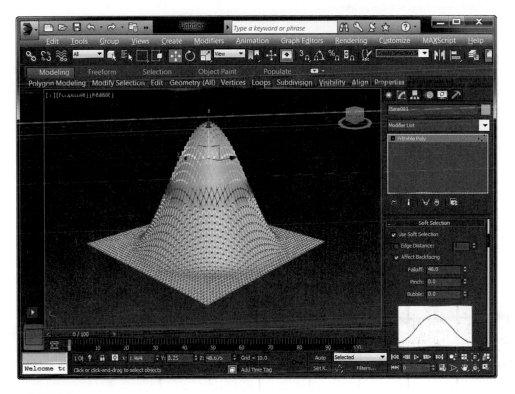

FIGURE 6.6
The *Soft Selection* tool can soften and smooth out the results of your pushing and pulling of sub-objects. It's kind of neat, I'm sure you'll agree!

The options in the *Soft Selection* rollout allow you to increase and decrease the amount of effect that a soft selection has on the full object. It's a great tool, as you'll see in the following Try It Yourself.

▼ TRY IT YOURSELF

Soft Selection

Using the *Soft Selection* tool is super easy, and a lot of fun, too. Follow these steps:

1. Create a standard primitive and convert it to an editable poly.

2. Drop into *Vertex* sub-object mode by clicking the *Vertex* sub-object mode button, and in the *Soft Selection* rollout, enable *Soft Selection*.

3. Use your mouse to select a *vertex* and use the *Move* tool to manipulate it until you have a smoother deformation. Note that surrounding vertices are also affected by your manipulation.

4. Increase the *Falloff* setting, select a new vertex, and manipulate it to see how the *Falloff* parameter affects the soft selection.

Contextual Rollouts on Editable Poly Objects

As you change your sub-object selection, you will notice that each sub-object level has its own unique rollout that appears in the *Modify* tab. These are the rollouts:

▶ *Edit Vertices*

▶ *Edit Edges*

▶ *Edit Borders*

▶ *Edit Polygons*

▶ *Edit Elements*

Each of these unique rollouts is contextual, meaning that it includes its own specific tools for editing and manipulating the sub-object level that you are currently working with. There are far too many tools included in these rollouts to discuss them all in this hour, but it is definitely worth taking some time to try out at least some of them. Of course, these unique rollouts are incredibly useful, and you will use some of their specific tools in upcoming hours.

The Edit Geometry Rollout

The *Edit Geometry* rollout appears in every sub-object selection mode. It includes some handy tools for editing and manipulating your geometry, and I advise you to try out some of its tools and options. You will use a few of these options in upcoming hours, but getting to know a few of these tools now will definitely help your understanding of the editable poly toolset.

Other Rollouts

Some other rollouts appear in the *Editable Poly* modifier. Although this hour doesn't discuss them, you can dig in on your own and work with them a bit. These other rollouts are definitely helpful, but I find them to be less important than both the contextual rollouts and the *Edit Geometry* rollout already covered in this hour.

Sub-Object-Level Shortcuts

As you become more confident using sub-objects, you will probably want a quicker way to access them than heading to the buttons each time you need to change the sub-object mode. And as with most other elements of 3ds Max, there are some handy keyboard shortcuts. Table 6.1 lists some of the handiest ones.

TABLE 6.1 Sub-Object-Level Keyboard Shortcuts

Keyboard Shortcut	Description
1	Vertex sub-object mode toggle
2	Edge sub-object mode toggle
3	Border sub-object mode toggle
4	Polygon sub-object mode toggle
5	Element sub-object mode toggle

Normals

What the heck is a normal, and why should you care about normals?

Well, *normals* tell you which way a surface is facing. In the most basic form, if a normal is pointing toward the camera, you can see it, and if it's pointing away, you can't see it. This will become super important when you get around to rendering (making pretty pictures) a bit later.

Generally speaking, normals should usually face outward and be perpendicular to the face of the geometry. This is not a rule or anything. It is simply a guideline and the default way normals are displayed when you first create a geometric object.

Figure 6.7 shows a sphere with its normals displayed in the viewport.

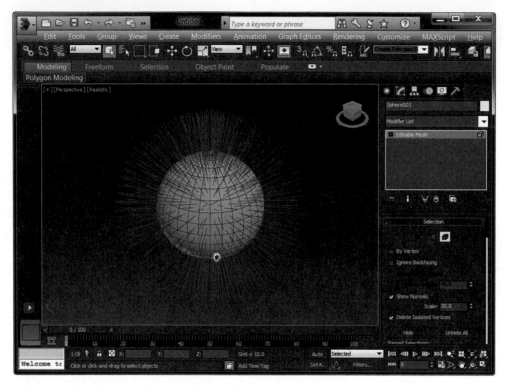

FIGURE 6.7
You can see the normals of an object within the viewports by adding an *Edit Mesh* modifier and enabling the *Show Normals* option in the *Selection* rollout.

NOTE

Visualizing Normals

If you put an *Edit Mesh* modifier onto an object, you can enable the *Show Normals* option in the sub-object modes (except *Edges*) to visualize normals on the object itself. You need to select the sub-object elements that you want to visualize, of course!

TIP

Flipping Normals!

There are a number of ways that you can flip normals so that they face the opposite direction. One way is to select the *Show Normals* check box in the *Normal* modifier. For an editable poly, you select the *Flip* button from either the *Polygon* or *Elements* rollout.

Summary

You've begun to get your hands dirty in this hour. I don't know about you, but I've enjoyed it a lot!

This hour, you've taken a good look at editable polys, learned some basic modeling concepts, and tried out the available sub-object elements. With all of this information, you're ready to start some real-world modeling tasks in the next hour.

Q&A

Q. How do I enable a sub-object mode?

A. You can convert an object to an editable poly, or you can attach an *Edit Poly* modifier to the object.

Q. What does the *Soft Selection* tool do?

A. It allows you to affect other sub-objects that are not in your main sub-object selection, using *Falloff* for a smoother effect.

Workshop

Sub-object modes open up a world of opportunities. By using them, you have taken your first steps into more complicated aspects of 3D. The following quiz and exercise will push your knowledge and understanding of sub-objects even further.

Quiz

1. How can you gain access to the editable poly tools without converting an object into an editable poly?

2. In what ways can you add to or remove from your current selection?

3. Which keyboard key allows you to duplicate objects and/or sub-objects?

Answers

1. You can add an *Edit Poly* modifier instead of converting an object into an editable poly.

2. You can add to or remove from your current selection by using the *Select* tool with the *Ctrl* and *Alt* keys.

3. The *Shift* key allows you to duplicate objects and sub-objects in 3ds Max. This is a little bit different from most other programs, in which the *Shift* key allows you to add to a selection.

Exercise

Experiment with multiple objects in a scene and convert them to editable polys. Try using the *Extrude* and *Attach* tools, which are found in the *editable poly modifier* under the Edit Polygons and Edit Geometry rollouts. Be sure to take your time with this exercise and thoroughly test the available tools while working with an editable poly object. This will help you better understand what you're doing in many of the upcoming hours.

3D Modeling

What You'll Learn in This Hour:

▶ Polygonal modeling techniques

▶ Editable poly conversion and modifier techniques

▶ Advanced sub-object-level editing

▶ How to use multiple objects for modeling 3D scenes

▶ Hands-on modeling of polygon objects

Polygon meshes are probably the most popular and most standard model type for most 3D applications out there. In my experience, using polygon meshes is the most popular modeling approach among 3D artists. Therefore, in this hour, you create some 3D polygonal models of your very own.

You've already learned pretty much everything you need to be successful with polygonal modeling. You're not going to be sitting around and learning concepts this hour; instead, you'll jump straight into the creation process.

In this hour, you will create three polygon models, each more complex than the last. As you work through this hour, you'll increase your knowledge of the modeling tools and techniques 3ds Max makes available.

Creating a Cartoon Face

A cartoon face is the first thing that I modeled when I was learning 3ds Max (see Figure 7.1). It was a great place for me to start, and I think it will be a good place for you to start, too. It's pretty simple but lots of fun.

You can create almost anything your mind can come up with by starting out with a sphere or a standard primitive, editing the sub-object levels, and using a few sub-object-level tools. Franklin is a neat example of what is possible with only a little effort, and now it's your turn to come up with your very own cartoon face creation.

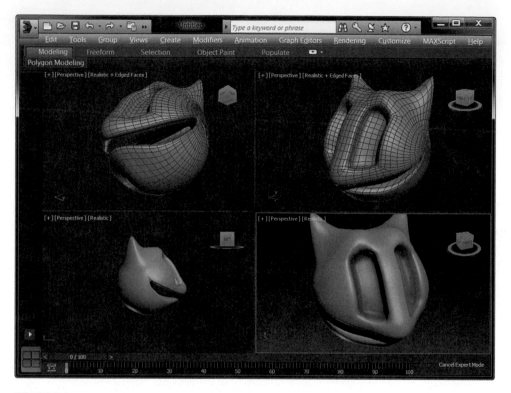

FIGURE 7.1
I edited a sphere to create a cartoon face. This awesome guy's name is Franklin.

You're going to use a few new tools and techniques in this section, and at first they might seem a little strange. But once you get used to working with them, you'll see that they're incredibly intuitive, and you'll wonder what you did without them! These are the new tools and techniques you'll use here:

▶ *Angle Snap Toggle*—The *Angle Snap Toggle* tool allows you to specify an incremental rotation amount so you can snap rotations to a specific increment. For instance, you can rotate something by exactly 45 degrees if you want to.

▶ *Edged Faces*—*Edged Faces* allow you to more easily see sub-object levels inside your viewports. The shortcut key for this tool is *F4*.

▶ *Shrink, Grow, Ring, and Loop*—As explained in Hour 6, "Sub-Object Exploration," these buttons apply to the sub-objects that you currently have selected. They help you refine the sub-objects so they are more specific to your needs.

- ▶ **Extrude**—The *Extrude* tool allows you to extrude a face along its normal to create a new face and add more geometry to a model.

- ▶ **Chamfer**—*Chamfer* refers to rounding off a sharp edge or corner, and in 3ds Max you can get this effect by using the *Chamfer* tool along with a selected edge.

- ▶ **Cut**—By using the *Cut* tool, you can cut additional detail into a model, creating more vertices, edges, and faces.

- ▶ **Soft Selection**—As explained in Hour 6, the *Soft Selection* tool allows you to affect an area of sub-objects using a falloff radius.

In the following Try It Yourself, you'll get going with some of these tools.

VIDEO 7.1

Modeling Franklin

Watch this video to see the steps I took to create Franklin's cartoon face.

TRY IT YOURSELF ▼

Creating Your Own Cartoon Face

In the following steps, you'll create your very own version of Franklin the cartoon face. This is just a guide, so feel free to change the design of this cartoon face and really make it your own. Be creative, go crazy!

1. Create a sphere. Use the *Move* tool to center this newly created sphere to the world origin [0,0,0]. (Remember the XYZ coordinates!)

2. Rotate the new sphere 90 degrees on its Y axis ([0,90,0]). To do this accurately, use the *Angle Snap Toggle* tool on the main toolbar (see Figure 7.2).

3. To make sure the sphere is the correct size, open the *Modify* tab and change the *Radius* setting for the sphere to *50.0*, as shown in Figure 7.3.

FIGURE 7.2
The *Angle Snap Toggle* tool is found on the main toolbar. To change the settings of this tool, simply right-click it.

4. Convert the sphere into an editable poly. To do this, make sure the sphere is selected and then right-click and select *Convert*, *Convert to Editable Poly*. Turn on *Edged Faces* in the viewport (by pressing *F4*) to more easily see the sub-object levels. Now that the sphere is an editable poly object, you have access to its sub-object levels.

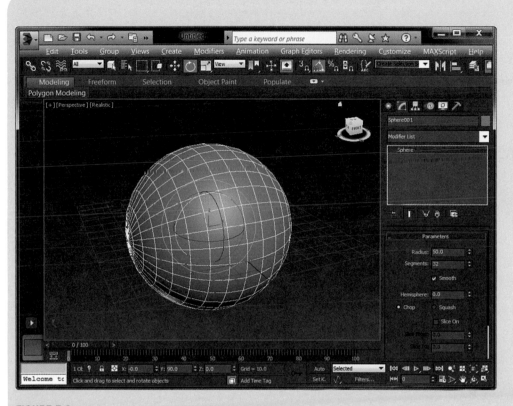

FIGURE 7.3
The sphere has been centered and rotated by 90 degrees, and its radius is 50.0 units.

5. Using a front viewport, select some polygons that will be suitable for the eyes of this character. With the polygons selected, use the *Extrude* tool to extrude the polygon selection inward to form eye sockets. To so do, open the *Modify* tab and find the *Edit Polygons* rollout; on this rollout, find the *Extrude* button. Click it and then click and drag in the viewport to extrude a polygon. Make sure you extrude inward, as shown in Figure 7.4.

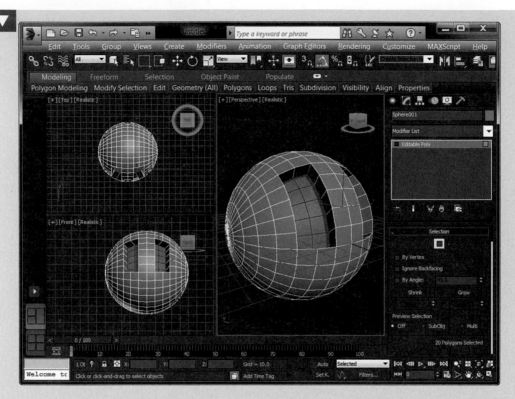

FIGURE 7.4
The selected polygons have now been extruded in-over to form the eye sockets of the character.

6. With the eye sockets created, go back to a front viewport and make a polygon sub-object selection where the mouth should be.

7. Using the same extrude in-over technique you used with the eye sockets, create the mouth of your character as shown in Figure 7.5.

8. Spend some time using sub-object selections in conjunction with the *Soft Selection* tool to refine the look of this character. Because you have no visual reference to follow, you have complete artistic freedom over how this character looks, so take your time and be creative for a while.

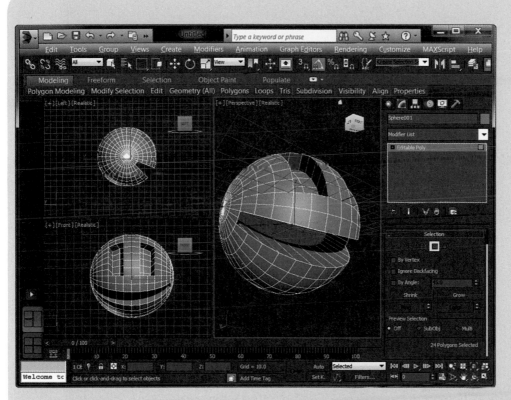

FIGURE 7.5
Your spherical friend now has eye sockets and a mouth. This little guy is starting to look pretty neat!

9. When you're happy with the overall look of your character, try some of the other options in the *Editable Poly* modifier. Figure 7.6 shows the Franklin character as his modeling is in progress.

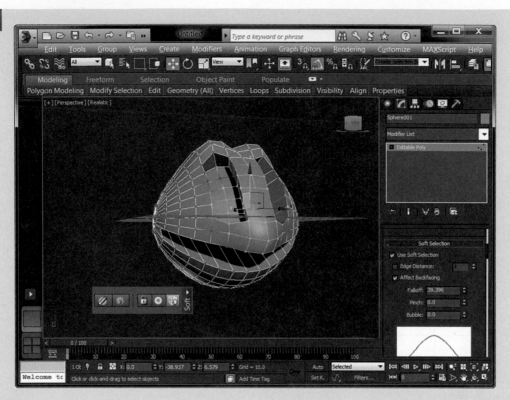

FIGURE 7.6
Franklin during his creation phase.

I created my final Franklin model (*SAMS_Hour7_Franklin.max*) by using a combination of the tools found in the *Editable Poly* modifier. It's important to just try different things and to not limit yourself to the tools you are familiar with. Stepping out of your comfort zone can really help you make excellent creations.

NOTE

Additional Tools Used While Creating Franklin

To get Franklin to his final stage, I used a combination of the tools found in the *Editable Poly* modifier. In particular, I made good use of the *Shrink*, *Grow*, *Ring*, and *Loop* selection options, as well as the *Soft Selection* tool and the *Extrude*, *Chamfer*, and *Cut* tools.

If you've made it this far, congratulations! You've now done some 3D modeling, and hopefully you have created and completed your first-ever 3D character head. Be sure to save your cartoon face and keep it safe. You will look back on it in a few years as an excellent reminder of where you started. I really wish I had kept my original sphere-head character. I'm sure it was terrible, but it would have been great to show you. Franklin will have to do.

Creating a Spaceship

After I created my first cartoon face, I modeled a spaceship. It was a great next step for me, so I'm going to have you take this next step, too. The techniques you just used to create a cartoon face are the same techniques you use to make a spaceship—or anything else, really. It's all about practice, practice, practice!

To start your spaceship model, you're going to use a box primitive, and once again you will convert it to an editable poly object so that you have access to the tools associated with it.

Once again, you are going to use a lot of the tools and techniques you have already been working with, as well as these two new tools:

▶ *Bevel*—A bevel, in 3ds Max terms at least, is an extruded area that can be scaled either larger or smaller.

▶ *Inset*—An inset is just like a bevel, but without the extrude effect.

VIDEO 7.2
_____

Spaceship Modeling

This video shows how to model a spaceship from a single box
primitive.
_____

TRY IT YOURSELF ▼

Creating a Spaceship: Blocking Phase

You are going to start with a box primitive and transform it into a super-cool spaceship. The first stage, or phase, is known as *blocking*—that is, getting the main shape and proportions of the model created. After you do the blocking, you can step into a secondary phase/stage where you detail the blocked-out shapes. Follow these steps to block your spaceship:

1. In a new scene create a box and center it in the world ([0,0,0]).

2. Use the *Modify* tab to change the *Length*, *Width*, and *Height* attributes so that they are all *25.0*.

3. Convert the box into an editable poly by right-clicking the object and choosing *Convert*, *Convert to Editable Poly*, as shown in Figure 7.7.

FIGURE 7.7
You can convert an object to an editable poly with only a few clicks.

4. Turn on *Edged Faces* in the viewports (by pressing *F4*) so that you can see the sub-object levels. Then jump into a front viewport and use the *Polygon* sub-object mode to select the polygon that will form the front section, or cockpit, of the spaceship.

5. Using a combination of the *Extrude*, *Move*, *Rotate*, and *Scale* tools, change the shape of the cockpit as you like. You have no reference to copy from here, so use your imagination to create something that will be appealing.

6. Using the same techniques, elongate the main fuselage section of the spaceship and extrude or bevel the tail section of the ship, reshaping things as you go along. Figure 7.8 shows how these changes to the spaceship might look.

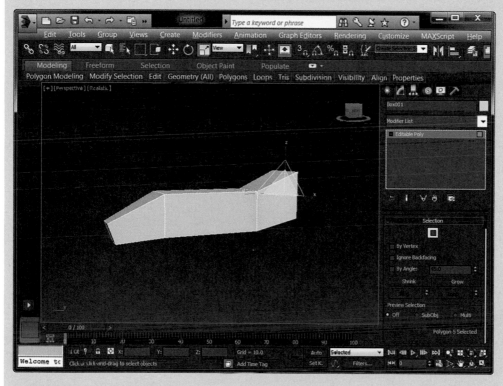

FIGURE 7.8
The front, middle, and rear sections of the spaceship are now in place.

7. Grab both sides of the fuselage by left-clicking one side and holding *Ctrl* and then left-clicking the other. Next, use a combination of the *Inset* and *Bevel* tools to create the wings of the craft.

8. When you're happy with the changes you have made and your creation is starting to look a little more like a spaceship, make sure to save so you don't lose any work.

You have now blocked out the main shape of the spaceship. For the sake of comparison, you can take a look at my spaceship model by opening the file *SAMS_Hour7_SpaceshipBlocking.max*. During this blocking phase, you have used a number of tools, including the *Inset* and *Bevel* tools.

The model is certainly not finished, but the main shape, style, and proportions are in place, and you can now go ahead and start adding in more detail.

During the detailing phase, you will be using yet another new tool and a new modifier:

▶ **Connect Edges**—By connecting edges with the *Connect Edges* tool, you can create a new edge between adjacent pairs of selected edges.

▶ **Symmetry**—The *Symmetry* modifier "mirrors" a mesh from one side to the other, using the X, Y, or Z axis.

NOTE

Symmetry Modifier Versus Mirror Modifier

You have the option of using either the *Symmetry* modifier or the *Mirror* modifier. They behave differently but give you very similar end results. Out of preference, I tend to use the *Symmetry* modifier more than the *Mirror* modifier.

▼ TRY IT YOURSELF

Creating a Spaceship: Detail Phase

You have already blocked a spaceship, and you'll use that here as a base to start detailing specific areas. Follow these steps to work on the details:

1. With your blocked spaceship scene open, select a central edge on the spaceship and ring the selection as shown in Figure 7.9.

2. With these edges selected, open the Edit Edges rollout and click the Connect button to connect all the selected edges.

3. Enter *Face* sub-object mode and select one side of the model. Then remove that selection by pressing the *Delete* key.

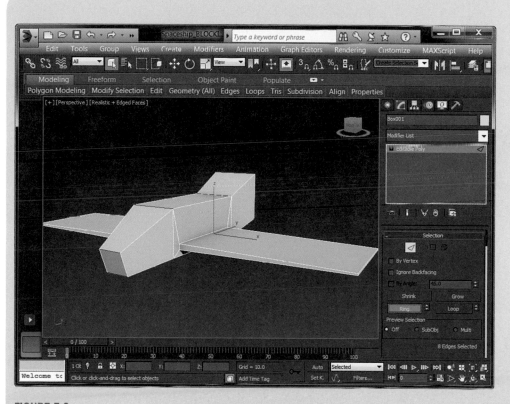

FIGURE 7.9
You can select a central edge and use the *Ring* selection tool to select all the central edges on the spaceship model.

4. With one side now missing, jump back to the object mode and add a *Symmetry* modifier to the spaceship. After you tweak the options in this modifier, the model should look complete once again, as shown in Figure 7.10.

5. Return to the *Editable Poly* layer in the modifier stack and start working on just one side of the spaceship. These updates will be automatically mirrored to the other side because of the *Symmetry* modifier. So get to work detailing your spaceship using the techniques you've already learned. If you want to see what both sides look like, click the *Show End Result* button, which is highlighted in Figure 7.11.

6. Once you're happy with your detailing, remember to save.

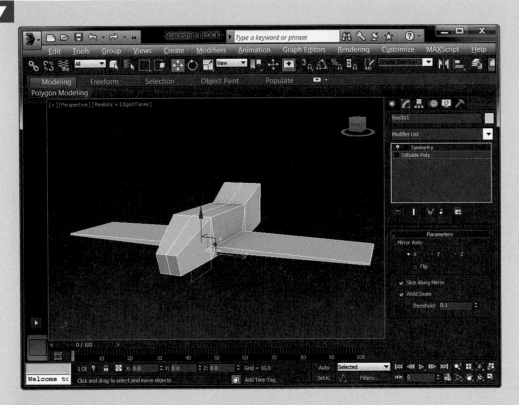

FIGURE 7.10
The spaceship model, with a *Symmetry* modifier applied to it, looks just like it did before you deleted one side of the thing.

FIGURE 7.11
The *Show End Results* button is found on the *Modify panel* just under the *Modifier Stack!*

At this point, you have blocked out your spaceship and detailed that block-out. You should have something that resembles what is shown in Figure 7.12, and you can take a look at my more detailed spaceship by opening the file *SAMS_Hour7_SpaceshipDetail.max*. Now you are ready for the final phase: refinement.

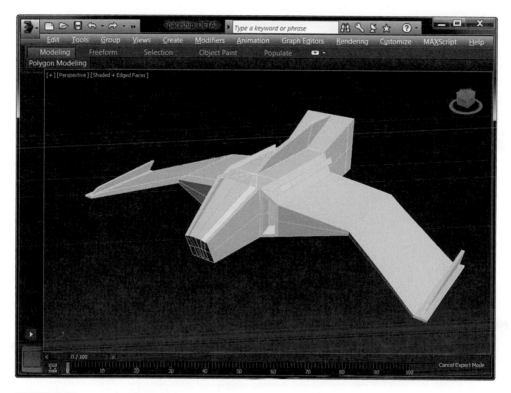

FIGURE 7.12
You have blocked out and detailed your spaceship, and you're ready for the refinement phase.

TRY IT YOURSELF ▼

Creating a Spaceship: Refinement Phase

Using all the techniques and tools you have already learned, you can refine the look of your spaceship. Instead of following a step-by-step guide here, I want you to just spend some time working on and refining your spaceship model.

When you're happy with the results, and you're sure you don't want to change it again, right-click in the modifier stack and click the *Collapse All* option. This removes all the modifiers and once again makes your spaceship an editable poly object while keeping all your changes and applying them to the base level.

When you're finished with your spaceship model, remember to save your work. You're going to need it a little later!

Check out my completed spaceship model by opening the file *SAMS_Hour7_SpaceshipRefine.max* and taking a look at Figure 7.13.

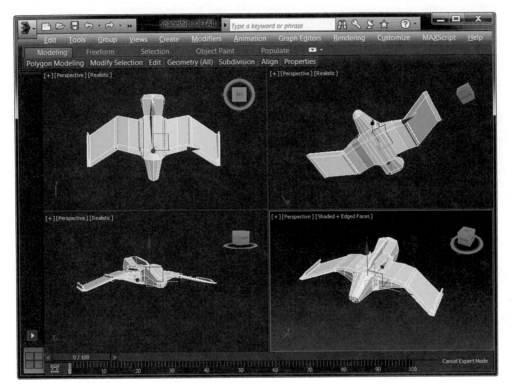

FIGURE 7.13
Using the techniques covered, we have successfully created a spaceship!

Creating a Futuristic City Planet

You've created a 3D spaceship, but you have nowhere for it to fly. Space would be a logical place, but that's kind of boring—what with the vast open spaces and random planets, which we all know are just big spheres. You are pretty much a sphere-making professional by now, so creating a planet wouldn't be as much fun as creating a futuristic city planet, so you'll do that instead.

VIDEO 7.3

Modeling a Futuristic City Planet

Watch this video to see me model a futuristic city planet.

Creating a Futuristic City Planet: Blocking, Detail, and Refinement

For your futuristic city planet, you will work on the blocking, detailing, and refinement phases in this one section. Follow these steps to see how it works:

1. In a new scene grab, create a box standard primitive. Center it ([0,0,0]) and change the *Length*, *Width*, and *Height* settings to *50.0*. Then change the *Length Segs*, *Width Segs*, and *Height Segs* settings to *10* instead of *1*.

2. With the box selected, apply the *Spherify* modifier. Leave the *Percent* parameter set to *100.0*, and you should have something that looks like Figure 7.14.

3. Instead of converting your spherified box to an editable poly object, apply the *Edit Poly* modifier to it. This modifier works in exactly the same way as the editable poly object, with just a few exceptions that really don't make a difference at this point. This spherified box will be your futuristic planet, to which you'll add roads and other goodies.

4. In the *Polygon* sub-object mode, start selecting polygons that you think would work well for the road structure of your futuristic city planet. This might take some time, but keep at it until you're happy with your selections.

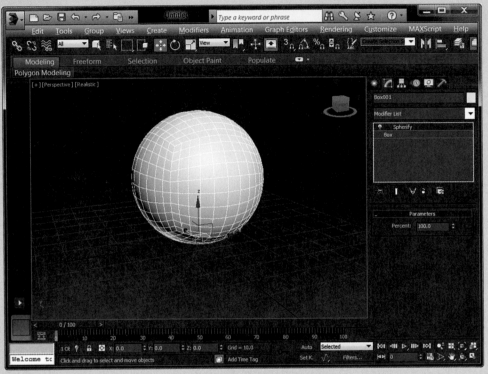

FIGURE 7.14
A box with its parameters adjusted and a *Spherify* modifier applied to it. The modifiers in 3ds Max are pretty amazing.

5. When you're done selecting polygons, click the *Extrude Option* button and make sure you're extruding by local normals. Enter a negative value in the *Extrude Amount* option, such as *-1*. With the options correctly set, click the checkmark icon to confirm the operation. Figure 7.15 shows this process.

6. With the road system in place, your futuristic city planet is already starting to look interesting. Now you can start adding skyscrapers and other buildings to it by using the *Polygon* sub-object mode and both the *Inset* and *Extrude* tools. Start to extrude the city buildings, varying the heights to keep things visually appealing. Don't forget that some open space is not a bad thing; you don't have to inset and extrude every available polygon.

FIGURE 7.15
The futuristic city planet now has a road structure.

By using all the skills you now possess, you have the ability to create a pretty cool futuristic city planet, as well as many other objects. Take some time to refine your futuristic city planet and be sure to save it when you're done as you'll need it later.

Figure 7.16 shows what your futuristic city planet might look like. You can grab hold of this model by opening the file *SAMS_Hour7_FuturisticCityPlanet.max*.

FIGURE 7.16
Now it looks like a futuristic city planet. Nice going!

Additional Modeling Techniques

You still have lots to learn when it comes to becoming a 3D modeling professional, but this hour should have you off to a good start. Before wrapping up this hour, I want to introduce you to two more things.

The *Graphite Modeling* tools are worth examining. Even though I find the interface a little disjointed, there are some very powerful tools hidden away in there, and you should take a look at them now.

Testing the Modeling Ribbon

Follow these steps to try out the *Graphite Modeling tools* found in the *Modeling* ribbon section of the 3ds Max user interface:

1. In a new scene, create a box and convert it to an editable poly.

2. Enter *Polygon* sub-object mode and take a look at the *Freeform* tab on the *Modeling* ribbon.

3. Test the *Strips* and *Branches* options to see what kind of awesomeness is available when you use these tools.

Finally, you need to create some text for your futuristic city planet. This text could be used to advertise products, as is done in many cities. The following Try It Yourself gives you a chance to use splines rather than standard primitives for a change.

NOTE

What Is a Spline?

A spline is a type of curve or line that has a starting point and an endpoint. It is very much like a line drawn on a piece of paper with a pencil. You can manipulate a spline object by using tangents. A tangent allows you to affect the curvature of the line. Using a spline is definitely a little more advanced and somewhat more confusing than modeling with a standard primitive, but splines can be extremely useful if used correctly.

Creating Text for Your Futuristic City Planet

In the following steps, you'll create text by using splines rather than the standard primitives you've been using so far:

1. Go to the *Create* tab and select *Shapes*, *Splines*, and then *Text*.

2. Change the *Text* creation parameter to something else, such as *Sams Teach Yourself 3ds Max in 24 Hours*.

3. Click in the viewport to create the text.

4. Go to the *Modify* tab and apply the *Extrude* modifier from the modifier list.

Summary

You've really started digging into 3ds Max now, and I hope you're starting to feel pretty confident in you modeling abilities. In this hour, you've learned about editable polys as well as the *Edit Poly* modifier. You have also looked at various tools, including *Extrude*, *Inset*, *Branch*, and *Strips*, all from various places within the 3ds Max UI. Oh, and you have used the *Shapes* category combined with the *Extrude* modifier to build some text.

Keep on working with all of the *Create* options and learn as much as you can. You've done some great work during this hour. I'm proud of you, and you should be, too.

Q&A

Q. How can I work on one side of my model and have the other side update automatically?

A. You can do this by using either the *Mirror* modifier or the *Symmetry* modifier.

Q. Should I convert an object to an editable poly, or should I apply the *Edit Poly* modifier instead?

A. This is really up to you! When you convert an object to an editable poly object, you lose the ability to restore your base object settings, so applying the *Edit Poly* modifier is typically a safer option. Personally, I use a mixture of the two. If I know that I won't need to go back to my base object, I go the conversion route; if I'm not sure, I use the modifier.

Workshop

The techniques you have learned in this hour form a good foundation for working with 3ds Max. This workshop forces you to really think about some of these techniques.

Quiz

You learned a lot of new tools and techniques during this hour. Let's see if you can answer a few questions related to all that new learning!

1. What does the *Extrude* tool enable you to do?

2. What are the differences between an editable poly object and the *Edit Poly* modifier?

3. How many sub-object levels do an editable poly object and an *Edit Poly* modifier have? Name them.

Answers

1. The *Extrude* tool allows you to extrude additional geometry along the local normal of the currently selected geometry.

2. An editable poly object and the *Edit Poly* modifier give you access to the same tools, but an editable poly object removes the object's base level, so you can no longer edit those parameters. When you use the *Edit Poly* modifier, you get to keep the object's base level; you can simply edit, turn off, or remove the modifier from the scene.

3. An editable poly object and the *Edit Poly* modifier have five sub-object levels: *Vertex*, *Edge*, *Border*, *Polygon*, and *Element*.

Exercise

You should have three models of your own by now: a cartoon face, a spaceship model, and a futuristic city planet. If you haven't followed the Try It Yourself sections in this hour, go ahead and do so right now.

Once you have completed your three models, use the techniques you've learned so far to create a robot. Remember that you can use more than one standard primitive to create the various sections of the robot. Keep in mind that your robot should be complex enough to be challenging but not so difficult that it is an impossible task to complete. Be sure to look for some reference and inspiration on what you would like your robot to look like—or even sketch out your own!

HOUR 8
Materials and Textures

What You'll Learn in This Hour:

▶ Working with materials and the *Material Editor*
▶ How to apply materials
▶ How to apply textures
▶ Basic *UVW* mapping

Soft, smooth, bumpy, orange, and green. These are all real-world properties you can use to describe a surface or material. *Materials* in 3ds Max are similar: They replicate, or mimic, materials found in the real world.

In this hour you are going to get to work with the materials available in 3ds Max and learn how you can change, edit, and apply these materials to your 3D objects. You are also going to take a look at how you can add textures to your materials as well as map those textures to objects within a scene.

The Material Editor

Every time you create an object in 3ds Max, a default object color is assigned to it. You have direct access to the default color in the *Name and Color* rollout, but you don't really have any options available. By using the *Material Editor*, you can add a whole lot more to an object. It provides a lot of options, and it can help you increase the realism and appeal of an object it is applied to—as long as it is used correctly, of course.

The *Material Editor* comes in two flavors: the *Slate Material Editor* and the *Compact Material Editor*.

VIDEO 8.1

Understanding the Material Editor

This video takes a look at both the *Slate Material Editor* and the *Compact Material Editor*, and it provides a brief introduction on how to use them.

In essence, both versions do exactly the same thing. However, the *Slate Material Editor* gives you access to a handy graph of nodes that show you how the materials are structured, and this is what is missing from the *Compact Material Editor*. Despite this difference, it really makes no difference which mode you use; your end result will be the same! Figure 8.1 shows both versions of the *Material Editor*.

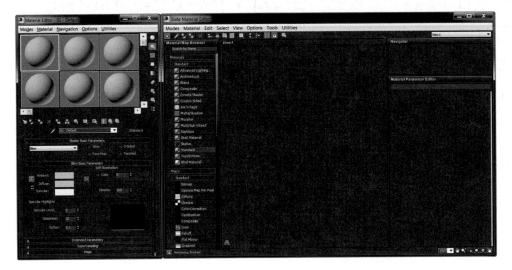

FIGURE 8.1
The *Compact Material Editor* (left) and the *Slate Material Editor* (right) are essentially the same. They just look and behave differently.

You can access both versions of the *Material Editor* by going to the main menu and selecting *Rendering, Material Editor*. You then see both the *Compact Material Editor* and *Slate Material Editor* options. Check them out for yourself right now!

TIP

Material Editor Shortcut

You can use the keyboard shortcut key *M* to toggle the *Material Editor* on and off. You can switch versions directly from the Material Editor menu; just head over to the *Modes* menu and choose your mode from there.

For clarity, this hour primarily discusses the *Slate Material Editor*, but don't be afraid to jump into the *Compact Material Editor* whenever you want to. In fact, it's a great idea to try it. You will probably notice the similarities right away. Remember that they pretty much do the exact same thing anyway.

The *Slate Material Editor* has its own floating window and contains eight sections:

- ▶ **Menu bar**—A menu bar contains various menus and options.

- ▶ **Toolbar**—The toolbar gives you access to the main tools in the *Material Editor*.

- ▶ *Material/Map Browser*—The *Material/Map Browser* shows various available materials. To edit a material, you simply drag it from the *Material/Map Browser* and into the active view.

- ▶ **Active view**—This is where you create your material trees, which consist of various nodes that are wired together. You can create numerous views to make navigating various material trees easier.

- ▶ **Navigator**—The navigator gives you a way to navigate larger views, which is handy if you have a number of materials.

- ▶ *Material Parameter Editor*—This is where all the attributes, parameters, and settings are located for the various maps and materials. You can double-click a material in the view to bring up the various parameters associated with that material.

- ▶ **Status area**—This area provides status information.

- ▶ **View navigation**—This area gives you direct access to tools available for navigating the active view.

Now that you have a basic understanding of the *Slate Material Editor*, you can start working with materials.

Click and drag a standard material from the *Material/Map Browser* into the active view, which in my case is *View1*. Then double-click the material in the active view. By doing this, you populate the *Material Parameter Editor* with lots of options related to that material. As you edit and change the options of a material, you update what the material will look like after it is rendered. (You'll learn more about rendering in Hour 12, "Rendering for Production.")

▼ TRY IT YOURSELF

Creating and Editing a Material

Follow these steps to create a standard material and edit its parameters using the *Slate Material Editor*.

1. Click and drag a standard material from the *Material/Map Browser* into the active view.

2. Double-click the material to bring up the parameters in the *Material Parameter Editor*.

3. Click the gray area next to the *Diffuse* parameter and select a different color. Notice that the sphere icon next to the material name updates with your color choice, giving an indication of what the material now looks like. Figure 8.2 shows an example of this.

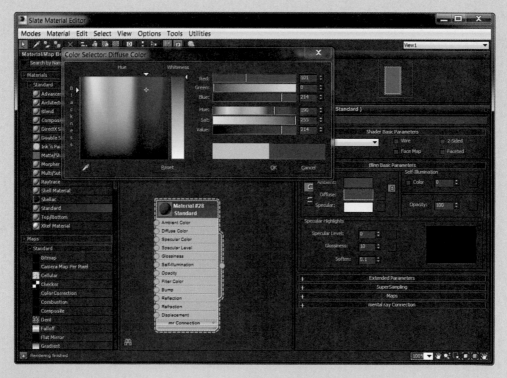

FIGURE 8.2
By editing the parameters of a material, you change its appearance.

Applying a material to an object is as simple as right-clicking the material and choosing the *Assign Material to Selection* option from the pop-up menu. Of course, you need to create some geometry and select it first, as shown in Figure 8.3.

FIGURE 8.3
Applying a material is as easy as selecting the object and then right-clicking the material and choosing the *Assign Material to Selection* option.

Creating, editing, and applying materials are the basics of material creation in 3ds Max. Obviously, there are many more materials available for you to use, and each one of them includes its own set of parameters. If this hour were to go through every single material and their parameters, I guarantee that both of us would not have any fun. A better way to learn about the materials and their parameters is to create an object and apply a material to it and then try out different things with it. Practical learning is way more enjoyable than theoretical learning, according to my brain!

There are some parameters and options that you'll use very often, so create an object and apply a standard material and then take a look at these options:

▶ **Material Name**—Just as you want to use a good naming convention in the main scene, it's important to correctly name your materials, too. Use descriptive words for the materials; for instance if it's a wood material, we probably want to include the word *wood* as part of the material name.

▶ **Shader Basic**—You use this parameter to change the base shader options, which affect the rest of the material's parameters dramatically.

▶ **Ambient**—You use this option to modify the background lighting for the material. This option is locked to the *Diffuse* color by default.

▶ *Diffuse*—This is where you specify the surface color of the material.

▶ *Specular*—This is where you specify the color of the highlights.

▶ *Self-Illumination*—If you want an object to glow, this is the parameter to change. Note that self-illuminating materials do not actually emit light themselves.

▶ *Opacity*—If you're looking for transparency (windows, glasses, etc.), this is the parameter you want.

▶ *Specular Level*, *Glossiness*, and *Soften*—Make your object shiny—or not! These three parameters affect the shiny and reflective options of the material.

NOTE

What Are All the Boxes?

The boxes that appear next to some of the parameters in the *Material Editor* allow for even more options for that particular parameter.

You now should have enough information to start digging into the *Slate Material Editor* and try out the various materials available to you. Next you need to start thinking about the textures of our materials.

Applying Textures to Objects

Textures are image files that can be applied to objects in a scene. They can affect the *Diffuse* color by wrapping an image onto an object. Think of a 3D model as a sculpture, the materials as the materials you used to sculpt the 3D model, and the texture as the paint or color for the model.

▼ TRY IT YOURSELF

Adding a Texture

Follow these steps to add a texture to an object in a scene by using the *Material Editor*:

1. Create a standard primitive and apply a material to it from the *Slate Material Editor*.

2. To apply a texture map, either double-click the material and click the *Diffuse* option box in the *Material Parameter Editor* or click and drag the circle on the left side of the *Diffuse Color* option in the active view to an empty area in the main view and choose *Bitmap*. Both of these *Diffuse* options are highlighted in Figure 8.4.

FIGURE 8.4
There are two ways to apply a *Bitmap* texture map to the *Diffuse* color channel of a material.

3. In the dialog window that has appeared, select an image from your computer to which you would like to apply this material and its object.

4. Take a look in the viewports, and you should see that your texture has not appeared, even though its texture has now been applied to both the material and the object it is assigned to. To rectify this, go to the toolbar section of the *Slate Material Editor* and click the *Show Shaded Material in Viewport* option. To find this button, simply hover over each of the icons and wait for a tooltip to help you out.

TIP

Quickly Applying a Diffuse Texture

You can drag an image from your desktop or a folder straight onto an object in 3ds Max, and it will be applied as a diffuse texture automatically.

You can even use textures to affect the surface of an object, such as the bumpiness of a brick wall. These are called *bump maps*, and you can create one of them by applying a texture to the bump of a material.

NOTE

Creating Textures

You can create textures by using a 2D application such as Adobe Photoshop. In addition, you can use specific 3D programs that allow for the creation of textures directly onto 3D geometry, such as Bodypaint 3D and Mari. Of course, this book focuses only on the use of 3ds Max, so using another application is out of the question!

3ds Max includes a tool called the *Viewport Canvas* that you'll find on the main menu, under *Tools*. This tool allows you to 3D paint directly in the 3ds Max viewport. Although it is a little bit limited in terms of functionality, it does allow you to create textures in 3D. Personally, I recommend using a 2D program rather than this, but the option is there if you'd like to explore it.

Assigning Multiple Materials

In *Polygon* sub-object mode, you can assign multiple materials to objects. This is as easy as creating a few materials, selecting the polygon faces, and assigning specific materials to them. Figure 8.5 shows a blue material and a red material, both of which have been assigned to the same object via the *Polygon* sub-object mode.

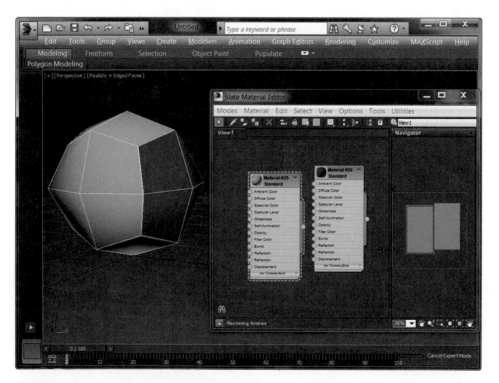

FIGURE 8.5
You can assign multiple materials and texture maps by selecting *Polygon* sub-objects.

You can also use material IDs in conjunction with a *Multi/Sub-Object* material to directly apply various materials to the same object.

Material IDs act as identification numbers for each face or polygon of an object. The *Multi/Sub-Object* material is a special material that allows you to link sub-materials to it. For instance, sub-material 3 would be applied to all polygons with material IDs of *3*. This is super easy to set up, and it's way easier to understand if you just go ahead and do it, so check out the next Try It Yourself.

VIDEO 8.2

Using Material IDs

This video looks at how to use material IDs to assign sub-materials to objects.

TRY IT YOURSELF ▼

Applying Multiple Materials Using Material IDs

You can use the *Multi/Sub-Object* material along with material IDs to specify what polygons get what material for an object. This is relatively simple to do, once you get the hang of it, so try it out:

1. In a fresh scene create a box with *Length*, *Width*, and *Height* all set to *50.0*. Center the box and increase the *Length Segs*, *Width Segs*, and *Height Segs* settings to 5.

2. Right-click the box and choose *Convert To*, *Convert to Editable Poly* to make the box an editable poly object.

3. Open the *Material Editor* (using the shortcut key *M*) and create a *Multi/Sub-Object* material by clicking and dragging the *Multi/Sub-Object* material from the *Material/Map Browser* into the main view (*View1*) area.

4. Double-click the newly created material and in the *Material Parameter Editor* section, find the *Multi/Sub-Object Basic Parameters* rollout and click the *Set Number* button.

5. In the new window, change the *Number of Materials* setting from *10* to *2*, as shown in Figure 8.6, and click *OK*. You now have a *Multi/Sub-Object* material that contains only 2 sub-object materials rather than the default 10 sub-object materials. This should make things a little easier to work with.

FIGURE 8.6
Creating a *Multi/Sub-Object* material and setting the number of sub-object materials to *2* instead of the default *10* makes life a little easier.

6. In the main view area, click and drag from the first circle labeled *(1)*, to a blank area of the screen main view. In the option menu that appears, navigate through *Materials* to *Standard* and click it. Figure 8.7 shows what this looks like.

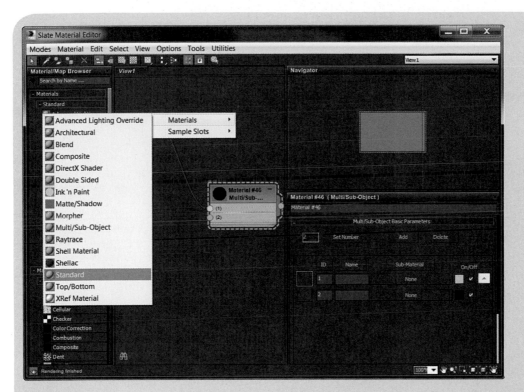

FIGURE 8.7
You click and drag from the circle to an empty area to bring up a menu where you can choose which material you want to assign to the sub-object material slot.

7. You have now created a standard material that is connected to the first *(1)* sub-object material slot of the *Multi/Sub-Object* material. To do the same thing for the second *(2)* sub-object material slot, click and drag from the second *(2)* circle and navigate through *Materials* to *Standard* and click it. You should end up with something that looks like Figure 8.8.

FIGURE 8.8
Two standard materials are now assigned to the two available sub-object material slots of the *Multi/Sub-Object* material.

8. Edit both of the standard materials however you like by double-clicking either of them and editing their parameters. For example, change the *Diffuse* colors to a neon green for sub-object material *(1)* and a neon pink for sub-object material *(2)*.

9. Before assigning the *Multi/Sub-Object* material to the box, assign material IDs to the polygon faces of the object. Back in the main viewport, select the box and enter *Polygon* sub-object mode. You have two sub-object materials to assign to your object, so you need to work with material IDs 1 and 2.

10. Select the polygon faces to which you would like to assign material ID 1. With the polygon faces selected, scroll down through the various rollouts in the *Modify* tab and find the *Polygon: Material IDs* rollout, which is shown in Figure 8.9. This is where you assign the material IDs. So, in the *Set ID* input box type *1* to assign it.

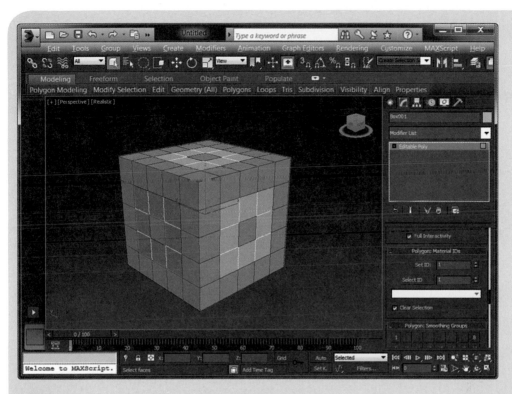

FIGURE 8.9
The *Polygon: Material IDs* rollout is where you assign specific material IDs to selected polygon faces.

11. Now that you have assigned the first ID, select the other polygons you missed last time and follow the same process as in step 10, but changing the ID number to 2.

12. With the material IDs set correctly, you can jump back into the *Material Editor* and assign the *Multi/Sub-Object* material to the box. Do this by making sure you have the box selected in the viewport and then right-clicking the *Multi/Sub-Object* material and choosing the *Assign Material to Selection* option, as shown in Figure 8.10.

FIGURE 8.10
You assign materials to an object by selecting the object and then right-clicking the material and choosing the *Assign Material to Selection* option.

In the viewport, the box object should now have updated with the *Multi/Sub-Object* material assigned to it. If you have set up the material IDs correctly, the box should now have two materials shown. Figure 8.11 shows what the box should look like at this point, and you can take a closer look at the box by opening the file *SAMS_Hour8_IDBox.max*.

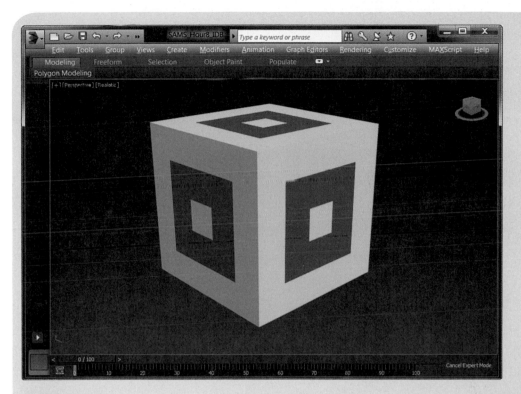

FIGURE 8.11
You have created a multicolored box by using the *Multi/Sub-Object* material.

UVW Mapping

Applying a texture to an object is easy, but defining how a texture is aligned to an object is a little bit more difficult because you can't paint textures directly onto 3D models in the viewport.

UVW mapping refers to the process you use to define how a 2D texture map is aligned to an object. You create these mapping coordinates by using a number of modifiers whose placement you can directly control so that you can successfully map textures to objects.

NOTE

What Is a UVW?

Mapping coordinates are expressed as *U* (horizontal), *V* (vertical), and *W* (depth) dimensions.

Think of *UVW* mapping as an arts-and-crafts exercise. For instance, if you were to make a cube out of a sheet of paper, you would need to sketch out a template, or "net," of the cube first. Then you would fold the net to create the cube. You're doing basically the same thing here, just the other way around. You already have the 3D model, and you need to cut up the geometry and place it onto a flat 2D page to make a template to color and map to our 3D geometry. Figure 8.12 shows a box with a finished texture and UVW map and how the net corresponds to the final textured 3D geometry.

FIGURE 8.12
A box with a finished texture and *UVW* map, including how the net corresponds to the 3D geometry.

You can take a look at this box in 3ds Max by opening the file *SAMS_Hour8_UVWBox.max.*

All this theoretical information can be difficult to understand, so it's time to stop talking about it and jump right into doing something.

Creating the UVW Mapping for a Box

To get used to working with *UVW* mapping, In the following steps you'll create a box and correctly map the box with a texture:

1. Create a box with *Length*, *Width*, and *Height* all set to *50.0* and center it.

2. Select your box and add the *Unwrap UVW* modifier to it.

3. Click the plus (+) button on the *Unwrap UVW* modifier to enable the drop-down menu. Select *Polygon* to drop into a sub object level. Alternatively, click the polygon button in the *Selection* rollout of the *UVW* modifier instead.

4. In the viewport, select every face of the box.

5. Find the *Projection* rollout in the *Unwrap UVW* modifier and click on the *Box Map* option, as shown in Figure 8.13.

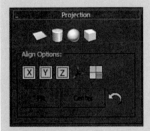

FIGURE 8.13
Inside the *Projection* rollout you can access the *Box Map* option, as well as a few other options.

6. Now that your box has a box map projection, edit the *UVs* by clicking the *Open UV Editor* button under the *Edit UVs* rollout. The *Edit UVWs* window opens up, and you're probably thinking something like, "Oh wow, even more icon buttons to learn! How exciting!" Don't worry; you don't have to learn about all the options here!

7. Click the *Mapping* menu from the top menu in this window. Then click the *Unfold Mapping* option, as shown in Figure 8.14.

FIGURE 8.14
There are way too many options and buttons to talk about in the *Edit UVWs* window. Luckily, you need only a few of these tools for this section.

8. Without changing any of the options in the *Unfold Mapping* window, simply click *OK*. You now have a net of your box laid out in the *Edit UVWs* window, and you need to get it out of 3ds Max and into some kind of 2D image file.

9. In the top menu, click *Tools, Render UVW Template*. Yep, another window opens. The *Render UVs* window allows you to specify the size of the 2D image file you want to output as well as a number of other options.

10. For now, simply click the *Render UV Template* button at the bottom of the *Render UVs* window. Figure 8.15 shows the *Edit UVWs* window, the *Render UVs* window, and the *Render Map* window.

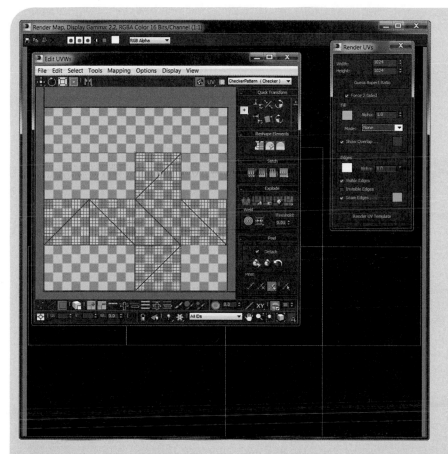

FIGURE 8.15
These are the three windows you have been using in the previous steps.

11. Save your image by clicking the *Save Image* icon at the top of the *Render Map* screen. Choose a format and save the image to a location of your choice. In terms of format, I prefer to use something that can handle alphas, such as PNG. You can now apply the saved image to the *Diffuse* color of a material and to the box. Any changes to that image will be updated in 3ds Max.

As you can see, you need to follow a particular process when creating and applying your own texture maps to an object in 3D. Figure 8.16 shows boxes with various textures applied, using the techniques you just tried.

FIGURE 8.16
You can apply an endless number of texture maps to the same box for different effects.

TIP

UVW Mapping Utopia

Consider these four best practices as you work with *UVW* mapping:

▶ Break your *UVW* map into as few pieces as possible. This makes it easier to understand which part of the model you're working on and gives you fewer seams to deal with.

▶ Minimize stretched areas so that your textures don't distort too heavily.

▶ Avoid overlapping areas because you can't paint two things on the same part of a map (unless you want them to be identical).

▶ Use the space you have available as efficiently as possible.

These best practices are just a guide, and there is no "perfect" *UVW* map. You just have to decide what is needed for a project and balance the time you have against the quality you want.

Summary

In this hour, you've taken a brief look at materials, textures, and *UVW* mapping. You haven't even scratched the surface of these topics but will return to some of them later, when you start building full 3D scenes that require multiple skills and techniques.

Q&A

Q. How can you quickly apply an image as a diffuse texture map?

A. You simply drag an image from your desktop or a folder straight onto an object in the 3D scene to apply it as a diffuse texture map.

Q. Can you use materials without textures?

A. Absolutely! Applying a material to an object does not mean that you need to apply textures to it as well. Sometimes just applying a material and editing its parameters is more than enough to get the look and feel of an object that you desire. However, by adding textures to a material, you can push the visual quality of an object further. Of course this takes a little more time and effort. How you handle this really comes down to how much time you have and the quality you need.

Q. Should you always use the *Box Map* option when creating *UVW* maps?

A. Not at all. You should use the projection option that best suits the needs of your object. Learning and understanding what to use to get the best *UVW* map takes lots of practice and some trial and error. Remember that at this stage, you still have a lot to learn about all aspects of 3ds Max, and you have learned about only the most basic options at this point.

Workshop

Adding materials and textures to 3D objects can enhance the appeal, realism, or stylization of your creations. This workshop should help you expand on what you've already learned.

Quiz

1. What parameter affects the main color of an object?

2. How can you make an object translucent?

3. What does *UVW* represent?

4. What are the two *Material Editor* flavors called?

Answers

1. The *Diffuse* parameter affects the main color of an object.

2. By changing the *Opacity* parameter value to less than 100, you can make an object translucent.

3. *UVW* refers to horizontal (*U*), vertical (*V*), and depth (*W*) dimensions.

4. The *Slate Material Editor* and the *Compact Material Editor* are the two *Material Editor* flavors.

Exercise

Based on what you've learned this hour, try adding a custom material to one of the objects you built in Hour 7, "3D Modeling." Once you have added a custom material to an object, try adjusting some of the parameters to see what effect your changes have on the look of the object. Experiment with a diffuse texture as well.

Using the "Creating the UVW Mapping for a Box" Try It Yourself section as a guide, attempt to correctly *UVW* map a sphere or another standard primitive. If you have access to a 2D program, try to create your own texture for it. Alternatively, test the *Viewport Canvas* tools included with 3ds Max.

HOUR 9
Computer Animation

What You'll Learn In This Hour:

▶ Animation concepts
▶ The 3ds Max animation tools
▶ Creating animation in 3ds Max
▶ Pivot points and their relevance to 3D

3ds Max gives you the ability to create amazing 3D computer animation for output into pretty much any digital media you can think of. Film, TV, video games, visualization, and technical product demonstrations come to mind right away, but there are many more industries and outputs where our 3D animations are needed.

This hour provides an overview of the world of 3ds Max animation and the tools it provides for giving motion to static objects.

Basic Animation Concepts

Animation boils down to a series of related still images shown quickly in sequence. Our eyes and brains are tricked by the quick succession of these images, and we perceive these still images to be continuous motion. This illusion is what we call *animation*, and each image we see in an animation is referred to as a *frame*.

You can animate just about anything in 3ds Max, and you do so by giving 3ds Max *keyframes* it can interpolate between. Keyframes are the "key" moments of a movement or an animation. For instance, the starting position and ending position of an animation would be keyframes. The interpolations between the keyframes are referred to simply as *frames*. When you use 3ds Max, you have complete control over all these different animation elements.

The term *computer animation* covers a wide variety of animation topics, from character animation to effects animation. There are just two main categories of computer animation:

▶ **2D animation**—2D, or two-dimensional, animation is the more "traditional" animation. Back in the day, 2D animation was created with pencils, paper, and paint. Thanks to computerization, 2D animations have been digitized.

▶ **3D animation**—3D, or three-dimensional, animation is created in a virtual 3D space like the one in 3ds Max.

Both of these types of computer animation use the same basic animation concepts, but they are accomplished using drastically different methods and various programs and applications.

Animation in 3ds Max

3ds Max is a 3D application, so it makes sense that the animation that you create in this program is 3D animation.

By using this program, you can create 3D computer animation for a variety of uses. For animating characters and vehicles for a video game, or creating visual effects for a film, or even making molecular illustrations for the medical industry, you have everything you need right here, all in 3ds Max.

The animation tools in 3ds Max are pretty incredible. You basically need to turn on *Auto Key* mode, move the time slider, and change the position, rotation, or scale attributes of an object over time. This gives you animation. In fact, you can actually animate just about any parameter or setting that affects an object's shape or surface in 3ds Max. You're going to take a more in-depth look into these tools in just a moment, but first you need to understand frames and their relationship to time. Read on!

Comparing Frames to Time

Frames and time are two separate things, but they are closely connected. The number of frames needed for each second of animation is called *frames per second* (*FPS*). The number of frames per second that are needed varies, depending on what the animation will be used for. In fact, the terms *frames per second*, *frame rate*, and *frame frequency* apply equally well to video cameras, computer animation, video players, and even motion capture systems.

If you are working in the entertainment industry, and in particular for film (cinema, and so on) or TV, it is good to know that the location where your animation will be broadcast will have an effect on the number of frames per second you will need. For example, the following are examples of fps rates for 1 second of animation:

▶ The traditional film (cinema, movie, tape) rate = 24 fps

▶ NTSC (National Television System Committee) standard (the format used in the United States and Canada) = 30 fps

▶ PAL (Phase Alternating Line) standard (the format used in Australia, parts of Asia, and some European countries) = 25 fps

The reasons for these differences come down to a number of technical reasons that are beyond the scope of this book. There is plenty of information out there on the Internet, of course, so if you are interested in the technical side of why the differences in FPS, then by all means take some time to research it.

Even if you don't really need to know the technical reasons for the FPS changes, you do have to understand in which broadcast locations these rules apply.

At its most basic, the film rate (24 fps) is what you see in most theaters throughout the world. More recently there have been experiments with different frame rates, but generally, we still use the tried-and-tested 24 frames per second in movie theaters.

Interestingly, video games don't pay too much attention to these "rules." Instead, the frame rates for a video game are dictated by the game development team and project. As I write this, frame rates between 30 and 60 fps are considered acceptable by most, but they can vary significantly from game to game. In fact, some games can run well in excess of 100 fps, although the frame rate within a game changes depending on what is happening at any given moment, or even with the hardware configuration the game is running on.

Again, the frame rate in video games is another technical aspect that this hour doesn't get into. After all, you do want to animate something eventually, right?

The Animation Tools

3ds Max provides many animation tools, and as you get more involved with computer animation, your need to use these tools increases (I know, that is kind of obvious). When working with animation in a 3D program, you use specific frames to set "keys" that define specific and definitive movements to your objects; these are known as "keyframes"—key frames of animation that set key movements! This will all start to make more sense as you use the animation tools and start animating for yourself.

As you get started, these are the main tools you'll need:

▶ **The time slider and track bar**—Below the viewports, you'll find the time slider and track bar combination (see Figure 9.1). The time slider allows you to slide around time, like a DJ with a turntable, scratch pad, and some vinyl. You can slide through the timeline (that is, "scrub") with ease. Keyframes are displayed in the track bar, and you can select them, move them, and delete them as needed.

FIGURE 9.1
You scrub through the timeline with the time slider, and you edit keyframes with the track bar.

▶ **Playback controls**—Figure 9.2 shows the playback controls, which are found in the bottom-right corner of the 3ds Max UI. The playback controls are very similar to those on a VCR...or DVR, if you're younger...or some other fancy playback device if you're too young for both of those examples. The playback controls in 3ds Max are pretty self-explanatory. You can play, stop, go to the start or end, and do a lot of the other things you're used to doing with a remote control. Oh, and this is the area where you can find the button to keyframe things.

FIGURE 9.2
The playback controls in 3ds Max are simple and elegant.

▶ **The track view**—The track view consists of the *Curve Editor* and *Dope Sheet*. You find them in the *Graph Editor* menu, which is accessible at the top of the UI on the main menu. These two graph-based editors allow you to view and modify existing animation data in your scenes. Figure 9.3 shows these editors.

▶ ***Motion* tab and *Hierarchy* tab**—These two tabs, which are found on the *Command Panel*, are pretty useful when you're working with animation objects, but they are a little more advanced than you need right now. The *Motion* tab allows you to adjust transform controllers that affect position, rotation, and scale animation. The *Hierarchy* tab gives you access to parameters that govern the linkage of two or more objects as well as pivot point adjustments. (You'll learn more about this in just a bit!)

NOTE

Many More Animation Tools

3ds Max has a lot more animation tools than are listed here. Check out the rest of the options in the *Graph Editors* menu, and don't forget that the *Animation* menu holds some great tools related to animation.

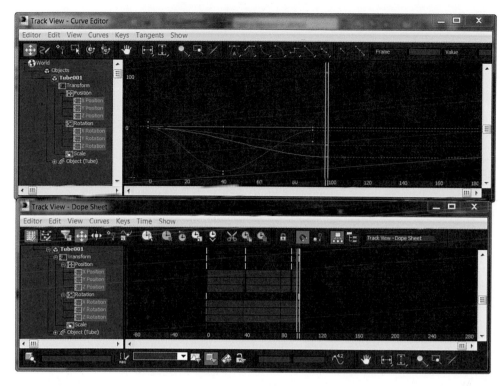

FIGURE 9.3
The *Curve Editor* and *Dope Sheet* are two graph-based editors that can really help 3D animators refine their animations.

First Steps into Animation

You could do a massive amount of theoretical study (and probably should) before undertaking any kind of animation, but time is often not a luxury that you have. So, against my better judgment, I'm going to have you skip to the good stuff and actually animate something now!

VIDEO 9.1

Basic Animations

This video shows how to create a standard primitive and describes some of the animation basics in 3ds Max.

▼ TRY IT YOURSELF

Creating a Basic Animation

You need to wrap your head around some basic animation techniques before you can create the next Hollywood animated blockbuster. Follow these steps to get started:

1. In a new scene, create a box with *Length*, *Width*, and *Height* settings of *50.0* and position it at the world center ([0,0,0]).

2. In the lower toolbar turn on *Auto Key* mode by clicking the *Auto* button. The interface is highlighted red to indicate that *Auto Key* is enabled. As long as you have *Auto Key* enabled, 3ds Max automatically creates keyframes for you as you manipulate the object.

3. With your box selected and your time slider set to frame 0, click the *Key Icon* button to set your first keyframe for this animation, as shown in Figure 9.4.

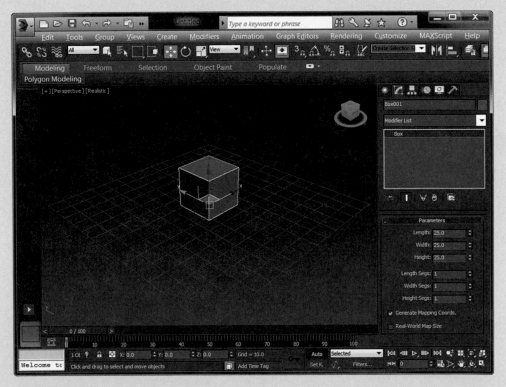

FIGURE 9.4
This is your first keyframe in 3ds Max! Notice that the interface is highlighted red to remind you that you have *Auto Key* enabled.

4. Move the time slider along to *50* (frames) and manipulate the box by using the *Move, Rotate*, and *Scale* tools.

5. Move the time slider to *100* (frames) and manipulate the box once more.

6. When you're finished animating, click the Auto button again to turn off *Auto Key*.

7. Scrub the timeline by sliding the time slider back and forth to see what your manipulations have created.

You should now have some animation right in front of you; it might look similar to my animation, shown in Figure 9.5. Remember that you can use the playback controls to see what the animation looks like when you are not scrubbing the timeline.

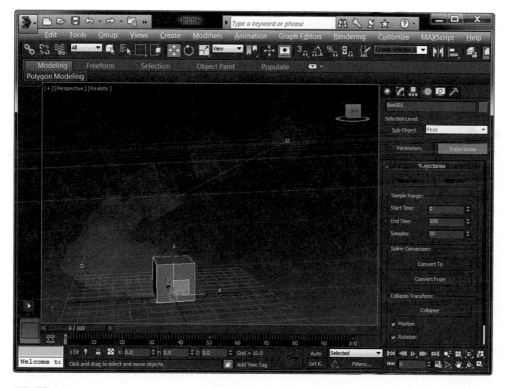

FIGURE 9.5
You just created some basic animation by using the time slider, *Auto Key*, the *Key Icon* button, and standard object manipulation tools.

CAUTION

Turn Off Auto Key!

When you're done animating, it is important that you turn off *Auto Key* mode because leaving it turned on will make 3ds Max keyframe things that you wish it hadn't.

This is a great opportunity for you to experiment with the manipulation of keyframes and using the *Curve Editor* to control animation that has already been created. After all, it's something that you're going to have to get accustomed to if you're working with 3D animation!

VIDEO 9.2

Teeny Car Animation

This video goes through editing keyframes and working with the *Curve Editor* to change some preexisting teeny car animations.

▼ TRY IT YOURSELF

Editing Keyframes and Working with the Curve Editor

By using keyframes and the *Curve Editor*, you can edit and manipulate existing animations to better suit your needs. The following steps introduce you to a new way of thinking about animation:

1. In a new scene, open the file *SAMS_Hour9_CarsStart.max*. Here you have five cars, each with two keyframes—one at the starting position, and one at the end. If you click the *Play* button or scrub the time slider, each car starts and stops at exactly the same time. This isn't exciting by any means, but it saves you from having to create your own animation for editing. Starting with this preexisting animation, you can edit the keyframes and work with the *Curve Editor* to learn how to edit animations.

2. Select the blue car and open the *Curve Editor*, which you find on the main toolbar (see the highlighted area in Figure 9.6). The *Curve Editor* allows you to see and edit the various animation curves for each transform, animated on a handy graph. Because you have already selected the blue car, you can see the animation curves for each of the animated transforms for it. Notice that you have all the position, rotation, and scale attributes selected on the left side, and their animation curves are shown on the right side. You can select specific attributes on the left side, and their animation curves appear on the right side.

3. At the moment, all the attributes are selected on the left, but you only need to work on one animation curve right now, so in the left side of the *Curve Editor*, click the *Y Position* attribute. The right side of the *Curve Editor* updates to display just a green line that represents the *Y Position* animation curve. Grab the small boxes (which are the tangents) at the beginning and end of the line to select them and drag this line around.

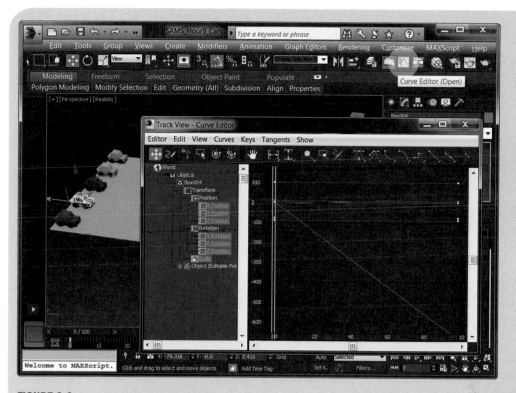

FIGURE 9.6
The *Curve Editor* is easy to access from the main toolbar.

4. With the tangents of the *Y Position* animation curve selected, click the *Set Tangents to Auto* button on the main toolbar of the *Curve Editor* (see the highlighted button in Figure 9.7). Notice that the animation curve tangents change after you click this button. Do you notice that when you set the tangents to auto, some little blue handles appear out from the tangents? Well these little guys allow you to edit the animation curve.

5. Go to your viewport and click the *Play* button to see how you have changed the animation of the blue car. You should notice that the little guy is now a slow starter, speeds past the other cars midway through, and slows down at the end. Interesting!

6. Now grab the green car and repeat steps 2 to 5 so that its animation is identical to that of the blue car.

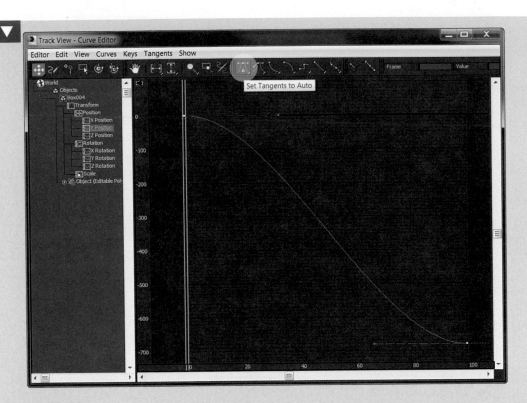

FIGURE 9.7
By clicking the *Set Tangents to Auto* button on the main toolbar, you set the tangents to auto, which affects the animation curve. In turn, it affects the animation that is shown in the viewport.

7. Grab the first tangent handle for the green car and move it downward, as I have done in Figure 9.8. To take a look at what this has done to the animation of the green car, click the *Play* button in your viewport. The little green car now shoots out at super speed from the start and then slows until the end, just like the blue car. Awesome, huh? Now both the green and blue cars have their own specific animations, and you only had to edit some animation curves.

8. Now, using the same techniques, grab the yellow, red, and pink cars and edit their animation curves by using the *Curve Editor*. Take some time to try out the other tangent options and see how your changes affect the animation. (Compare what you end up with to the file *SAMS_Hour9_CarsEdit.max*.) Your cars should now all have different animations; however, the cars still start and stop all at the same time because their keyframes take place on frames 0 and 100. You could change this by moving the tangents in the *Curve Editor*, but you can also do this from the time slider area.

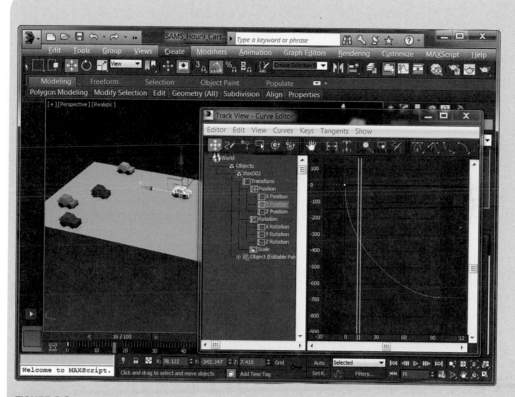

FIGURE 9.8
You can edit the animation curves more accurately by using the tangent handles.

9. Select the pink car, which has keyframes at frame 0 and frame 100. Click and drag the keyframe from frame 0 and to frame 8. Play the animation now and notice that the pink car does not start its animation until frame 8.

10. Edit the start and end keyframes for each of the cars. Get the cars to start and end at different frames, and you should get a more interesting animation. You can check out my final animation by opening the file *SAMS_Hour9_CarsEnd.max*.

Pivot Points

A *pivot point* is the central point of an object—the position around which an object always rotates. Think of a see-saw. It is attached to a support in the center, and this support acts as the pivot point.

Every object you create in 3ds Max has a pivot point that represents its local center and local coordinate system. The pivot point is the transform center for an object; it dictates the location from which you animate, where the rotation takes place, and to and from where a scale occurs.

You can use pivot points for a number of purposes, and they are incredibly important for animation. These are the main uses for pivot points:

▶ A central point for movement, rotation, and scaling.

▶ The default location of a modifier's center.

▶ The transform origin for linked children in a hierarchy.

▶ The joint location for inverse kinematics (IK).

You can display and adjust the position and orientation of an object's pivot point in the *Hierarchy* tab on the *Command Panel*.

VIDEO 9.3
_____

Working with Pivot Points

This video takes a look at pivot points and how they affect object transformations.

_____

These terms may seem a little abstract at the moment, but you will learn all you need to know about pivot points, hierarchies, and IK in Hour 14, "Rigging Objects for Easier Animation." However, that doesn't mean you shouldn't take some time right now to get started with using pivot points, so take a look at the file *SAMS_Hour9_PivotPoints.max*. This file contains five boxes, and each of them has had its pivot point edited in the *Hierarchy* panel. Grab each box and use the *Rotate* tool to check out how the pivot point can drastically affect an object's manipulation.

Summary

This hour, you have briefly jumped into the world of animation. After taking a quick look at some of the animation concepts, you looked over the various animation tools available in 3ds Max. You put these tools to good use and created your very own animation. It's a very basic animation, but it's a step in the right direction.

Next, you used the *Curve Editor* to edit a preexisting animation and drastically change the look of similar animations into something new. You will be using what you have learned here during Hour 16, "Character Animation," when you return to the world of animation and apply these tools and techniques to character animation. Remember that you can apply animation to just about anything and everything in 3ds Max, so keep experimenting and take these fundamentals with you on your journey!

Q&A

Q. How do frames relate to seconds?

A. An animation has a frame rate that expresses the number of frames that appear in 1 second. As a rule of thumb, you generally use 24 frames for each second of animation in film, 30 for NTSC format, and 25 for PAL format.

Q. What can you animate in 3ds Max?

A. You can animate pretty much anything and everything in 3ds Max.

Q. Is it possible to do 2D computer animation in 3ds Max?

A. The short answer is no. However, you can "fake" 2D animation inside the 3D world by keeping your animation on a two-dimensional plane, as if you're looking through an orthographic camera. You are still animating in a 3D world, so technically you will still produce 3D computer animation, even though it may look 2D.

Workshop

Animation can take a lifetime to master, and this hour only lightly scuffs the very deep surface of what is possible. This small workshop should help you put the concepts and techniques you've learned into practice.

Quiz

1. What is another name for a *frame* of animation?

2. What does *fps* stand for in relation to animation?

3. During this hour you edited some preexisting animation. What are the two techniques you used to do it?

Answers

1. A still image is a frame of animation; multiple related still images (frames) create the illusion of animation.

2. Fps stands for frames per second.

3. You used the *Curve Editor* in conjunction with moving keyframes to edit preexisting animation.

Exercise

In this hour you spent some time editing preexisting animation on some teeny cars. Take what you learned in that exercise and apply it to something you create yourself. Open your spaceship model from Hour 7, "3D Modeling," and add some flying animation to it. You could even model an environment for your spaceship to fly around in, or at least add some standard primitives that represent an environment.

When you're done with the animation on your spaceship, use the *Curve Editor* to edit your created animation to perfection. Try adding something like a *Noise* modifier to your spaceship model to see how it affects your animation.

HOUR 10
Illuminating Scenes Using Lights

What You'll Learn in This Hour:

▶ An introduction to lighting in 3ds Max

▶ Lighting and shadow basics

▶ Accessing and changing ambient light

▶ Standard versus photometric lighting

▶ Lighting scenes in 3ds Max

You are able to see an object because light reflects from the object into your eyes, which send the data to your brain so it can process the data and form an image. You can't see without light—honest! Just as in nature, illumination in 3ds Max happens through a complex interaction of lights and objects.

Light can come from a number of sources, the most obvious being the sun, our source of natural lighting, and from bulbs, which handle our real-world artificial lighting. It makes sense, then, that 3ds Max also provides a number of lighting options that allow you to replicate both natural and artificial lighting within scenes.

This hour, you are going to take a look at the various lighting options available to you and how you can use them to illuminate your 3D worlds and scenes.

3ds Max Lighting Introduction

Lights in the real world allow you to see things, and the lights in 3ds Max do exactly the same thing. In addition, you can assign qualities to the lighting tools available in 3ds Max to enable them to cast shadows, project images, and even manipulate the atmospheric lighting effects.

The basic lighting tools are located in the default creation area in 3ds Max—the *Create* tab of the *Command Panel*. The *Lights* category is the third icon from the left, which looks like a studio spotlight; this category is home to the lighting tools.

Two main subcategories of lights are available: standard lights and photometric lights. You can create lights just as you do any other objects, and you can also transform them by using the *Move*, *Rotate*, and *Scale* tools.

Before you jump in and start creating lights, it's important that you know that 3ds Max automatically provides a default lighting setup when you start the program. Read on to learn more.

Default Lighting

3ds Max provides you with default lighting if you have not specified (created) any lights yourself. This allows you to view any objects you create without having to worry about lighting the scene first. The default lights disappear as soon as another light is created, and they magically reappear if all other lights in the scene are deleted.

Shadows

Shadows are areas where light is obstructed by an object, causing a darker area than its surroundings. 3ds Max supports various types of shadow-casting options, and unlike in real life, you have the ability to make only some lights cast shadows and others not. Work through the following Try It Yourself to get a taste of this.

▼ TRY IT YOURSELF

Casting Shadows Using Default Lighting

Follow these steps to see how the default lighting in 3ds Max casts shadows on objects you create:

1. In a new scene, create a plane (a standard primitive, not an aircraft).

2. Create a sphere.

3. Move the sphere around to see how the default lighting in 3ds Max casts shadows onto objects.

Ambient Light

Ambient light is general lighting that affects an entire scene; it is also called global ambient. It has no source or direction but affects everything in a scene uniformly. Because ambient light has an effect on everything, you can use it to your advantage to create a specific atmosphere or simply to adjust the overall color of a scene.

Figure 10.1 shows the *Environment and Effects* window, where you can manually adjust the ambient light for a scene.

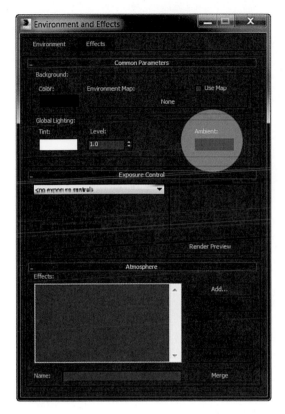

FIGURE 10.1
The *Environment and Effects* window gives you access to the ambient light properties for each scene.

NOTE

Changing the Global Ambient Light Settings

You can press the *8* key to bring up the *Environment and Effects* window, where you can adjust the *Ambient* setting. Alternatively, you can open this window by selecting *Rendering, Environment* from the main menu.

TRY IT YOURSELF ▼

Changing and Manipulating the Global Ambient Light Settings

It is incredibly simple to change the *Global Lighting* options in a 3ds Max scene, and these steps show you how to do just that:

1. In a new scene, create some standard primitives or simply open a scene that you have worked on previously that includes some geometry.

2. Open the *Environment and Effects* window by either pressing the *8* key on your keyboard or selecting *Rendering, Environment* from the main menu. As shown in Figure 10.1, the *Environment and Effects* window contains two tabs that separate the *Environment and Effects* options. You need to worry about only the first tab (*Environment*) for now.

3. Ensure that the *Environment* tab is open and find the *Common Parameters* rollout, which should be right at the top. The first section of this rollout contains options for changing and affecting the background of the main scene.

4. Scroll down the *Common Parameters* rollout until you come to the *Global Lighting* options.

5. Find the *Tint* option under *Global Lighting* and click the white square to bring up a color picker.

6. Manipulate and choose a color by using the color picker. Notice that your scene objects are tinted in the color you are choosing. As you can see, changing this color can have a dramatic effect on the visual look of a scene.

7. Change the *Level* option in this section to intensify or decrease the effect that the tint has on the scene. Also try out the *Ambient* option, which behaves just like the *Tint* effect. (The effect of the *Ambient* option is hard to see in your viewports, but you can see it in renders quite easily. You'll learn about renders and rendering in Hour 12, "Rendering for Production," so make a note of where this ambient light setting is so you can find it again in a few hours.)

Standard Lights

These standard lights are the "standard" lighting solution available for 3ds Max. Yeah, I know, you kind of worked that one out for yourself, didn't you? These lights are truly "3D" lights—that is, they are created in 3D (of course), but they have no comparison to real-world lighting solutions. Sure, a spotlight is something that you know from the real world, but the spotlight solution available in the *Standard Lights* list doesn't compare to any real-world parameters. This might not seem like a big deal right now, but when you start having to think about realistic lighting solutions and how the temperature of a light affects its color, you'll see that these real-world parameters would come in pretty handy!

To create lights in 3ds Max, you have to head over to the *Create* tab, just as we usually do when you want to create something. In the *Create* tab, under the *Lights* category, we see two subcategories, *Standard* and *Photometric*, as shown in Figure 10.2.

The *Standard* subcategory in 3ds Max give you a few good options to choose from:

▶ **Target Spot** and **Free Spot**—Spotlights cast a resizable beam of light either toward a target or in a general direction.

▶ *Target Direct* and *Free Direct*—Direct lights cast parallel rays of light in a single direction, just like the sun. You can target these rays to a specific direction or simply rotate the *Free Direct* version.

▶ *Omni*—Omni lights cast rays in all directions from a single source, just like a real-world light bulb. In fact, the default lighting uses two of these omni lights in its setup.

▶ *Skylight*—The skylight replicates daytime lighting for your scene.

▶ *mr Area Omni* and *mr Area Spot*—These two lights are similar to the omni and spotlights you've already seen; however, you use them specifically when you're using the Mental Ray (mr) rendering system. If I were you, I would just forget about these lights for the moment, until you dip your feet into Mental Ray rendering in Hour 20, "Mental Ray Rendering."

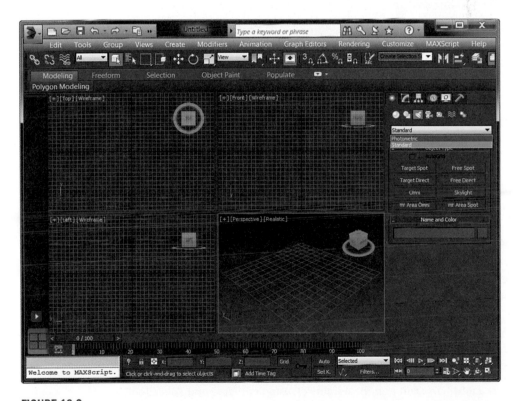

FIGURE 10.2
Standard lighting is available in the *Lights* category on the *Create* tab. There are eight standard lights to choose from!

Figure 10.3 shows the options available in the *Standard* subcategory.

FIGURE 10.3
The *Standard* subcategory offers a total of eight lighting options.

Photometric Lights

Choosing the *Photometric* subcategory limits the number of different lights you can create. However, unlike the lights in the *Standard* subcategory, lights in the *Photometric* subcategory behave like real-world lighting solutions.

The photometric lights have settings that relate directly to real-world light measurement values, such as *Intensity* and *Temperature*. These values are often easiest to understand if you're used to a bit of DIY or just general real-world lighting, although using them can take a little more time to set up correctly than using the standard lighting options. However, 3ds Max comes with a number of templates that can help you out, and they make it as easy as choosing *40W Bulb* for a 40-watt bulb. Nice!

These are the options in the *Photometric* subcategory:

▶ **Target Light**—You can aim a target light at a specified target, using the target sub-object provided with this light.

▶ **Free Light**—You can aim these lights by using the *Move* and *Rotate* tools.

▶ **mr Sky Portal**—Once again, this is a Mental Ray–specific lighting option, and I advise you to leave it alone for now as it's a little too complex for your 3ds Max experience.

Figure 10.4 shows the few options you have available in the *Photometric* subcategory.

FIGURE 10.4
You have only three options available when you use the *Photometric* subcategory, but they allow you to use real-world lighting measurements.

Adding Lights to a Scene

Now that you know about both the standard and photometric lighting solutions, as well as some background on shadows and ambient light, you can start lighting your scenes. In fact, creating a light is as simple as clicking the button for the light you want, clicking in the scene, and changing some options. Give it a go!

VIDEO 10.1

Creating a Flashlight Beam

This video shows you how to create a flashlight beam, using the *Omni* and *Free Spot* standard lights.

TRY IT YOURSELF ▼

Using Standard Lights to Create a Flashlight Beam

Creating standard lights is incredibly simple. In the following steps, you will use a spotlight to create a beam of light that is emitted from a flashlight:

1. Open the file *SAMS_Hour10_TorchStart.max*. In this scene, a battery-operated flashlight is pointed directly at a gray wall. You need to add lights so that the flashlight illuminates the wall as you would expect.

2. On the *Create* tab, click the *Lights* category, and then move to the *Standard* subcategory. You will use a spotlight for the flashlight.

3. Click the *Free Spot* button and then click once in the scene to create it. Right-click to end the creation process. (If you don't right-click, you'll be creating spotlights.) By adding a spotlight to the scene, you force 3ds Max to remove the default lighting setup that it usually uses. This leaves your scene completely dark. However, if you move and rotate the spotlight around, you should notice that it now casts light. You need to position the spotlight correctly, but it's going to be a little difficult to do that with the scene being in total darkness.

4. Open the *Create* tab once again, and in the *Lights* category, stay in the *Standard* subcategory and click the *Omni* button. Click in the scene to create an omni light. Your scene brightens up once again.

5. Position your spotlight as shown in Figure 10.5.

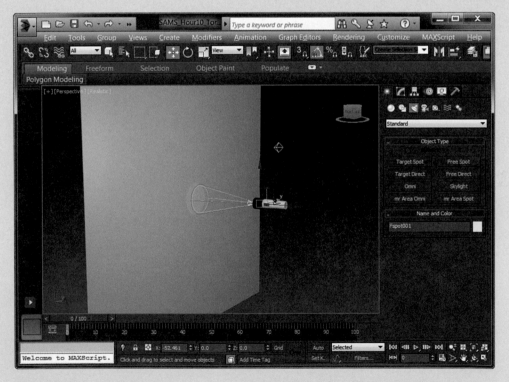

FIGURE 10.5
The spotlight is correctly positioned in the scene so that it illuminates from the flashlight beam.

6. With the lights in place, edit some of their parameters to improve the look of the scene. Click the omni light in the scene and then open the *Modify* tab.

7. Scroll down and expand the *Intensity/Color/Attenuation* rollout so that you have access to the *Multiplier* parameter. Change the *Multiplier* setting to *0.1*. This makes the scene a little darker than it was before.

8. In the viewport, click the spotlight and open the *Modify* tab.

9. Scroll down the *Modify* tab and expand the *Intensity/Color/Attenuation* rollout. Time change the *Multiplier* parameter to *5.0*. This should make the spotlight super bright.

10. Still in the *Modify* tab, find and expand the *Spotlight Parameters* rollout. Change the *Horspot/Beam* parameter to *1.0*. Also change the *Falloff/Field* parameter to 95.0. You should now have something that looks a little like Figure 10.6.

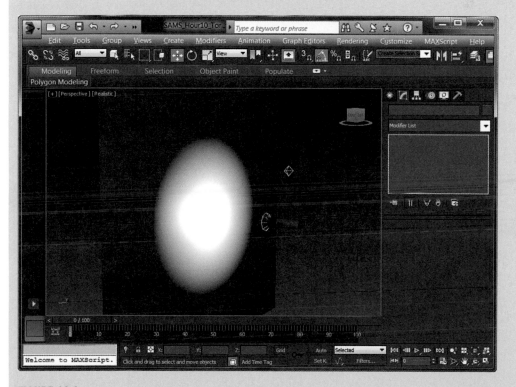

FIGURE 10.6
By editing the lighting parameters, you have enhanced the look of the scene and the spotlight beam of the flashlight.

11. As an optional step, use the *Select and Link* tool (the first button on the main toolbar) to link the spotlight to the yellow section of the flashlight. To do this, you grab hold of the yellow flashlight section and use the *Move* and *Rotate* tools to manipulate the flashlight and the light. Be sure to check out the final flashlight file, *SAMS_Hour10_TorchEnd.max*, for an example.

CAUTION

Don't Go Lighting Crazy!

With each light you add to a scene, the computational costs of the scene increase. Got one or just a few lights in your scene? No problem! Got way too many lights? At best, your scene's performance will suffer. In a worst-case scenario, it could crash 3ds Max or possibly your whole computer system. Adding another light to a scene increases the calculations 3ds Max has to do. I'm not saying you shouldn't use as many lights as you need. Just be aware that there are some limitations in terms of performance at a system level.

Summary

Lighting can really impact the visual appeal of a scene you are working with. This hour covers the lighting options in 3ds Max, and you've even tried out some lighting for yourself. You should be armed with enough skills and information to be able to light your own scenes way better than the default lighting does.

Q&A

Q. Why is lighting so important in 3D?

A. In 3D, just like in the real world, lighting can have a dramatic effect on both the look and feel of a scene or environment. It can help set the tone and mood for a whole animation or just a single still frame.

Q. Why are there two subcategories, *Standard* and *Photometric*, for lighting in 3ds Max?

A. Photometric lights contain real-world parameters, which can be a little daunting for those new to lighting in 3d Max; however, using them is the preferred method for lighting more realistic or explicitly lit scenes. Standard lights give you non-real-world parameters that are easier to use and can still give great effect, but in a less-daunting way. In general, photometric lights are more complex but give more accuracy, and standard lights are simpler to use but require more trial and error to get something to look exactly how you want it to.

Q. **How many lights can you add to a scene?**

A. It depends on your computer's hardware. Each light you add increases the calculations that 3ds Max has to perform. The more lights you have in a scene, the longer it takes for the calculations to complete. With better hardware, 3ds Max can do more calculations, but there will always be a limit to the calculations a computer system can do. A good rule of thumb is to use the lowest number of lights possible to achieve the results you are looking for.

Workshop

Lighting can dramatically improve the look and feel of a scene. This workshop asks a few questions that you should now be able to answer, and it includes an exercise that challenges you to create a lighting setup that requires the use of photometric lights.

Quiz

1. When is the 3ds Max default lighting available?

2. What does ambient light do?

3. What are shadows?

4. What two lighting subcategories are available in 3ds Max?

Answers

1. The default lighting is available in 3ds Max when the program starts or when no other lights are in the scene.

2. Ambient light controls the overall lighting for a whole scene.

3. Shadows are areas where light is obstructed by an object, causing an area to be darker than its surroundings.

4. 3ds Max provides standard and photometric lighting options.

Exercise

Getting used to photometric lights can take a little while, and the small number of creation options may seem limiting at first. However, their real-world parameters can make the application of these kinds of lights a better choice for more realistic or precise lighting simulations.

Open the file *SAMS_Hour10_StreetLighting.max* and light the scene using only photometric lights. Try creating a day scene and a night scene, which both have different challenges. This will give you a greater understanding of how lighting can dramatically affect the mood of a scene.

Adding and Editing 3D Cameras

What You'll Learn in This Hour:

- ▶ Camera basics
- ▶ An introduction to 3ds Max cameras
- ▶ Creating and viewing cameras
- ▶ Adjusting camera lenses and options
- ▶ Animating cameras

If you want to create your own movie in the real world, you have to invest in a camera so that you can record the action and show those recordings to others. When you're using 3D to create a movie, you also need a camera so that you can show others what you have created.

This hour covers the creation and use of cameras within a 3D scene. Cameras in the real world and cameras in 3ds Max have the same characteristics, and if you're into photography or videography, then you will probably find the terms in this hour familiar.

Camera-Based Concepts

A camera shows a scene from a specific point of view (POV), just like a viewport in 3ds Max does. With 3ds Max, the POV is the angle from which your audience views your scenes.

3ds Max gives you access to both a target camera and a free camera, and these cameras, just like real-world cameras, have "lenses" that change the field of view (FOV) when you look through them. Much like the photometric lighting solutions you looked at last hour, 3ds Max's cameras come with some stock lenses that mimic real-world camera lenses (see Figure 11.1), giving you some quick-access presets to work with.

There are many options available to you for both of the available cameras, including effects such as depth of field and motion blur, which can enhance the visual appeal of your 3D scenes (see Figure 11.2).

6mm

18mm–200mm

FIGURE 11.1
Stock lenses included with the cameras in 3ds Max mimic real-world lenses and provide handy templates for you to work from.

FIGURE 11.2
Depth of field is a handy camera effect that blurs out-of-focus areas to draw attention to particular areas of a scene.

3ds Max Cameras

In 3ds Max, you can create cameras directly by going to the *Create* tab and clicking the *Cameras* category. Although the *Cameras* category has a drop-down menu for subcategories, you actually only have access to the *Standard* subcategory cameras, which include two options:

▶ *Target Camera*—You can aim a target camera at a specific area in 3D space, or at a specific object. This allows you to easily keep focus on a specific point in a 3D scene even while moving the camera.

▶ *Free Camera*—You use a free camera to view the area where the camera is aimed. Because there is no target for this type of camera, you are free to manipulate it as you like.

Figure 11.3 shows both of these types of 3ds Max cameras.

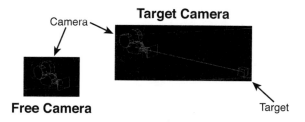

FIGURE 11.3
A target camera and a free camera, as displayed in the viewports of 3ds Max.

These camera objects are representations of the cameras that you have created. They are visible to you in the viewports unless you specifically choose not to display them. They are there to act as a visual guide to show you where a camera is located and how it is oriented. These representative icons are not actually visible once you render your scenes for display to an audience. (You'll learn more about renders and rendering in Hour 12, "Rendering for Production.")

VIDEO 11.1

3ds Max Camera Basics
This video covers the basic creation, manipulation, and viewing of cameras.

▼ TRY IT YOURSELF

Creating and Viewing Cameras

Creating and viewing cameras in 3ds Max is pretty simple, but it requires you to adjust your viewport layouts to accommodate the new views that you are creating. Follow these steps to see what I mean:

1. Open *SAMS_Hour11_CityScene.max* or another scene of your choice, as long as it includes some geometry that you can focus on.

2. Open the *Create* tab and select the *Cameras* category. Choose *Free* and add this camera to your scene by clicking in a viewport. Right-click after the camera is created to exit creation mode.

3. Use the *Move* and *Rotate* tools to position the camera in such a way that it is aimed toward the geometry.

4. Choose a viewport that will be your camera view and click the viewport name. In the drop-down menu, go to *Cameras* and choose the name of the camera that you just created (which should be *Camera001* if it is the first camera in your scene). The view changes so that you can see through the lens of that camera, as shown in Figure 11.4.

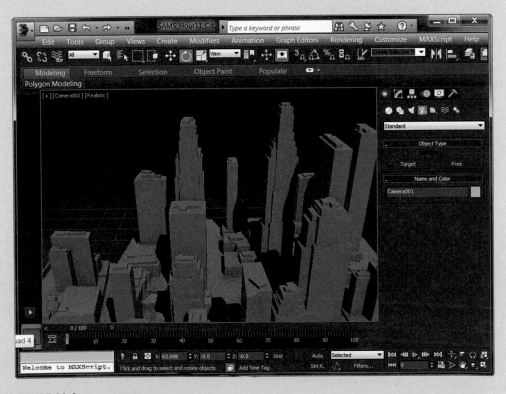

FIGURE 11.4
You can now see exactly what the camera sees!

TIP

Changing a Viewport to a Camera View

You can use the default keyboard shortcut *C* to display a camera view in the viewport. If you have more than one camera in your scene, a handy pop-up window appears, allowing you to select which camera you want to view.

Now that you know how to create a camera, you have access to all the options that are available when working with the selected camera. As you might guess, you can find those options by selecting the camera and opening the *Modify* tab.

TIP

Creating a Camera from Your Current Viewport

By pressing *Ctrl+C*, you can automatically create a camera that matches the view of your currently active viewport. This is a quick and easy method to create cameras from the viewport you are currently looking through!

Interestingly, both the free camera and target camera share exactly the same rollouts and parameters. You can even switch between types of camera by using the *Type* drop-down menu, as shown in Figure 11.5.

FIGURE 11.5
The parameters for both target and free cameras are identical. You can even change which type of camera you are currently using by using the *Type* drop-down menu.

Also in Figure 11.5 you can see the *Stock Lenses* section. In this area, you can click a specific lens, and it will be instantly applied to your camera, which is super helpful to say the least. The size of the lens you choose to use can drastically change how you view your 3D scenes through the camera. It's worth noting that the smaller the lens size, the wider the angle of view, and the larger the lens size, the narrower the view.

▼ TRY IT YOURSELF

Adjusting Camera Options

With cameras created in a scene, you can access and edit their options and parameters as well as change the camera lens to get the best look for a shot. Follow these steps to try it out:

1. Open the file *SAMS_Hour11_CityScene.max* once again.

2. Manipulate the *Perspective* viewport until you find an interesting shot from the current viewport. Figure 11.6 should give you an idea of what I mean.

FIGURE 11.6
An interesting shot in the *Perspective* viewport.

3. Create a camera from this view by using the default keyboard shortcut *Ctrl+C*.

4. Now that you have a camera created and are currently looking through it, open the *Modify* tab and check out the *Stock Lenses* section in the *Parameters* rollout. Click through each of the various *Stock Lenses* options and see how the size of each lens affects what the camera sees.

5. After you've had some fun checking out the stock lenses, pick one that you like and then in the same rollout, enable the *Orthographic Projection* option to see how it affects the camera view. Pretty crazy, right?

6. Disable the *Orthographic Projection* option and change the viewport layout so that you can see both the *Camera* view and the *Perspective* viewport

7. In the *Perspective* viewport, grab hold of the camera target box and use the *Move* tool to manipulate it, as shown in Figure 11.7. Be sure to check the *Camera* viewport to see how this is affected!

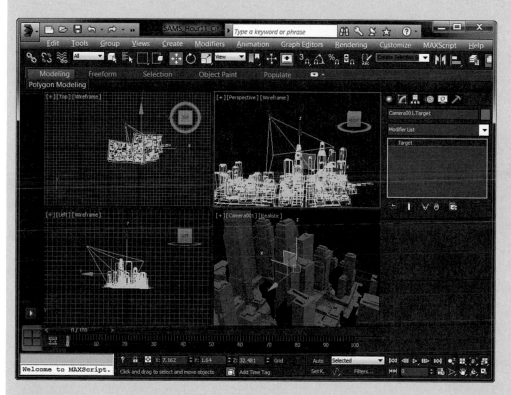

FIGURE 11.7
Grabbing hold of the camera target and moving it allows the *Camera* viewport to focus on a different area. Alternatively, you could move the camera, and you would continue to focus wherever the camera target is positioned.

Animating Cameras

You use the same tools for animating cameras as you would for animating any other object in 3ds Max. So, just as when you're animating objects, you can use the *Set Key* or *Auto Key* button in conjunction with the transformation tools (*Move*, *Rotate*, and *Scale*).

You haven't yet seen how to animate the creation parameters of an object. The creation parameters are the parameters you edit when you're first creating an object. The creation parameters for cameras are the *Stock Lenses* settings and other parameters that you find in the *Modify* tab.

A difficult part of animating cameras is making your animations feel realistic and cinematic. By using a 3D application, you are able to manipulate and animate a camera in unrealistic ways. By not keeping real-world restrictions in mind, you run the risk of creating camera animations that are ridiculous and unrealistic.

VIDEO 11.2

 Animation Cameras in 3D

This video shows the creation and animation of cameras in 3ds Max.

▼ TRY IT YOURSELF

Animating Cameras

There is not really much to animating cameras, but there are a few tips and tricks you can use to make your camera animations feel dynamic and cinematic. Follow these steps to get a feel for them:

1. Open the file *SAMS_Hour11_CitySceneCamAnimated.max*. This scene has a camera (*Camera001*) already animated.

2. Check out *Camera001* by looking through the camera and clicking the *Play* button. Look at the parameters in the *Modify* tab as you play through the animation.

3. Notice that the *Lens* and *FOV* (field of view) parameters change as you play through the animation. The spinners for these parameters are also highlighted in red on frames 0 and 100, showing that these parameters have keyframes, and they have ben animated. Cool!

4. Head back over to the *Create* tab and create a free camera in the scene. Position and set your new camera however you want it. You are going to animate this camera flying through the city.

5. Tell 3ds Max that you want to keyframe more than just the position, rotation, and scale of this camera. To do this, head to the lower toolbar and click the *Filters* button to open the *Set Key Filters* window, shown in Figure 11.8.

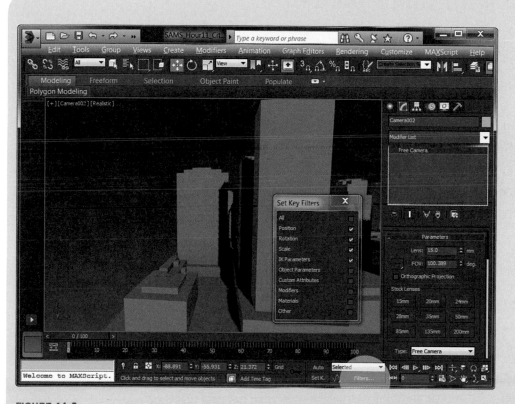

FIGURE 11.8
The *Set Key Filters* window can be found by clicking the *Filters* button on the lower toolbar.

6. Click the *All* option in the *Set Key Filters* window to allow keyframes to be set on everything for this camera object.

7. Make sure your time slider is set at frame *0* and turn on *Auto Key*.

8. Click the *Key* button to set your first keyframe for the camera.

9. Scrub the time slider to frame 100 and manipulate the camera so that it flies through the city scene. 3ds Max sets a keyframe on whichever transformations you made, but you want to set a keyframe on everything, so be sure to click the *Key* button once again.

10. With *Auto Key* still on and the time slider at frame 100, click on a different stock lens from the one your camera currently has.

11. Turn off *Auto Key* and press the *Play* button to check out your camera animation. Congratulations, you have just animated a camera and its parameters!

Cameras and Modifiers

Hang on a second! Modifiers? With cameras?! I know: What an absolutely crazy idea. Imagine being able to add a modifier to a camera. Well, you really can. For instance, if you select a camera and then add a *Noise* modifier to it, you can make the camera jitter and jump around by turning on *Animate Noise* and increasing the *X, Y,* and *Z Strength* parameters.

This can be loads of fun, and the effects you can create from adding a modifier to a camera can be dramatic, shocking, and totally cool. Take some time and try experimenting with modifiers and cameras. You will quickly find which modifiers actually work and which ones have no effect at all.

TIP

Camera Correction Modifier

If you right-click a created camera, you can find the option *Camera Correction* modifier. This modifier applies a two-point perspective to the camera rather than the standard three-point perspective that is the default with every created camera. This is a rather advanced camera option for those who are already comfortable with cameras and their terminology.

Summary

The cameras in 3ds Max replicate real-life cameras quite closely. Prior knowledge of real-life cameras, camera equipment, and photography is a transferrable skill that will help you work the cameras in your 3D scenes. If you are new to cameras and their terminology, you might need a bit of time to get up to speed, but as you can already tell, working with cameras isn't too difficult.

Q&A

Q. Why are there only two camera creation options available in 3ds Max?

A. Both of the available cameras in 3ds Max contain more than enough parameters and settings to allow you to create realistic shots. Start digging into all the parameters and settings of these cameras, and you will soon realize that you don't really need any additional cameras.

Q. Are there any specific settings or techniques to use when animating cameras?

A. Nope, not really. It's always good practice to keep in mind general cinematography rules and/or techniques, but that is entirely up to you. Go crazy, have fun, and just try things out!

Q. Do all modifiers work with cameras?

A. Nope. Some do, some don't. In fact, some do work but don't have any effect. Nuts!

Workshop

Creating and using cameras in 3ds Max is incredibly simple, and despite the many parameters and settings, it is not too difficult to get the shot that you want. The theory of staging, composition, and shot setup is a rather advanced topic that is beyond the scope of this book, but that doesn't mean you can't work with cameras right now. This workshop should get your brain thinking about some of the various points covered in this hour as well as challenge you to create your own dynamic camera movement in a 3D scene.

Quiz

1. This hour uses a number of acronyms and abbreviations. What do *FOV* and *DOF* stand for in the world of cameras?

2. Why would you want to switch lenses on a camera?

3. What should you do if you want to enable the keyframing of the creation parameters of a camera or object during animation?

Answers

1. *FOV* stands for *field of view*, and *DOF* stands for *depth of field*.

2. A smaller lens gives you less zoom but more vision, whereas a larger lens gives you more zoom and less vision. Both distort the view somewhat. Which lens you use depends on what you need in a shot.

3. You need to make sure that the correct key filters are set. You can do this from the lower toolbar by clicking the *Filters* button and choosing which key filters are applied in the *Set Key Filters* window.

Exercise

Open *SAMS_Hour11_CityScene.max* and create a camera. With the camera created, add transformation animation and creation parameter animation so that you get a dynamic shot that sweeps through the city. When you're happy with your animation, experiment even further by adding a *Noise* modifier to your camera and edit the parameters so that it gives the appearance of a handheld camera. Remember to save your scene when you finish.

HOUR 12
Rendering for Production

What You'll Learn in This Hour:

▶ An introduction to rendering
▶ Creating a quick render
▶ Rendering tools
▶ How to render still images
▶ How to render animation

"Lights! Camera! Action!" People tend to associate these three words with live-action filming for TV and film. These words are also applicable to 3D. In fact, Hour 10, "Illuminating Scenes Using Lights," introduced you to illuminating scenes using lights. Then during Hour 11, "Adding and Editing 3D Cameras," you worked with cameras and lenses to get specific views, or shots, of your 3D scenes. In Hour 9, "Computer Animation," you learned about animation, which I guess is the "Action!" element. So, that should be everything, right? Well, not exactly. When it comes to 3D, you need to do one more step: "Render!"

Rendering is a process that takes the scene's geometry, lighting, materials, animations, settings, parameters, and everything else and saves them as a final image or video that can be shared with friends, family, enemies, and random people on the street.

An Overview of Rendering in 3ds Max

Rendering is one of the major subtopics of computer graphics, and as with most other things in 3D, it is a complex subject that directly connects with and influences other disciplines. When it comes to 3D computer graphics, rendering may be done in one of two ways:

▶ **Real-time rendering**—The most common example of real-time rendering is 3D video games. Each image, or frame, is rendered in real time, or as it happens. This allows users to interact with the 3D worlds as stuff is happening.

▶ **Pre-rendering**—Pre-rendering relates to any content that is not rendered in real time, and it is the default rendering of 3ds Max and most other 3D applications. Pre-rendered images are previously rendered in full before being displayed to an audience.

It's important not to mistake what you have been seeing in the viewports as renders. Although relatable to real-time rendering, the viewports themselves let you view and manipulate a 3D scene in any way that you want, but that is not a true representation of how the scene will actually look in a final render.

To fully understand the process of rendering in 3ds Max, and in particular creating and rendering an animated video, you need to remember that a video is simply related individual frames (pictures/images) played in sequence at a specific speed. This is usually a rather fast rate, such as 24 frames per second (fps), which creates the illusion of motion.

Various rendering engines are available, and 3ds Max uses the *Default Scanline* renderer as its generic rendering engine. The engine itself is basic, but it includes enough options, settings, and parameters that you can get some nice-looking renders from it with relatively little trouble.

Rendering requires a substantial amount of processing power from your computer system. To help with the load, modern computers have graphics processing unit (GPU) devices, occasionally named visual processing units (VPUs), that assist the central processing unit (CPU) in performing complex rendering calculations. This, of course, can become very complicated very quickly. Luckily, you don't have to jump into the complexities of rendering at that level just yet or even at all if it's not your thing. 3ds Max allows you to render your scenes without needing too much technical knowledge of the rendering process.

Quick Rendering

3ds Max provides an incredibly fast way to render the viewport you are currently working in: Simply press *F9*.

VIDEO 12.1

 Quick Rendering in 3ds Max
This video provides a brief introduction to rendering and using the quick rendering method shortcut key (*F9*).

If you have nothing in the scene you're currently working on, you are probably staring at a *Render Preview* window that is completely black. Don't worry, that's how it should be! For now, close the *Render Preview* window and add some geometry to your scene. Then press the *F9* key once again, and that geometry appears in the *Render Preview* window.

For example, if you open the futuristic city planet scene from Hour 7, "3D Modeling," (the file *SAMS_Hour7_FuturisticCityPlanet.max*) and press *F9*, you should see it rendered as in Figure 12.1.

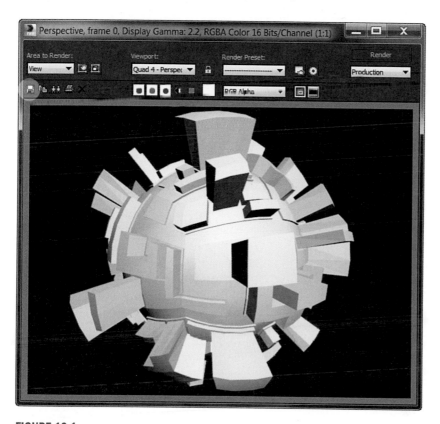

FIGURE 12.1
This is a rendered version of my futuristic city planet from Hour 7. I have highlighted the *Save Image* button to indicate what you need to click if you want to save your render as an image file.

I use this method a lot, to get a quick test of what my final scene or shot will look like as I work through the lighting and rendering for a project. This is by far the easiest and quickest way to render scenes. Remember that this method allows you to look at the scene in its final form via the *Rendered Frame* window. If you want to save a render as an image file, you need to click the *Save Image* button, which is highlighted in Figure 12.1.

Rendering Tools

3ds Max includes many tools to help you get the best possible renders. To find them, go to the main menu and click the *Rendering* menu to see a whole list of rendering tools, as shown in Figure 12.2.

FIGURE 12.2
3ds Max contains many helpful rendering tools that you can access from the *Rendering* menu in the main menu.

The *Material Explorer* tool allows you to browse and manage all the materials in the current scene, and *Print Size Assistant* is a handy tool when you want to print a rendered image and need to specify output size, resolution, and other parameters.

You could spend hours looking into each and every option, but as in many other cases, you really want to be more selective and spend your time where it matters most. In this case, you really need to know about three rendering tools that are the most practical and useful to you as you start experimenting with rendering: *Render Setup*, *Render Frame Window*, and *Render Production/Iterative/Active Shade*. You find these three tools on the main toolbar, as shown in Figure 12.3.

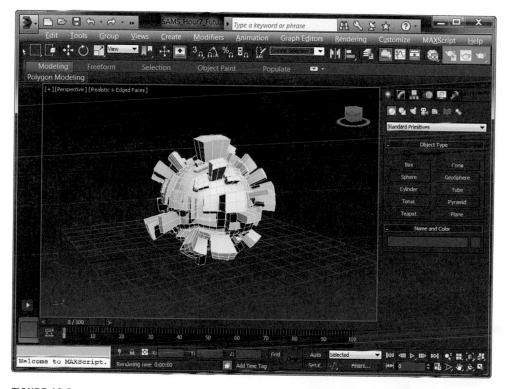

FIGURE 12.3
The three rendering tools you are checking out are found on the main toolbar, highlighted in the top-right corner of this image.

Of course, you can also find these tools in the *Rendering* menu on the main menu as well. The main toolbar is a little more accessible than that, though, so that's where I like to go to work with these tools. You can hover your mouse over each of these icons, and a tooltip will appear to let you know which one is which. For clarity, I've pointed out each specific tool in Figure 12.4.

Render Setup

Render Setup is the most complicated of the three rendering tools discussed here. The *Render Setup* dialog has a lot of tabs, and they change, depending on the active rendering engine you are currently using. Figure 12.5 shows an example of the default interface of the *Render Setup* dialog.

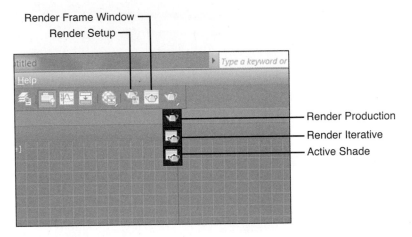

FIGURE 12.4
The three main rendering tools on the main toolbar. Notice that the *Render Production/Render Iterative/Active Shade* tool is a drop-down menu.

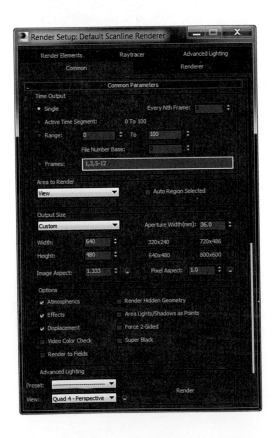

FIGURE 12.5
The *Render Setup* dialog can be complex because the tabs change, depending on the selected rendering engine. Only the *Common* and *Renderer* tabs are always present.

Because you are only using the *Default Scanline* rendering engine at the moment, you do not need to worry about the various tabs changing on you just yet. However, it's good to note that at least two of these tabs are always present, no matter which engine you decide to use:

▶ **Common tab**—This tab contains all the main controls related to rendering. This is where you find the options for setting the resolution of your renders, whether you want a single frame (image) or an animation. You can also choose the location where your images are saved.

▶ **Renderer tab**—This tab contains all the main controls for the current renderer.

Figure 12.6 highlights both the *Common* and *Renderer* tabs.

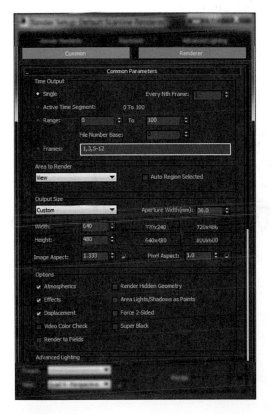

FIGURE 12.6
The *Render Setup* dialog contains various tabs. The *Common* and *Renderer* tabs are the only tabs that do not change when you switch rendering engines.

The bottom section of the *Render Setup* dialog gives you access to various rendering presets, the option to change which view is being rendered and to lock it so it cannot change, a big *Render* button, and a drop-down menu that gives us quick access to the rendering method used. Figure 12.7 shows where you find these options.

FIGURE 12.7
The bottom section of the *Render Setup* dialog gives you access to a few more options that are always available, no matter which tab you are currently working in.

Render Frame Window

The *Render Frame Window* dialog displays the rendered output of the current scene, and you already took a quick look at it when you used the quick render (*F9*) technique earlier (refer to Figure 12.1).

This dialog gives you access to various options, such as the area rendered, which viewport to render from, which render preset to use, the ability to save the image, and so on. Figure 12.8 shows an example of what the *Render Frame Window* dialog looks like. If you are missing any of the options shown in this image, click the *Toggle UI* button, which is at the far right side of this window. Remember that you can hover over the various icons to see a tooltip if you are having trouble figuring out what the buttons in 3ds Max do.

FIGURE 12.8
The *Rendered Frame* dialog shows the rendered output of a scene and includes some quick-access additional options.

Render Production, Render Iterative, and Active Shade

You can access the *Render Production/Render Iterative/Active Shade* rendering methods from either the main toolbar (refer to Figure 12.3) or directly from the *Render Setup* dialog (refer to Figure 12.5). Both of these options open a drop-down menu that reveals the various rendering modes from which you can choose, as shown in Figure 12.9.

FIGURE 12.9
You can access the options for the various rendering modes from the main toolbar or from the *Render Setup* dialog window (at the bottom).

The final option in this drop-down menu, the *Submit to Network Rendering* option, allows you to render on multiple computers at the same time but is more of a networking topic than 3ds Max specific. The three rendering modes in this drop-down allow you to output renders that are suited to your needs:

▶ **Production Render Mode**—This highest-quality rendering option is also the slowest option of the three. You generally use this option for final rendered output.

▶ **Iterative Render Mode**—This is a modest-quality, modest-speed rendering option. It gives you quicker rendering at the expense of quality. This option is great for testing renders quickly.

▶ *Active Shade Mode*—This is the lowest-quality rendering option but also the quickest. It is great for super-fast previews of rendered scenes.

Depending on the complexity of your scene, you might be able to use the *Production Render Mode* option even for quick render tests. However, as you start adding more complex geometry, lights, cameras, effects, and all that extra eye-candy, your rendering speed will slow down, and those other rendering modes may be very useful.

Still Image Rendering

By using the quick rendering technique (*F9*) covered earlier this hour, you have already rendered an image. Saving that rendered image is as easy as clicking the *Save* icon in the *Rendered Frame* dialog.

▼ TRY IT YOURSELF

Rendering and Saving an Image

Saving an image file from a render in 3ds Max is super simple, and very quick to do:

1. Render your scene, either by pressing *F9* or clicking the *Rendered Frame* button on the main toolbar. Actually, you could even click *Rendering* on the main toolbar and then *Render*, or you could use the keyboard shortcut *Shift+Q*. As with everything else in 3ds Max, here you have multiple ways to do the same thing.

2. With the *Rendered Frame* dialog open, click the *Save* icon and choose the format and location for saving the image. Easy!

Animation Rendering

Animation rendering requires you to choose where you want to save the rendered output, as well as what type of animated file(s) you want to save.

A common output method is to render each frame (image) separately and put them together in a composite, using an external program (such as Adobe After Effects or Nuke); after that, you can make additional changes and enhancements in the external program. You also have the option of simply saving an animated file directly from 3ds Max. Often, this is not the desired, or best, way to render a scene, but it's great for quick tests, especially if you're not working in a production environment, which typically requires that separate frames be rendered.

VIDEO 12.2

Rendering Animation in 3ds Max

Watch this video to learn about rendering an animation in
3ds Max.

 TRY IT YOURSELF ▼

Rendering an Animation

Rendering an animation is somewhat more complicated than simply rendering just an image.
Follow these steps to learn how to do it:

1. Open the file *SAMS_Hour9_CarsEnd.max.*

2. Open the *Render Setup* dialog from the main menu, from the main toolbar, or by
   pressing *F10*.

3. In the *Common* tab change the *Time Output to Active Time Segment* setting or the *Range*
   setting if you want to specify which frames are rendered.

4. Scroll down and in the *Render Output* section, click the *Files* button to open the *Render
   Output File* dialog (see Figure 12.10). In the dialog, select a location to store this animation file, give the file a name (such as *SAMS_Hour12_CarRace*), and choose *AVI File (*.avi)*
   for the file type.

5. Click *Save*, and the *AVI File Compression Setup* dialog appears, as shown in Figure 12.11.
   Leave everything in this dialog set as it is and click *OK*.

6. Click *Render*. 3ds Max renders each frame, saving it to the AVI file you have just created.
   When this process is finished, navigate to your AVI file and check out your animation.

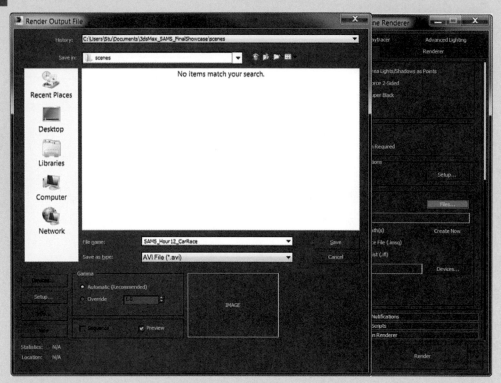

FIGURE 12.10
Saving the file type as an AVI allows you to render directly to an animation movie file, which you can watch when the rendering is complete.

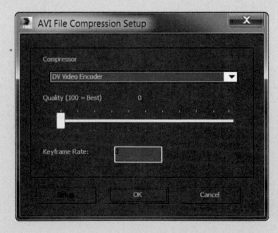

FIGURE 12.11
You leave the *AVI File Compression Setup* settings at their defaults and click the *OK* button to continue.

Rendering directly to an animated video file allows you to quickly get access to your rendered animations so that you can show them to others. Figure 12.12 is a single frame from my finished animation, and you can take a look at the whole finished animation video by opening the file *SAMS_Hour12_CarRace.avi* in a video/movie player on your computer.

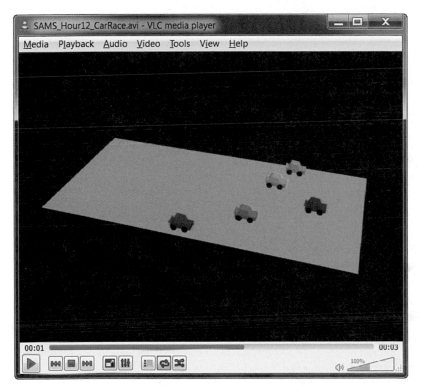

FIGURE 12.12
The car animation created in Hour 9 has now been rendered and saved as an AVI video file that you can share with others.

Summary

Rendering is another one of those complex topics that can take a while to fully understand. Changing rendering engines can also be confusing, but to keep things relatively simple, you can stick with the *Default Scanline* renderer that ships with 3ds Max.

The *Default Scanline* renderer does not produce the best results, and it is not a rendering engine that most advanced users would use. However, getting going with it is quick and easy, and it gives you access to some basic rendering techniques that will be helpful when you dig into more complex rendering engines. You will learn about these more advanced engines in Hour 20, "Mental Ray Rendering."

Q&A

Q. **Do you need to render your scenes? What if you can already see what you have created?**

A. You do need to render your scenes if you would like others who do not have 3ds Max to see your work. Rendering can also improve the visual quality of the scenes.

Q. **Why are there so many buttons, tabs, and options for rendering?**

A. You can tweak, change, and tamper with everything in 3ds Max to get great results. Rendering is the final result that most people see, and the related options give you a chance to make everything look amazing.

Q. **Do you need a fantastic computer system to render images?**

A. Not at all. If you are able to run 3ds Max, you should be able to render basic scenes. However, as 3D scenes increase in complexity, the processing power required to render the scene also increases and therefore requires a more powerful computer system.

Workshop

Rendering is a complicated subject, and although you've learned about the main tools this hour, there are many more options and parameters, and you are far from being a rendering expert just yet. This workshop should help reinforce some of the information you have learned during this hour.

Quiz

1. What rendering options are available in 3ds Max?

2. What is the quickest way to render a single frame, image, or picture in 3ds Max?

3. What file type do you use this hour for rendering out your animation?

Answers

1. The following rendering options are available in 3ds Max: *Render Setup*, *Render Frame*, *Render Production*, *Render Iterative*, and *Active Shade*.

2. The quickest way to render a single frame, image, or picture in 3ds Max is to use the quick rendering technique: pressing the *F9* key.

3. During this hour you use the AVI file type to save out your animations into a format that can be viewed by others who do not have direct access to 3ds Max.

Exercise

Open *SAMS_Hour12_StreetRendering.max*. This file uses some of the techniques covered in the previous hours to create a very short street scene with a car driving by. Using the supplied camera in the *SAMS_Hour12_StreetRendering.max* file and the techniques outlined in this hour, render this shot as an AVI animation movie that you can share with others.

Once you have the animation rendered to a movie file, open the file *SAMS_Hour12_StreetDIY.max* and create a new animated shot, using the animation you just rendered as a guide. Create your own cameras, lights, and car animation and see what you can come up with. Remember to save the animation as an AVI file when you are finished so that you can show the whole world what you have been working on.

Combining Techniques to Create a Showcase

What You'll Learn in This Hour:

▶ Working with and merging multiple scenes

▶ Lights, cameras, and rendering working together

▶ A practical approach to creating a showcase of your work

You are just over halfway through your 24-hour adventure into the amazing world of 3ds Max, and you've covered a crazy amount of ground already. I think this is a great time to create a showcase of the work you have already completed so that you have something to show people who don't have access to 3ds Max. In addition, this is a great way for you to work through a complete project and combine all the separate skills and techniques covered over the past 12 hours.

During this hour you are going to combine your various scenes into one mega-awesome scene. You are then going to add some animation, light everything, and then render it so that you can show and display it for the whole world to see what you have been up to. Doing this will give you a chance to solidify the knowledge you have gained over the previous hours as well as introduce you to working with multiple scenes and more complex scenes with more geometry, some lights, cameras, animation, and rendering.

Stages Explained

This hour changes things up a little. Instead of working on specific topics this hour, you are going to work in stages to create your final showcase. Think of this hour as one big Try It Yourself section. It's up to you to follow along with the stages and use them as a guide for creating your very own showcase.

TIP

Save, Save Often, Save Iteratively

It should go without saying that you should save your work often. In addition, you should be saving your work iteratively. This may mean that you will have multiple files containing your scene at various points of progression, but it will allow you to backtrack to an earlier version if anything goes wrong. After all, it's better to lose a bit of your work than to lose all your work!

VIDEO 13.1

Showcase Creation

This video goes through each stage of the showcase creation process, from beginning to end.

Stage 1: Preparation

All right! Are you ready to begin? The first thing you need to do is to choose which files you want to showcase, and I think that your spaceship and futuristic city planet are the winners here. You need to prepare your scene by combining the spaceship and futuristic city planet into the same scene—and doing this is relatively simple.

Open the file *SAMS_Hour7_FuturisticCityPlanet.max* (or your own file, if you want). Do a quick check to see if the model is placed in the world center ([0,0,0]) and move it there if it isn't.

With the futuristic city planet in place, it's time to bring the spaceship model into the same scene. Click the *Application* button and then slide down and hover over the *Import* option. In the new menu that appears, click the *Merge* button to merge the spaceship scene with the futuristic city planet scene you already have open.

Navigate to your finished spaceship file, or to the file *SAMS_Hour7_SpaceshipRefine.max*. When you try to merge the file, you see a *Merge* dialog. All you have to do here is choose the object you want to merge into the scene and click the *OK* button. Figure 13.1 shows where you find the *Merge* option and what the *Merge* dialog looks like.

You might notice that the spaceship object is called *Box001*. There's a problem: The futuristic city planet is also named *Box001*. Uh oh!

Luckily, 3ds Max is clever enough to realize that this could be a problem, and it therefore prompts me with the *Duplicate Name* dialog, as shown in Figure 13.2.

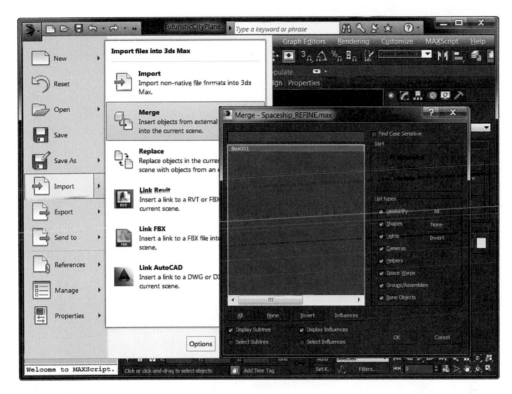

FIGURE 13.1
You can access the *Merge* option from the *Application* button. When merging, you are prompted with the option of merging only what you want from a specific scene.

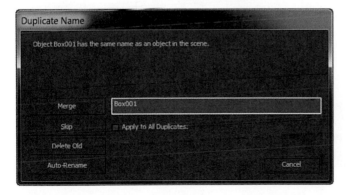

FIGURE 13.2
Whoops! Duplicate names are not good and are not recommended. I should really know better...

This window allows you to do a number of things, one of which is rename your object. For example, you can rename *Box001* to *Spaceship* so that it is easier to identify as you work in the new scene. This issue highlights the importance of naming things well in your scenes. To make sure you don't have any more problems like this, you should select your futuristic city planet object and rename it *FuturisticCityPlanet!*

Great stuff! You now have both of the objects in the same scene, and they are named correctly. This is a good point to save our work, so under the *Application* button, choose *Save As.* (You want to use *Save As* here instead of *Save* so that you can create a new file rather than overwrite your original file.) Choose a name for the new file, such as *SAMS_Hour13_Showcase.max*, and click the *Save* button.

Back in the scene, as Figure 13.3 shows, there's a problem with the scale of things. The spaceship should be tiny compared to the futuristic city planet, but that's not the case.

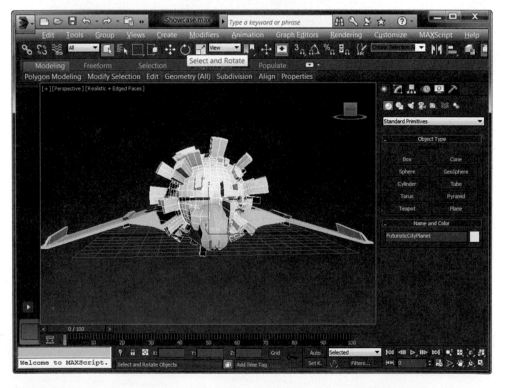

FIGURE 13.3
This looks like a scale problem!

Until this point, you haven't worried about the scale of the objects you have been creating. If the current scale problem were a production environment, you would have some very real problems to deal with. However, in this case, it's a simple matter of scaling the spaceship down or scaling the futuristic city planet up. Go ahead, give it a try and judge for yourself how big the objects should be.

With the scale of the objects taken care of, all that is left to do at this stage is to place the spaceship somewhere next to the futuristic city planet. Figure 13.4 shows how I scaled the spaceship compared to the futuristic city planet and also where I've positioned the spaceship.

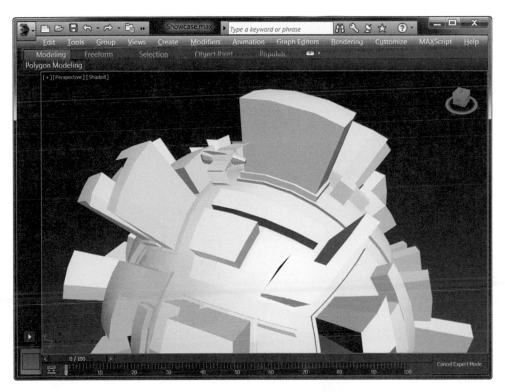

FIGURE 13.4
The spaceship is now positioned and has been rescaled to fit the scene.

You're now ready for stage 2—as soon as you save your progress so far. You can take a look at my progress on the project to this point by opening the file *SAMS_Hour13_ShowcaseSTAGE1.max*.

Stage 2: Materials

Right now the spaceship and futuristic city planet models are a little bit dull looking. A lick of paint would spruce them right up. To that end, you're going to create some materials to change the colors of both models.

Go to the *Slate Material Editor* (by pressing the shortcut *M*) and create a *Multi/Sub-Object* material in the *Standard Materials* section.

Now that you have created a *Multi/Sub-Object* material, you can assign it to the spaceship by selecting the spaceship geometry and right-clicking the material and choosing *Assign Material to Selection*.

The spaceship is now a fully black color, showing that the material has been successfully applied. You can add even more materials. Click and drag from the first input of the *Multi/Sub-Object* material—labeled (*1*)—and choose *Materials, Standard* to create a standard material, as shown in Figure 13.5.

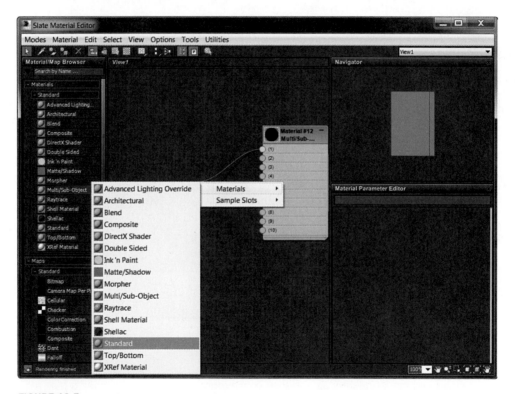

FIGURE 13.5
You can add a standard material to the first input of the *Multi/Sub-Object* material.

Back in your main scene, you may have noticed that some areas of the spaceship now have a gray color applied to them. What has happened is that any polygon with a material ID of 1 has been assigned the (*1*) input material from the *Multi/Sub-Object* material that is applied to it. So it makes sense that any polygon with a material ID of 2 will be assigned the second input material—labeled (*2*)—and so on.

Now that you understand more about *Multi/Sub-Object* materials, you need to assign material IDs to your spaceship geometry. This is actually incredibly simple: You just select your spaceship and jump into *Polygon* sub-object mode. Then you scroll down the *Modify* tab until you find the *Polygon: Material IDs* rollout. This is where you can set and select the various material IDs of the geometry. For now, select all the polygons in your spaceship model and use the *Set ID* parameter to set all the polygons to a material ID of *1*. When you deselect the polygons, you should see that your spaceship is fully assigned the gray standard material that you just put into *Multi/Sub-Object* material input (*1*), as shown in Figure 13.6.

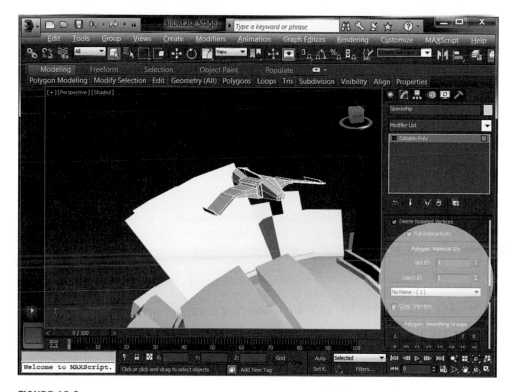

FIGURE 13.6
The *Polygon: Material IDs* rollout is where you can assign material IDs to your geometry.

Now it's time to set material IDs for all the different sections of the spaceship as well as create materials for all those sections/IDs. Oh, and when you finish up with the spaceship, remember that you have to do the futuristic city planet, too.

This is probably going to take you some time, so go and grab a drink and get to work. You can see my final results in Figure 13.7 and the file *SAMS_Hour13_ShowcaseSTAGE2.max*, which should give you some ideas and help.

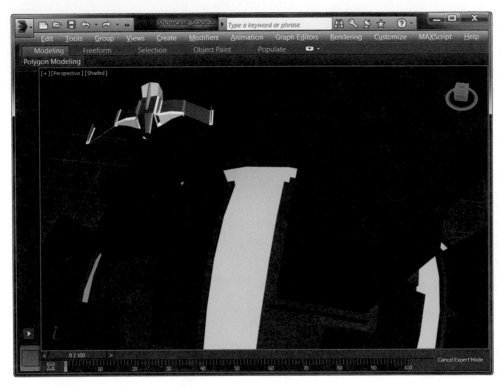

FIGURE 13.7
Multi/Sub-Object materials have now been applied to both the spaceship and the futuristic city planet.

Stage 3: Camera

You need to create a camera and position it so that it shows the action as you'd like the audience to see it. You should ensure that the scene includes both the spaceship and the futuristic city planet. You might also want to change the lens to a 15 mm stock lens.

You should also open the *Render Setup* dialog (using the shortcut key *F10*) and change the *Output Size* setting to something like *HDTV (Video)* and *1920x1080* so that you get a good-sized render. In addition, while you're looking through your camera view, turn on *Show Safe Frames* (using the shortcut *Shift+F*) so that you can frame your camera view correctly, as shown in Figure 13.8.

NOTE

Show Safe Frames

Show Safe Frames provides a visual guide to help you visualize which portions of a viewport will be visible when you render a scene.

FIGURE 13.8
The *Safe Frames* appear depending upon what *Output Size* you have chosen. Set this to *HDTV (video)* with a resolution of *1920x1080* for some great results.

That's all you need to do for this stage. *SAMS_Hour13_ShowcaseSTAGE3.max* shows the progress to this point.

Stage 4: Animation

You can keep the animation of this scene very simple, as discussed in this section, or you can feel free to push your animation further.

Say that you want to be able to rotate the futuristic city planet and have the spaceship come along for free. To do this, you need to use the *Select and Link* tool from the main toolbar to link the spaceship to the futuristic city planet. When you do this, the spaceship becomes a child of the futuristic city planet, and it now moves, rotates, and scales along with it. Nice!

Now that both the futuristic city planet and the spaceship can be animated together, it's time to turn on *Auto Key* and set a keyframe on frame 0. When you're done with that, move the time slider to frame 100 and rotate the futuristic city planet as much as you want on the *Z* axis.

I am making my planet rotate around a full 360 degrees on just the *Z* axis, but you can do whatever crazy animation moves you would like to do. Take a look at the file *SAMS_Hour13_ ShowcaseSTAGE4.max* if you'd like to see what I came up with for this stage.

When you're happy with your animation in the camera view, save your work to finish up the animation stage.

Stage 5: Lighting

In this case, you're going to focus your attention on standard lights only, completely ignoring the photometric lights that you also have available. I want to warn you that this stage could take you a lot of time! Lighting can dramatically change the look, feel, and atmosphere of a scene, and it deserves your time and respect. It can be hard to achieve the desired visuals you want, but keep at it: It's worth the effort.

First, you need to establish a main light source in the scene that will replicate a kind of sunlight. You can use a free direct light to simulate this, and by turning on *Shadows* and choosing the *Ray Traced Shadows* option, you get some pretty nice hard-edged shadows, as shown in Figure 13.9.

FIGURE 13.9
By adding a free direct light to the scene, you can simulate sunlight. Also, by turning on *Ray Traced Shadows*, you get hard-edged shadows on your objects from this light source.

As you work through this section, changing the lighting setup, periodically use the quick render (*F9*) technique to check how your scene is looking. Remember that what you see in your viewport is not necessarily a clear representation of what you will see in the render.

Now that you have a sort of simulated sunlight and some hard-edged shadows, you can continue lighting the scene using various standard lighting solutions. There are no hard-and-fast rules for this, so start adding lights to your scene, start tweaking light parameters and settings, and get your scene lit. Take your time and keep working on it!

It's important that you start to really look into all the various options and settings that are available for each light you create. Doing so will increase your understanding of what is possible when using standard lights in 3ds Max. In particular, by using the *Atmosphere & Effects* rollout, you can add various interesting effects to your lighting setups. Be sure to check this out on the *Modify* tab while you have a light selected.

To get the effects shown in Figure 13.10, you use three volume lights and two lens effects. As with many other areas of 3ds Max, these effects have an immense number of options and can get complex pretty quickly. You should learn how different things work by just trying them out. You will soon get accustomed to their uses, and if you get stuck, be sure to turn to the built-in help files (shortcut key *F1*).

Keep adding various lights and checking your results by pressing *F9*. When you are happy with the results, you might have something similar to the image in Figure 13.10.

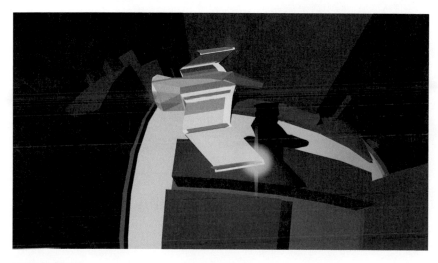

FIGURE 13.10
Final lighting for the spaceship and futuristic city planet showcase scene.

Check out *SAMS_Hour13_ShowcaseSTAGE5.max* to see what my work looks like through this stage.

Stage 6: Final Changes

Scenes merged and geometry scaled and in position—check!

Materials applied to the geometry—check!

Camera added—check!

Basic animation added—check!

Finished with lighting using standard lights—check!

Final checks—umm, time to check!

This stage is all about fixing any problems, sorting out any errors, and making refinements to your nearly completed scene. The first problem with this scene that you might notice is that if you scrub through the animation, all the lights in the scene stay in the same place. This causes some problems as the spaceship moves away and its lights stay behind, floating in midair, as shown in Figure 13.11.

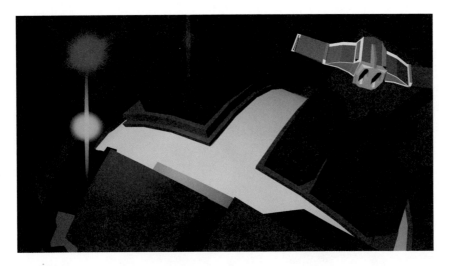

FIGURE 13.11
The spaceship's lights need to be linked to the spaceship, or they won't follow along during animation, as shown here.

Fixing this is simple: You just make sure the time slider is at frame 0 and then you can use the *Select and Link* tool to link the lights to the spaceship.

The next issue is with the spaceship model itself and the smoothing groups assigned to it. To fix this, you go to the *Polygon* sub-object mode and select all the polygons of the spaceship model. From there you need to locate the *Polygon: Smoothing Groups* rollout in the *Modify* tab and click the *Auto Smooth* button. Figure 13.12 shows the spaceship geometry before and after *Auto Smooth* is applied.

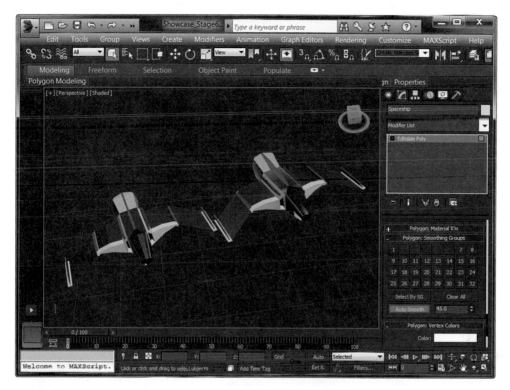

FIGURE 13.12
Smoothing groups affect the apparent "hard edges" of a model, and not having them set correctly can lead to some strange results. The spaceship on the left has incorrect smoothing groups; the one on the right has had *Auto Smooth* applied to it.

When you apply *Auto Smooth* to a model, any two adjacent polygons are placed into the same smoothing group if the angle between their normal is less than the threshold angle. You set this threshold angle by using the *Auto Smooth* spinner. Feel free to change this and experiment with it. You may also want to try applying *Auto Smooth* to your futuristic city planet.

Finally, you can refine any other elements that you want to. You can do things like add more lights, think about camera movement and effects, and change the animation. It's really up to you at this point, so go for it!

To see what my final showcase looks like inside 3ds Max, open the file *SAMS_Hour13_ShowcaseSTAGE6.max*.

Stage 7: Rendering

All that's left to do is create a final render of your showcase animation. You just learned how to do this in Hour 12, "Rendering for Production," so I will leave you alone to sort out the rendering for yourself! If you get stuck, be sure to refer to Hour 12, and then if something still isn't working, jump back to "Stage 6: Final Changes" in this hour and refine your scene.

Take a look at my final showcase animation by opening the file *SAMS_Hour13_Showcase.avi*.

Good luck!

Summary

This hour has been unlike any other so far. The techniques covered in the previous 12 hours have been brought together in this hour of your 3D adventure. You've combined all your new skills and applied them to a showcase piece that you can use to show the world how super-amazing-awesome you are at 3D. This is something that 3D folks actually do quite often: They get together their best work and compile it into a showcase for others to see. This is usually called a demo reel or show reel, and it's a common item that you need to have to get yourself a job in the industry. You never know, this could be the first step into your 3D career, and you now have the skills and expertise to create your very own show reels.

Hold on for a second, though! We're only just over halfway through this book, so maybe you should finish the upcoming hours first, before you jump ahead to landing a 3D job. After all, you never know what other tips and tricks await you. You are sure to find treasures along the way that can enhance your already pretty neat showcase.

Q&A

Q. What is this hour all about?

A. It is a chance to compile all your skills, expertise, and techniques into one project—a showcase.

Q. What is the purpose of a completed showcase?

A. You can use a completed showcase to show others what you have been creating in 3D. It is also very much like creating your own show reels, which can help you land a job in the 3D industry.

Workshop

This whole hour is one super-huge workshop, but there's still more to learn—and no time to rest!

Quiz

1. What should you do often while you work in 3D to protect your work?

2. What does a *Multi/Sub-Object* material allow you to do?

3. What can you do if you want to combine two scenes together into one scene?

Answers

1. You should save often while working in 3D. It's a useful habit to get into, and frequent saving can prevent a lot of frustration that would result from something going wrong, like the program or your computer crashing. Losing hours of work is possibly one of the most annoying things in the world—ever!

2. A *Multi/Sub-Object* material allows you to assign different materials to the sub-object level of your geometry.

3. To combine two scenes into one scene, you can use the *Merge* command, found under the *Application* button and in the *Import* section of the 3ds Max user interface.

Exercise

Okay, this is going to be a big exercise: I want you to design and model your own 3D creation. Apply materials and texture to your creation, use light, and render to create an additional showcase. With two items in your showcase, you can really start to say you have your first show reel!

Rigging Objects for Easier Animation

What You'll Learn in This Hour:

▶ Basic rigging concepts and tools
▶ Forward kinematics (FK) and inverse kinematics (IK)
▶ Built-in rigging solutions
▶ Custom rigging solutions

Rigging is essentially the process of creating special helper objects that make the animation process as easy as possible. It is often a simple idea that relies on a complex process, and it is a blend of artistic and technical endeavors. In fact, most, if not all, 3D characters have some kind of character rig that makes animation easier and keeps the articulations realistic (or not, if preferred).

Think about the human body. It contains a skeleton, a muscle system, and skin, among other things. We often replicate these elements in 3D, and usually this is referred to as *character rigging*.

During this hour, you're going to look over some basic rigging concepts, explore some built-in rigging solutions, and create your own custom rigs so that you get the flavor of a few different rigging techniques.

Hierarchies and Linking

Rigging is basically a bunch of objects working together either by being linked in a hierarchy or through some other means, such as linked/shared attributes. What exactly do I mean by *hierarchies* and *linking*?

A *hierarchy* is a structure of objects that are linked together. For instance, take a look at your arm. Your hand is linked to your forearm, and that is linked to your upper arm, with the upper arm linked to your clavicle and shoulder blade. This is a hierarchy.

The *links*, or connections, within a hierarchy are often referred to as either *parents* or *children* (child), with the parent controlling a child and being higher up in the hierarchical structure. The shoulder blade/clavicle is the parent of the upper arm, which is the child of the shoulder blade/clavicle. The upper arm is the parent of its child, the lower arm, and so on. So, if the upper arm moves, so does its child, and so do the rest of the children. However, if the hand moves, nothing happens to the parents because the hand is the lowest child in the hierarchy. The same thing happens with a leg: The upper leg is the parent of the lower leg, and the ankle is the child of the lower leg, and so on. Hopefully, Figure 14.1 makes all this clearer than my words do on their own.

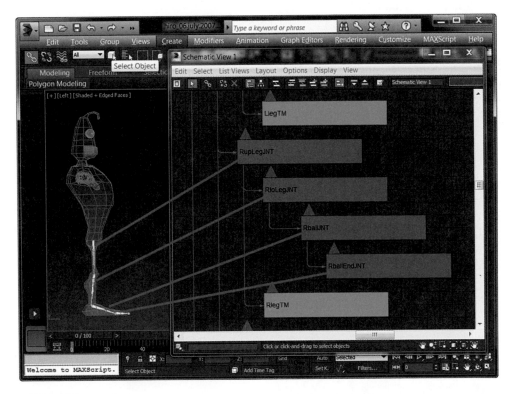

FIGURE 14.1
A leg can be thought of as a hierarchical structure, with the elements linked together.

To create the links shown in Figure 14.1, you use the *Select and Link* tool, and to break links, you use the *Unlink Selection* tool. You can access both of these tools from the main toolbar.

To visualize linked hierarchies, I like to use the *Schematic* view, which helps me work out both basic and complex hierarchical structures. Figure 14.2 shows what the *Schematic* view looks like.

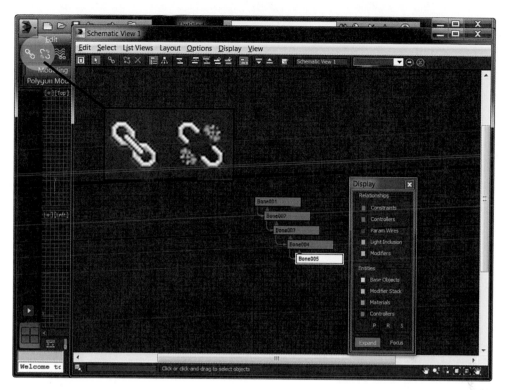

FIGURE 14.2
You can use the *Select and Link* tool to create hierarchical structures and the *Unlink Selection* tool to break linked hierarchies. The *Schematic* view helps you visualize these hierarchical structures.

You can access the *Schematic* view by clicking the *Schematic View* button on the main toolbar or by using the *Graph Editors* menu and clicking the *New Schematic View* option (see Figure 14.3).

VIDEO 14.1

Basic Hierarchies
This video explores the *Select and Link* and *Unlink Selection* tools, the *Schematic* view, and how hierarchies affect the objects in a view.

FIGURE 14.3
You can access the *Schematic* view by clicking the *Schematic View* button on the main toolbar or by using the *Graph Editors* menu and clicking the *New Schematic View* option.

▼ TRY IT YOURSELF

Linking and Unlinking Object Hierarchies

Linking objects together to form a hierarchy is incredibly simple, and so is unlinking objects. Follow these steps to see just how simple these tasks are:

1. In a new scene, create four objects. They can be anything you want—spheres, boxes, whatever.

2. Click the first button on the main toolbar, *Select and Link*. Then click and drag between one of your objects and another to link them together.

3. Open the *Schematic* view to see the connection. (You can easily find the *Schematic* view on the main toolbar by hovering your mouse cursor over the icons until you find the tooltip for the *Schematic* view.)

4. Link the other two objects to the object lowest in the hierarchy. Your *Schematic* view should now have something like Figure 14.4.

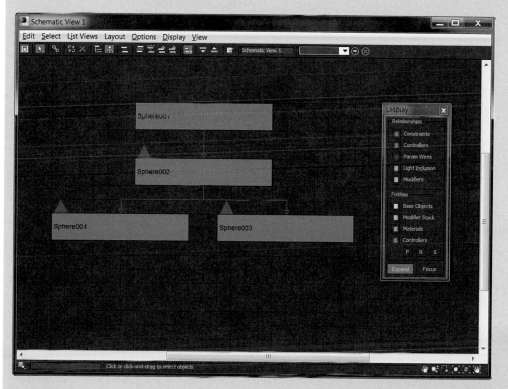

FIGURE 14.4
The *Schematic* view shows the linked hierarchy you just created.

5. To unlink an object from the hierarchy, select that object and use the *Unlink Selection* tool, which is right next to the *Select and Link* tool on the main toolbar.

Bone Tools

Every human has a skeleton. This skeleton is the main structure that keeps us together and allows us to move around. 3ds Max allows you to build skeletal structures by using *Bone* tools.

The *Bone* tools automatically create hierarchies as you use them in the viewports. Bones are often the first element you create when you're rigging characters (see Figure 14.5).

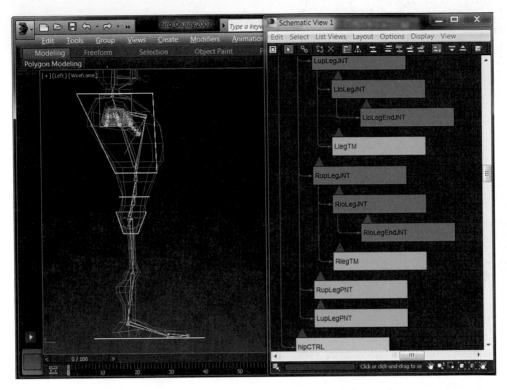

FIGURE 14.5
The *Bone* tools automatically create linked hierarchies.

You can access the *Bone* tools from either the *Command Panel* or by using my preferred method, from the *Bone Tools* dialog, which you access through the main menu. The *Bone Tools* window gives you access to all the options you could ever need when creating and editing bones. It also has options to change the appearance of the bones, so it's better to use it than to use the *Command Panel*.

▼ TRY IT YOURSELF

Creating Some Bones

Bones in 3ds Max, like our human bones, make up skeletons. Follow these steps to create some bones:

  1. In the main menu, click *Animation*. Then scroll down and click *Bone Tools* to toggle on the *Bone Tools* dialog.

2. Click the *Create Bones* button and create bones in the viewport. When you're finished, right-click to exit bone creation mode and then right-click again to exit the tool. That's all you have to do to create some bones. Note that for accuracy, you can use orthographic viewports, such as the *Front* and *Left* and *Right* viewports, to help place bones more easily than you can in the *Perspective* viewport.

TIP

Bones in All Things

You can use bones for anything and everything you need to rig—not just for character rigging. For instance you could use bones to rig a car, from its suspension to its doors—the possibilities are endless!

Forward and Inverse Kinematics

Kinematics describes the motion of objects from a specific point, without consideration of the causes of that motion. In turn, forward kinematics (FK) and inverse kinematics (IK) basically refer to how you interact, manipulate, and give motion to objects in 3D.

Think back to the earlier arm example. If you rotate your upper arm, the lower arm and hand come along for free with that movement (see Figure 14.6). We call this FK.

You get access to FK for free, and whenever you place something into a hierarchy, or simply create some bones, when you rotate the objects, you affect the children in that hierarchy.

To take advantage of IK, on the other hand, you need to create an IK solver, which gives you something to control the inverse movements. The IK solver also does some of the calculations for you, so you don't have to rely on your mathematical knowledge. Yay!

VIDEO 14.2

FK and IK

This video takes a look at FK and IK as control solutions for animation.

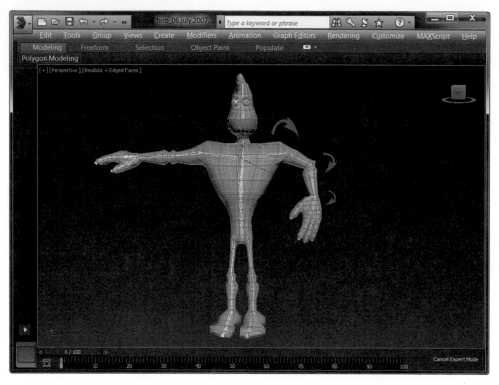

FIGURE 14.6
FK works by rotating from the top to the bottom of a hierarchy.

▼ TRY IT YOURSELF

Creating and Manipulating Forward Kinematics and Inverse Kinematics

Follow these steps to check out the differences between FK and IK interaction:

1. Open the file *SAMS_Hour14_FKIK.max*. This file includes two identical bone hierarchies. The first is FK and the second is IK—or at least it will be!

2. Select the top bone of the IK chain.

3. In the main menu, select *Animation, IK Solvers* and choose *HI Solver*, as shown in Figure 14.7. A dotted line appears from the bone in the viewport, and it follows your cursor. This indicates where the IK solver will be created.

4. Click the last bone in the hierarchy to create the IK.

FIGURE 14.7
Select the first joint in the IK joint chain and then, from the main menu, select *Animation*, *IK Solvers*, *HI Solver*.

5. Experiment with both the FK and IK chains to see how they behave. Notice that you can rotate the bones of the FK chain but not the IK chain bones. However, you can move the IK handle (created at the end of the bones where you clicked), and this affects the bones in the IK chain. Neat! You can take a look at my finished FK and IK joint chains in the file *SAMS_Hour14_FKIKComplete.max*.

So what exactly is an IK solver? Well, at its most basic, it is a goal-based solution where 3ds Max calculates the position and orientation of a hierarchy from the bottom to the top (rather than the top-to-the bottom order that FK uses).

You have probably noticed that there are a number of IK solvers to choose from. Why did I have you choose to use the *HI Solver* instead of the rest? Because each type of IK solver has its own behaviors and workflows, as well as its own set of specialized controls and tools, and I find the *HI Solver* the best IK solver to work with...at least most of the time!

Four IK solvers are available in 3ds Max:

- ▶ **HI** (**History-Independent**) *Solver*—This is my preferred IK solver, and the preferred IK solver for character animation. As the name says, this IK solver is history independent, which means it doesn't "remember" anything. This also means that it is as fast to use on frame 0 as it is on frame 80,000. Oh, and you can use this solver over multiple objects, which can come in handy.

- ▶ **HD** (**History-Dependent**) *Solver*—Because this solver is history dependent, it actually does "remember." This solver is therefore ideally suited to short animation sequences because its performance is affected over time. Don't write it off as something you'll never want because this solver can be useful for animating machines that have sliding parts.

- ▶ **IK Limb Solver**—Like the *HI Solver*, the *IK Limb Solver* is history independent, meaning that it has a consistently fast performance. This solver is limited to only two objects but it can be exported into game engines, so it can be extremely useful.

- ▶ **Spline IK Solver**—The *Spline IK Solver* is very different from the rest of the IK solvers. This solver uses a spline to determine the curvature of a series of linked objects. It is a far most flexible animation system than the other IK solvers, but it does require specific setup and is not ideal for every situation.

You've just gotten a lot of information. To help it sink it, it's time to create your own custom rig.

Creating a Custom Rig

You have already learned the main tools that you need to create your very own custom rig. Creating a rig is simply a case of using the *Bone* tools, linking, the Schematic view, and FK and IK. The following Try It Yourself shows you how.

▼ TRY IT YOURSELF

Creating a Custom Rigging Solution

As you've already learned, to create a custom rigging solution, you use the *Bone Tools* window along with some IK and the *Schematic* view. Follow these steps to create a rigging solution of your own:

1. Open the file *SAMS_Hour14_BoxDude.max*, which includes the basic geometry for a character.

2. Use the *Bone Tools* window to allow you to create the bones for this basic character. Keep in mind that this is a human-type biped character, so the bones should mimic our own!

3. When you have placed the bones, start adding in the inverse kinematics. Keep the arms of the character in FK and use IK for the legs so that you are able to "plant" the feet of this character.

4. With the bones and IK in place, use the *Select and Link* tool to link the geometry to the various bones that you have created.

The custom character rig you just created may not be the most advanced rig, but going through these steps has certainly improved your ability to pose and animate a character. If you hadn't done any rigging at all, posing and animating would be next to impossible.

For a completed custom rigging solution, check out *SAMS_Hour14_BoxDudeRigged.max*. It should give you some ideas for creating your own rig. Figure 14.8 shows a posed version of this custom rig.

FIGURE 14.8
This rig is posed and ready for action!

Using Character Studio (Biped)

Custom rigging is by far the best way to get the kind of rig that you want. However, it's also the most time-consuming and tedious method. Wouldn't it be amazing if you had access to something that could create a humanoid (bipedal) rig for you, with great features already built-in? You'll be happy to hear that 3ds Max provides this option already.

Yep, *Character Studio* (often referred to as *Biped*) is a system that allows you to build a bipedal (humanoid) rig without any hassle.

VIDEO 14.3
___

Creating Biped Rigs

Check out this video to see how easy it is to create a biped rigging solution.

___

▼ TRY IT YOURSELF

Creating a Rig with Character Studio

With *Character Studio*, you can create a complex character rigging setup with very little effort. These steps show you how easy it is to create a biped rig of your own:

1. In a new scene, open the *Create* tab and take a look at the *Systems* category.

2. Click the *Biped* button and then click and drag in your viewport. You have just created a biped rig.

3. To change or tweak any part of the biped, open the *Motion* tab (not the *Modify* tab, which you would usually use). From this tab, experiment with making changes.

There are some limitations and problems with using *Character Studio*, but as you can see, using it is an incredibly fast way to get a pretty nice biped rig up and running quickly and easily.

Using CAT (Character Animation Toolkit)

Like *Character Studio*, CAT *(Character Animation Toolkit)* is another built-in rigging solution in 3ds Max. *CAT* is a quick and easy solution that actually has more options than *Character Studio* but still ships with its own limitations and problems. For now, these issues shouldn't bother you, but be aware that using any kind of built-in (easy) system is never going to be as robust as a custom solution—but it is way quicker and easier!

VIDEO 14.4

CAT Rigging

This video covers the setup of a basic *CAT* rig.

TRY IT YOURSELF ▼

Creating a Rig with CAT

Creating a rig with *CAT* is a little more difficult than using *Character Studio*, but it's still nothing compared to a custom rig. Follow these steps to create a rig with *CAT* for yourself:

1. In a new scene, go to the *Create* tab, click the *Helpers* category, and change the subcategory to *CAT Objects.* You see three options: *CATMuscle, Muscle Strand,* and *CATParent.*

2. Click the *CATParent* option.

3. Click and drag in the viewport to create a *CATParent* object. Right-click to exit the tool.

4. Open the *Modify* tab. Toward the bottom of the *CATRig Load Save* rollout, click the *Create Pelvis* button to create the pelvis of the character rig.

5. Select the newly created pelvis object and then use the *Modify* tab to add legs, arms, spines, tails, bones, and your own rigging. That's all there is to creating a basic *CAT* rig.

NOTE

Loading a Predefined Rig

When you click the *CATParent* button, you get the option of loading a predefined rig that has already been created by selecting one of the options from the *CATRig Load Save* rollout. Check it out, and test it out!

Figure 14.9 shows a *Character Studio* rig and a *CAT* rig side by side.

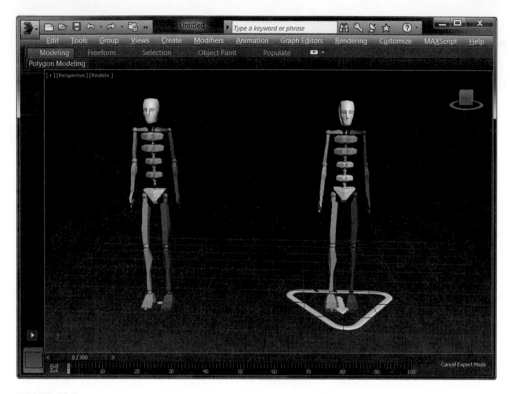

FIGURE 14.9
Rigs created in *Character Studio* and in *CAT* look almost identical. The *CAT* rig can be easily seen, as it has an arrow and triangle at its base, indicating its root, the top-most parent in its hierarchy.

Summary

This hour covers a lot of rigging basics. You've tried your own custom rig, and you've worked with the built-in 3ds Max rigging options. It's important to realize that rigging is not just for characters but can be for any object or item that you need to pose or animate. Choosing the correct solution is half of the battle!

Q&A

Q. **There are built-in rigging solutions, so do you really need to learn about custom rigging?**

A. Nope! As with learning any other 3D disciplines, everything is optional. Using a custom rigging solution is time-consuming, and the built-in solutions are great for many different scenarios, so if you don't need to go that in-depth, then don't worry about learning custom rigging.

Q. In a production environment, are built-in solutions used instead of custom rigging?

A. Many productions use built-in solutions. However, most large-scale productions and any production that requires complex character rigs move to custom rigging due to its flexibility and customization.

Workshop

You've already applied a custom rigging solution to a character, and in this workshop you're going to start with that same character and apply a *Character Studio* and *CAT* rig to him

Quiz

1. What are the names of the built-in rigging solutions in 3ds Max?

2. What do FK and IK stand for and what do they mean?

3. What are the names of the four IK solvers that are available in 3ds Max?

Answers

1. *Character Studio* (aka *Biped*) and *Character Animation Toolkit* (*CAT*) are the two built-in rigging solutions in 3ds Max.

2. *FK* stands for *forward kinematics*, and *IK* stands for *inverse kinematics*. They both relate to how you interact, manipulate, and give motion to objects in 3D.

3. The four IK solvers in 3ds Max are *HI* (History-Independent) *Solver*, *HD* (History-Dependent) *Solver*, *IK Limb Solver*, and *Spline IK Solver*.

Exercise

Using the *Try It Yourself* sections in this hour as a guide, open *SAMS_Hour14_BoxDude.max* and create a *Character Studio* rig for this character. When you're happy with your *Character Studio* rigging solution, make sure to save your file with a new name.

Once again open file *SAMS_Hour14_BoxDude.max* and this time create a *CAT* rig for him. When you have everything set up as you want it, make sure to save the file with a new name.

Analyze both your *Character Studio* and *CAT* rig files. Experiment with and test the rigs by posing them in different positions. Which solution do you prefer?

Influencing Geometry Using Skinning Techniques

What You'll Learn in This Hour:

▶ An introduction to skinning

▶ Influence and envelopes

▶ The *Skin* modifier

▶ Manual skin weighting techniques

▶ Setting up characters for animation

Geometry that is affected by a skeletal structure of some kind is called a *skin*. Skinning is the process you use to define the area of a model that is affected by a skeletal structure or specific bone or influence object.

The skinning process can be confusing to those who are new to it, and for any complex object or character, skinning can take up a whole lot of time. You're going to spend this hour looking at a few of the skinning tools and a couple techniques that should make this process easier for you.

What Is Skinning?

Just as your own human skin is moved by the motion of your bones and muscles, geometry in 3ds Max can be moved by bones or other objects, which are sometimes referred to as *influence objects*. You use various tools and techniques to associate geometry with specific influence objects, in a process called *skinning*.

Skinning, along with the movement of geometry by way of influence objects, is achieved by using one of two built-in 3ds Max modifiers: the *Physique* modifier and the *Skin* modifier. Both of these modifiers can achieve the same results, but the *Skin* modifier is the one I prefer, and it's more advanced.

The *Physique* modifier is actually a legacy (really old) modifier that I personally don't recommend using, and I therefore don't mention it again during this hour or in the rest of the book!

Influence Area and Envelopes

In 3ds Max, each bone (or influence object) that affects the skin has an influence area. This influence area is automatically assigned and has a capsule-shaped *envelope*. Vertices of the object that are within the boundaries of these envelopes move along with the bones, and where the envelopes overlap, vertices in this area blend between the envelopes. Figure 15.1 shows an example of what these envelope areas look like.

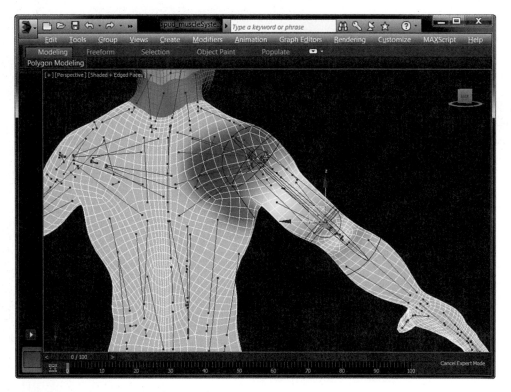

FIGURE 15.1
Envelopes help you visualize and edit the area where a bone has an effect on the geometry.

Skin weights are what you call the influence amount that each vertex inherits from the *Skin* modifier. These numbers run from 0 to 1, and you can think of this as a percentage from 0% to 100% (or a fraction, if you prefer, as it all adds up to the same thing). So if a vertex is weighted to 1 (or 100%) to a bone, it will move along only with that specific bone. If a vertex is weighted 0.5 (50%) to one bone and 0.5 (50%) to another bone (50/50), it will move half with one and half with the other. This weighting information is shown in the viewports visually by color, running from red (100%) through orange, yellow, and blue and to gray (0%). It's a little hard to explain, but Figure 15.2 should help clarify this.

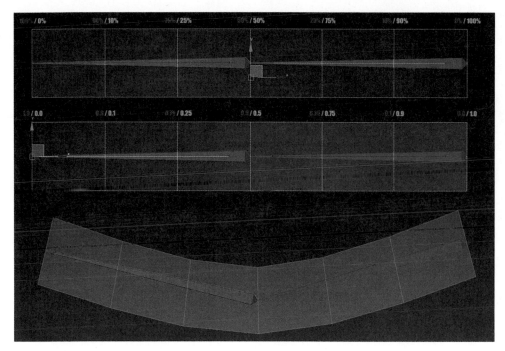

FIGURE 15.2
A visual look at how skin weighting works. Notice that, as the bones rotate, the geometry also moves (deforms) depending on the weighting influence of the skin.

The Skin Modifier

The *Skin* modifier allows us to deform and affect geometry using another object (often bones). We do this by using envelopes and weighting information in which we control the level of influence the *Skin* modifier has over the geometry, in turn changing the affected geometry's deformation.

In this section, you'll use the *Skin* modifier to apply skin to an object. It gives you direct access to the envelopes as well as many advanced options that can help you create some great skin deformations. Figure 15.3 shows the effects of adding a *Skin* modifier to geometry after some tweaking.

At its most basic, the *Skin* modifier is a deformation tool that lets you deform one object with another object. By applying the *Skin* modifier to an object, and then assigning influence objects to the modifier, you can control the deformations of one object by that of another—or multiple others.

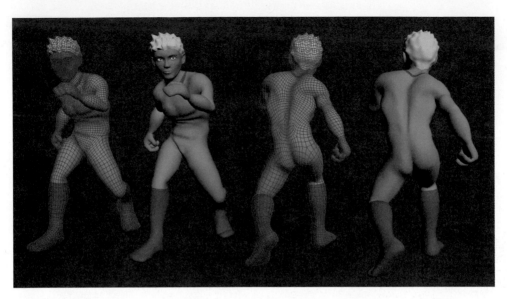

FIGURE 15.3
The *Skin* modifier applies skin to objects to allow for skin deformations of characters and objects.

Once you apply the *Skin* modifier and influence objects to an object, we can access the envelopes by expanding the *Skin* modifier or by clicking the *Edit Envelopes* button in the *Parameters* rollout. You'll find five main rollouts in the *Skin* modifier:

▶ *Parameters*—The *Parameters* rollout is where you access the main tools and options for the *Skin* modifier. You will spend much of your 3ds Max skinning time in this rollout.

▶ *Display*—You use this rollout to change the various display options for the *Skin* modifier.

▶ *Mirror Parameters*—Working on an object that needs the same skin information on both sides? This rollout allows you to mirror the skinning information from one side to the other, which can cut your work in half.

▶ *Advanced Parameters*—The options in the *Advanced Parameters* rollout give you access to additional parameters that affect the skin you have applied. As you get more accustomed to using the *Skin* modifier, the options on this rollout will start playing a bigger role as you deform geometry with skin.

▶ *Gizmos*—The *Gizmos* rollout allows you to deform the geometry according to the angle of a specific bone. This is particularly useful when you start thinking about things like muscle bulging and other more advanced skin deformation techniques.

VIDEO 15.1

Basic Skinning

This video takes a look at basic skinning concepts and using the *Skin* modifier.

TRY IT YOURSELF ▼

Applying Skin and Editing Envelopes

In just a few clicks, you can apply a *Skin* modifier and start editing envelopes. Follow these steps:

1. Open the file *SAMS_Hour15_BasicSkinning.max*. As you can see, this is an incredibly simple file, but the techniques you'll use here are directly transferable to more complex files.

2. Select the geometry, open the *Modify* tab, and add a *Skin* modifier to the object.

3. In the *Parameters* rollout of the *Skin* modifier, click the *Bones: Add* button. The *Select Bones* dialog appears. (Figure 15.4 highlights where the *Bones: Add* button is on the *Skin* modifier.)

4. In the *Select Bones* dialog, select all the bones (that is, influence objects) that appear in the list and then click *Select* (see Figure 15.4). You have now successfully added skin to this character, and you can test it by selecting a bone and rotating it.

5. To edit the envelopes, click the geometry once again, and in the *Parameters* rollout, click the *Edit Envelopes* button. The geometry switches to colors that define the influence areas.

6. Select the various bones (influence objects) that are affecting the skin by using the *Bones* table on the *Skin* modifier and move the small squares/dots on the envelopes in the viewport to change the affected areas for each of the envelopes individually, as shown in Figure 15.5.

FIGURE 15.4
You can find the Bones: Add button on the Skin modifier. This opens a new pop-up window that allows us to choose the influence objects from the scene.

7. When you're finished with your changes, click the *Edit Envelopes* button to disable it and then click the bones and rotate them to see what changes you have made to the skin deformations of the object.

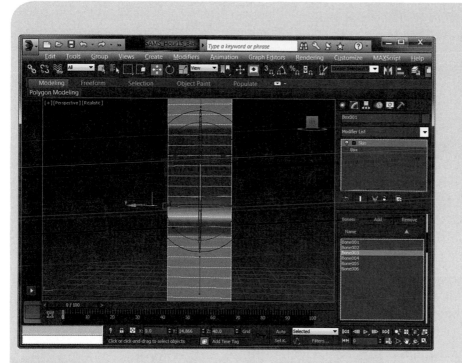

FIGURE 15.5
You use the small squares/dots to edit the envelopes in the viewport, and this updates the influence area of the specified bone.

Manual Skin Weighting

To manually weight skin, instead of using envelopes to change the skin weighting on the object, you manually adjust the weighting information for each vertex. This method is extremely time-consuming, but it does give you an additional level of control that you often need on complex or realistic skin simulations. In fact, even though it takes longer to do it this way, it is my preferred method of skinning because it gives me complete control over the weighting information.

3ds Max provides two tools for editing weights manually:

- ▶ *Weight* **tool**—You access the *Weight* tool by clicking the *Spanner* icon on the *Skin* modifier. The *Weight Tool* dialog provides tools to manually select and assign weighting information to specific vertices (see Figure 15.6). This dialog also allows you to copy and paste weights, as well as blend between influences.

FIGURE 15.6
The *Weight Tool* dialog is a handy floating window that really helps you out when you're manually skin weighting an object.

▶ **Skin Weight** table—The *Skin Weight* table provides access to several vertices and bones (influence objects) at the same time (see Figure 15.7). Vertex numbers appear in the left column, and bone and influence object names appear along the top, with their weighting information in the rows and columns below. This table also gives you access to a few more advanced features, such as normalized weights and rigid weights.

VIDEO 15.2

Manual Skin Weighting

This video looks at manual skin weighting techniques and the tools associated with directly editing the weights of vertices.

FIGURE 15.7
The *Skin Weight* table gives you access to several vertices and bones at the same time, and it includes some advanced skin weighting features.

Manually Weighting Skin

Skinning an object manually takes a lot more time than just editing envelopes, but you can get much higher-quality final skin deformations because you have absolute control over everything. No finished skinning is perfect by any means, but this method gets you as close to perfect as possible:

1. Open the file *SAMS_Hour15_ManualSkinning.max*. As you can see in Figure 15.8, this scene contains two identical objects. On the left is the object you will be working with, and on the right is an example of an object that has already been skinned.

2. Rotate the bones of the already skinned object to see what is possible with manual skin weighting.

FIGURE 15.8
The file you are working with contains the object that you will be skinning on the left, and a sample object that has already been skinned on the right.

3. Select the geometry of the object you are going to skin and add a *Skin* modifier to it.

4. To add the bones (influence objects) for this object, click the *Bones: Add* button and be sure to select only the bones that include the word *SKIN* in their name. Figure 15.9 shows what you should be selecting.

5. Now that the bones have been added to the object, ensure that the default skin weighting is assigned to the object. You do this by rotating the bones. Be sure to set them back to their original rotation when you finish testing.

6. In the *Parameters* rollout of the *Skin* modifier, click the *Edit Envelopes* button and then directly under it, select the *Vertices* check box. Doing this gives you direct access to the vertices of the model, and you can edit the specific weights for each vertex.

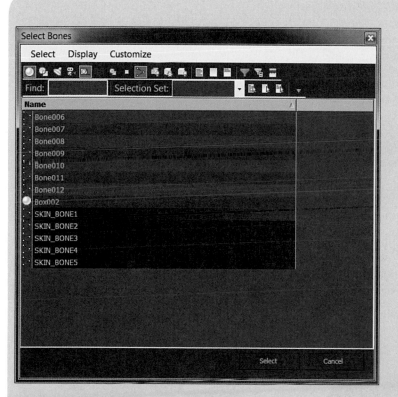

FIGURE 15.9
Add only the bones that include the word *SKIN* in their name.

7. Open the *Weight Tool* dialog by scrolling down and clicking the *Spanner* icon button, which is right next to the *Weight Table* button. You should not be in the dialog shown back in Figure 15.6.

8. Select a vertex or multiple vertices to enable the tools in the *Weight Tool* dialog.

9. With the tools now available, manually edit the vertex weighting for the object. At the very top of the *Weight Tool* dialog you see some familiar tools, such as *Shrink*, *Grow*, *Ring*, and *Loop*. Just under these are some number buttons that allow you to assign specific weight amounts to the selected bones in the *Weight Tool* dialog. Under this are some additional weighting options, as well as buttons to copy and paste and so on. Grab all the vertices on the object and click the *Blend* button about 20 times to see how the *Blend* tool affects the vertex weighting. The *Blend* tool blends the weights for the currently selected bone and vertices. You can see this in the color change of the object's geometry.

10. Try using the *Blend* tool for all the other bones that are accessible in either the *Weight Tool* dialog or the *Modify* tab. Figure 15.10 shows the coloring for a blended influence object that spans the whole object.

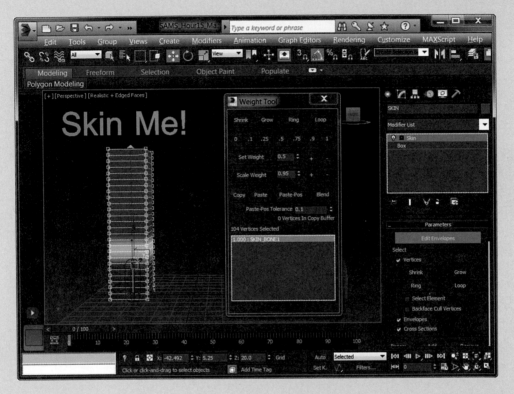

FIGURE 15.10
The colors of the object indicate the amount of influence an object has over the various vertices. This ranges from red (100%) to gray (0%), with orange, yellow, and blue in between.

11. Spend some time using the *Weight Tool* dialog, and then open the *Skin Weight* table and explore its interface. This table gives you access to all the bones and vertices, as well as their influence amounts, which you are free to change and edit as you wish.

Setting Up Characters for Animation Use

When you're setting up a character for animation purposes, a number of concepts and theories revolve around multiple areas of 3D. From the conceptual phase, to modeling, through rigging and of course skinning, there are a number of things that you need to be mindful of.

Character Concepts

Designing a character is definitely one of the most exciting and fun parts of creating a character. What will it look like? How will it move? What should it be? The possibilities are endless...or are they?!

You see, you have to really think about how a 2D sketch of a character and/or the concept art will translate into 3D. You have to think carefully about the design, as well as the limitations when it comes to creating 3D characters; both the application and you yourself can become hurdles at this point.

Character Modeling

We have already looked into a bit of modeling, but character modeling requires you to have a deep understanding of the tools and processes needed in order for character animation to be successful. Sensible topology (the looping and flowing of edges), correct scale for the character geometry, and the correct position and pose for the character come into play.

Character Rigging

As you know, rigging is the process of creating objects and bones to more easily control the movements of an object or a character. 3ds Max provides amazing built-in rigging solutions, and you can also create your own custom rigging solutions.

When it comes to creating rigs for characters, it is extremely important that you understand anatomy, hierarchies, and animation itself.

Character Skinning

Skinning involves the binding of vertices to influence objects, and you've spent this hour figuring out how to use the *Skin* modifier that is available in 3ds Max. The initial setup is typically automated but usually not very good, and you need to spend time manually weighting the geometry to ensure satisfactory results.

All these phases are a little more technical and complex than the rest of this book, but having even just this basic knowledge will put you on the right path for creating good character setups for animation.

▼ TRY IT YOURSELF

Skinning a Character

Skinning a character is just like skinning any other object. It requires time and dedication, as well as good knowledge of the tools available. You may have to do a lot of trial and error during this process, and there are no shortcuts or hidden tricks to make it any easier. Only hard work and dedication will pay off, so get started by following these steps:

1. Open the file *SAMS_Hour15_CharacterSkinning.max*. This scene contains a very basic character model, all the bones required for some character animation/poses, and two IK chains for the legs (see Figure 15.11).

2. Use the techniques covered earlier in this hour to skin this character correctly.

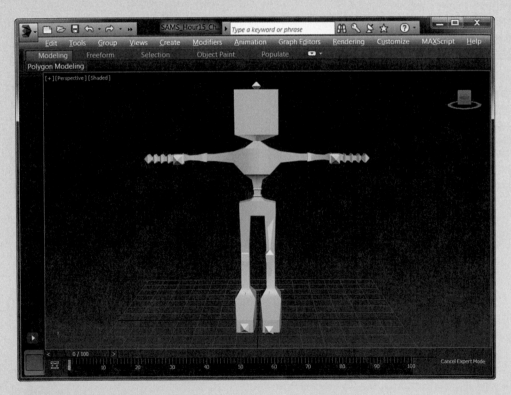

FIGURE 15.11
This is a very basic character model, but it has all the bones needed for you to start skinning it and getting it ready for animation.

Be sure to check out the file *SAMS_Hour15_CharacterSkinningFINAL.max*, which shows my finished version of the character skin.

Summary

Skinning and rigging techniques combined form the basis of workflows dedicated to character systems. This hour has taken you through the fundamentals of skinning and the process behind it. With this foundation, it's now up to you to keep developing your skills and start thinking about how to incorporate advanced deformation and muscle systems for added believability with skin deformations.

Q&A

Q. What exactly is the skinning process, and how do you start skinning an object?

A. Skinning is a technique used to allow objects, such as bones, to affect the geometry, or "skin," of a character or another object. Applying the *Skin* modifier to an object enables you to start skinning.

Q. Should you use envelopes when skinning a character?

A. An envelope defines the influence area of the skin from a specific bone or object; envelopes are quick and easy to use, but they are not particularly accurate. You can use envelopes as a starting point for your skinning, but I suggest switching to manual skin weighting if you're working with a character designed for use in animation. The added control will allow you to get better skin deformations overall.

Workshop

Skinning is a difficult skill to master. It can be super frustrating and boring, and it can also be mega-artistic and satisfying. This workshop will push your skinning skill to its limits.

Quiz

1. Why should you use the *Skin* modifier rather than the *Physique* modifier?

2. What are the two tools that 3ds Max provides for manual skin weighting?

3. Which technique gives you better results for skinning: enveloping or manual weighting?

Answers

1. The *Physique* modifier is a legacy (old) modifier that is no longer supported. The *Skin* modifier is bigger and better in every way!

2. 3ds Max provides the *Weight* tool and the *Skin Weight* table tools for manual skin weighting.

3. Manual weighting gives you more fidelity and better control over each and every vertex weight on a skinned object, which means you can tweak and edit to perfection...or at least close to perfection.

Exercise

Using the file *SAMS_Hour15_GreenMan.max* as a starting point, add bones and IK or use one of the built-in methods to create a rig for the character.

With the rig in place, apply the *Skin* modifier and skin the character to the best of your ability. Remember to keep testing your skinning by putting the character in various poses or even by animating some of the bones so that you can scrub through the animation as you skin him. When you're happy with your work, make sure to save the file.

HOUR 16
Character Animation

What You'll Learn In This Hour:

▶ What character animation is

▶ The 12 principles of animation

▶ How to create a bouncing-ball animation

▶ How to edit animation curves

▶ How to use modifiers to enhance animation

Character animation is a specific area of animation that focuses on characters. (I know, you worked that out already, didn't you?) Basically, a character animator is actually an actor, and it is his or her job to give life to the characters he or she is animating—creating the illusion of life, thought, personality, and emotion. You've already looked at creating animations, but mastering the process and skills needed to translate those basic animation techniques into character animation can take a long time.

You learned some basic animation back in Hour 9, "Computer Animation," but that was mostly an introduction to the tools and how to animate the movement of objects. In this hour you are not just giving movement to objects but giving them character. You are going to learn about some of the principles of character animation, which will give you a grounding in more animation techniques. You'll also work through a few exercises that will improve your understanding of what it takes to do some great character animation for yourself.

The 12 Principles of Animation

Two Disney animators, Ollie Johnston and Frank Thomas, introduced 12 basic principles of animation that animators all around the world have adopted widely. These principles were originally intended to apply to traditional, hand-drawn animation, but they still have relevance if you're using computers to create animations; they just need a little adaptation. The following sections describe all 12 principles.

Squash and Stretch

Figure 16.1 shows an example of squash and stretch. This principle enables you to enhance the illusion of weight and volume to an object as it moves. The level of the squash and stretch of an item depends on what is required of the scene or animation. This is probably the most important element you need to use and master.

FIGURE 16.1
Squash and stretch is possibly the most important of the 12 principles.

Anticipation

Figure 16.2 shows an example of anticipation. Any action that occurs before the main action can be classed as the anticipation of that movement. Think about jumping. You first crouch (anticipation), then you jump (action), and finally you land (reaction). The anticipation prepares the audience for what is about to happen and also helps keep things weighted and realistic.

FIGURE 16.2
The action before the action is the anticipation of a movement.

Staging

Figure 16.3 shows an example of staging. *Staging* refers to the communication of an animation. Often the staging of a character, a set, lights, or objects enhances the visuals of an animated scene by drawing the viewer's eye and allowing viewers to read the scene easily and clearly.

Straight Ahead and Pose to Pose

Figure 16.4 shows an example of straight ahead and pose to pose. These both refer to the approaches one can take to the actual drawing process with traditional 2D (hand-drawn) animation. *Straight ahead* refers to drawing an animation frame by frame, from beginning to end. *Pose to pose* means drawing the keyframes of the scene and filling in the gaps with more drawings later. In 3ds Max, you can use both of these techniques by either keyframing each frame or by keyframing just the main poses and letting the computer fill in the gaps (which you can edit later). Most animators prefer the pose to pose method.

FIGURE 16.3
Staging directs the audience's eye and allows a scene to be read quickly and easily.

FIGURE 16.4
This principle refers to the actual drawing process that traditional 2D animators undertook, and those same principles can be replicated in 3D.

Follow-Through and Overlapping Action

Figure 16.5 shows an example of follow-through and overlapping action. When a character's movement comes to an end, not all elements of that character stop at the same time; things like long hair or clothing continue after the main motion stops, and we refer to this as *follow-through*. *Overlapping action* is the continuation of a movement when the movement is changed. When a character turns around quickly, his or her hair or clothing continues in the first direction before catching up to the turn and continuing in the new direction; it overlaps the new action with the previous action.

FIGURE 16.5
Follow-through and *overlapping action* refer to the continuous movement after an action is stopped or changed.

Slow In and Slow Out

Figure 16.6 shows an example of slow in and slow out. Hardly anything moves at a linear pace. When you run, you start slowly (slow in), you reach your desired momentum, and then as you come to a stop, you slow down (slow out). You don't instantly go from stationary to full speed to immediate stop.

Arcs

Figure 16.7 shows an example of arcs. Arcs, or slightly circular paths of motion, take place in just about all movements (with a few exceptions, such as some mechanical devices). It is important that arcs be apparent in your character movements.

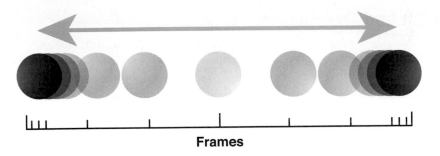

Frames

FIGURE 16.6
Slow in and slow out means go slow at the start and slow at the end.

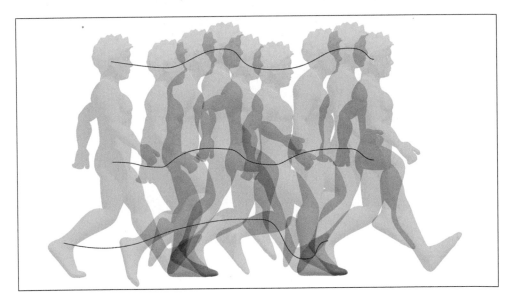

FIGURE 16.7
Arcs appear in just about all movements.

Secondary Action

Figure 16.8 shows an example of secondary action. The main action may be something like a walk cycle. However, the character may be feeling remorse, or extreme happiness, and you want to show this as well (via the walk itself and via facial expressions or in some other way). These feelings can be thought of as secondary to the main action, or secondary actions.

FIGURE 16.8
A walk can be angry, sad, or happy. These feelings and expressions are secondary to the main action.

Timing

Figure 16.9 shows an example of timing. The time taken for an action and the time between keyframes or movements have to do with timing. It's important to get the timing right, or your animations will look unrealistic.

Exaggeration

Figure 16.10 shows an example of exaggeration. *Exaggeration* is the pushing of a pose or an action past what is realistic. Just the right amount of exaggeration can help sell an animation; too much, however, and it can look theatrical and over the top.

Solid Drawing

Figure 16.11 shows an example of solid drawing. Solid drawing directly relates to a good drawing for the purpose of an animation. In 3D, I like to reword this principle as "solid rig and deformations."

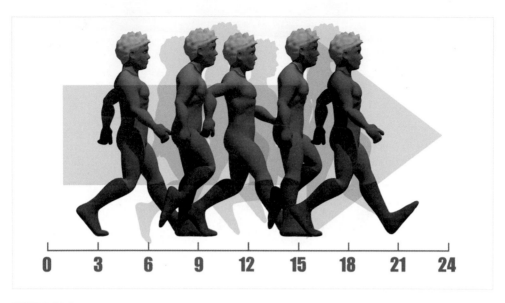

FIGURE 16.9
The time between keyframes or movements is important. Actions that are too quick or too slow won't feel right and will look unrealistic.

FIGURE 16.10
The exaggeration of a pose or an action can help sell an animation to the audience, but if you push it too far, you can totally break your character and animation.

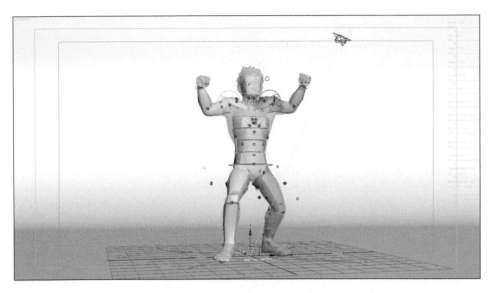

FIGURE 16.11
In 2D, this principle simply refers to a good drawing. In 3D, it's more about our rigs and deformations.

Appeal

Figure 16.12 shows an example of appeal. Appeal of something can change from person to person, but animations are usually there to appeal to a certain audience or to work within a scene. Do they do that? Do they work for your needs?

FIGURE 16.12
The final principle is appeal. Does the audience like the animation? Does it work for the scene?

The Bouncing Ball

Now that you know about the 12 principles of animation, you can start applying them to some animations of your own making. The bouncing-ball exercise is a total animation cliché, but it holds so much value that pretty much no one will pass over it—me included! Figure 16.13 shows a completed bouncing-ball exercise, and you can take a closer look at it in the file *SAMS_Hour16_BouncingBallExample.max*.

VIDEO 16.1

An Introduction to Animation with Character

This video talks about the 12 principles of animation, looks at creating a bouncing-ball animation, and explains where to look for further information on character animation.

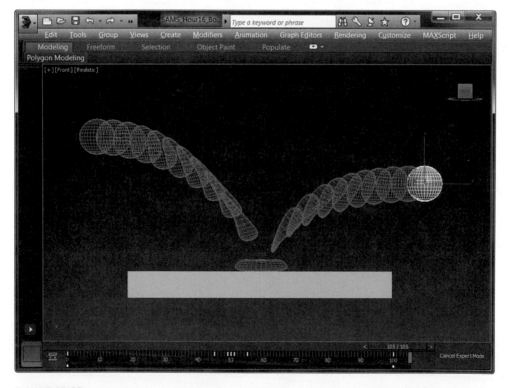

FIGURE 16.13
The bouncing-ball exercise may be overused, but it teaches skills and techniques that you can apply to all character animation.

You can use all 12 principles when you animate a bouncing ball. Timing is a big aspect when it comes to the feel and weight of the ball's animation. This kind of character animation requires you to gain a deeper understanding of the *Curve Editor* tool as well as the individual axes (*X*, *Y*, and *Z*) for the various manipulation tools available (*Move*, *Rotate*, *Scale*, and so on).

Due to the complexities of this animation, I've split it into stages, so you can focus on specific areas of the animation rather than try to combine everything and get more confused than you have to.

Stage 1: Bouncing-Ball Animation

If you've never tried to animate a bouncing ball, you might think it's a simple task. However, when you start working on any character-based animation, each and every one of the 12 principles comes into play, making things a little more difficult. Along with considering those 12 principles, you have to start using the available tools (both animation-related tools and others) at a more advanced level.

In the following Try It Yourself, you'll work on animating the bouncing ball.

TRY IT YOURSELF ▼

Animating a Bouncing Ball

Follow these steps to see what I mean about the difficulty of animating a bouncing ball:

1. Open the file *SAMS_Hour16_BouncingBallAnimStart.max*.

2. In a front viewport, move the *BouncingBall* sphere to the left and up so that you can see the *BouncingBall* object in its entirety and at the start of its bounce, as shown in Figure 16.14.

3. Turn on *Auto Key* and click the *Key* button to set a keyframe at frame 0.

4. Move the time slider to frame 50, and with the *BouncingBall* object still selected, click the *Align* icon on the main toolbar (highlighted in Figure 16.15). Your cursor does not change, and if you click on the *Ground* object, the *Align Selection* tool pops up.

5. Using Figure 16.15 as a guide, align the X position and Y position using the *Minimum* option for the current object (*BouncingBall*) and the pivot point of the target object (*Ground*). Click *OK* to exit the tool and the alignment. The *BouncingBall* object heads to the center of the *Ground* object, and does not intersect it.

6. With the *BouncingBall* object still selected, click the *Key* button to make a keyframe at frame 50.

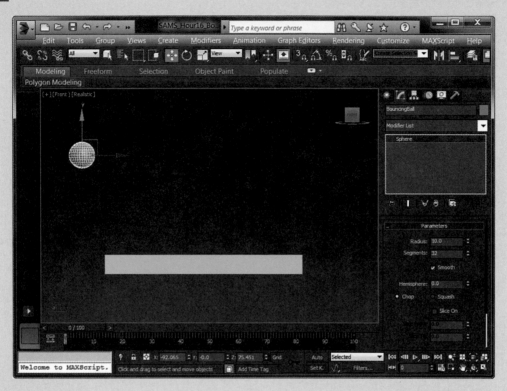

FIGURE 16.14
Using a front viewport, you move the *BouncingBall* object to the left so that you can see it fully.

7. Move the time slider to frame 100 and move the *BouncingBall* object to the right and up, to indicate the final position of the *BouncingBall* object after it has bounced. When you're happy with its end position, remember to click the *Key* button once again to set a keyframe at frame 100.

8. Turn off *Auto Key* and click the *Play* button to check your animation.

FIGURE 16.15
The *Align* tool, which is on the main toolbar, allows you to align one object to another using a variety of parameters.

You can take a look at the file *SAMS_BouncingBallAnimEnd.max* to see what my bouncing-ball animation looks like to this point.

I'm sure you will agree that the animation you have just created is not exactly looking too great. But fear not! You are going to work some magic into this animation in the next stage of this process.

Stage 2: Bouncing-Ball Animation Curves

You're going to fix your basic animation by using the *Curve Editor* to manipulate the animation curves rather than spend time attacking loads of keyframes.

▼ TRY IT YOURSELF

Editing Animation Curves

When you create animation, you are also creating animation curves. The animation curves control the flow of animation over time, and you can access and edit them by jumping into and using the *Curve Editor*. Here's what you do:

1. Continue from your last bouncing-ball animation file or open *SAMS_BouncingBallAnimEnd. max* to work along on my file.

2. Open the Curve Editor from the main toolbar or by right-clicking the *BouncingBall* object and choosing the *Curve Editor* option. Figure 16.16 shows both of these ways of getting to the *Curve Editor*.

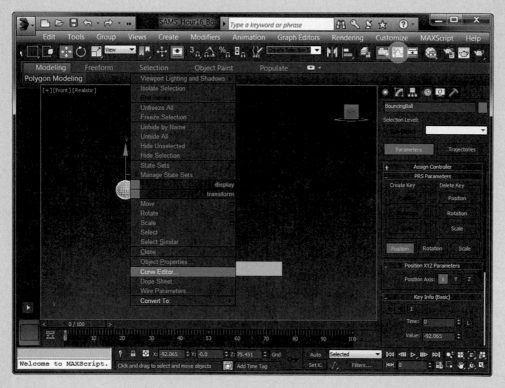

FIGURE 16.16
You can open the *Curve Editor* either from the main toolbar or by right-clicking an object and selecting the *Curve Editor* option.

3. With the *Curve Editor* window open, make sure the *BouncingBall* is selected and you can see its animation curves. All these animation curves are now displayed for the *BouncingBall* object's position, rotation, and scale parameters. You want to focus on the "up and down," or "bounce," of the ball right now, so you need to select only the *Z Position* parameter from the *Controller* section on the left side of the *Curve Editor*. Figure 16.17 provides a visual reference on how to do this. With only the *Z Position* animation curve displayed, you should have an easier time viewing and manipulating that animation curve.

4. Inside the *Curve Editor* select the keyframe that appears on frame 50, and the tangent handles for this keyframe appear, as shown in Figure 16.17.

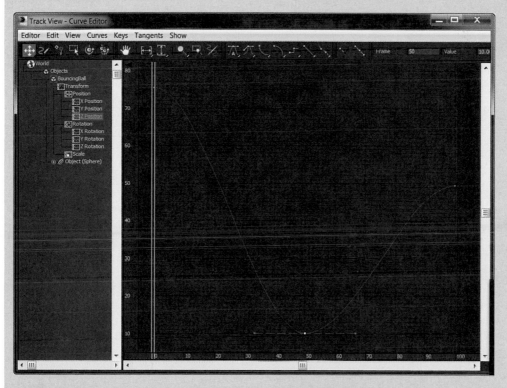

FIGURE 16.17
You can select the specific animation curves you want to access by clicking the relevant attribute in the *Controller* section on the left side of the *Curve Editor*. By selecting a keyframe in the main *Key* window at the right side of the *Curve Editor*, you can display the tangent handles and edit them as needed.

5. Hold down the *Shift* key and drag the left tangent handle upward in the *Key* window. Using the *Shift* key allows you to manipulate the left handle independently from the right handle. You should have a curve that looks something like what is shown in Figure 16.18.

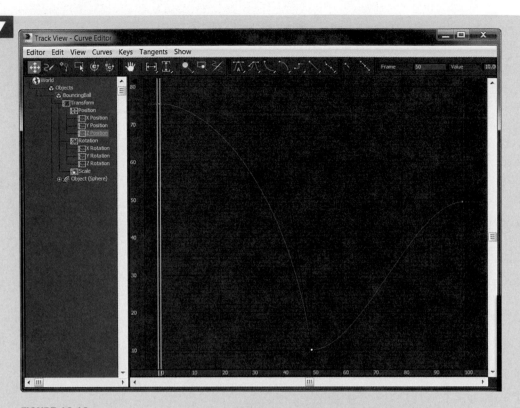

FIGURE 16.18
Editing tangent handles is as easy as clicking them and dragging. You can control the left tangent handle independently from the right tangent handle by holding the *Shift* key.

6. Click the *Play* button to take a quick look at your animation and see how the changes you have made to the animation curve have affected it. When you're ready, jump back into the *Curve Editor* and repeat the same process that you just did for the right-side tangent handle (that is, hold *Shift* and click and drag the tangent handle upward).

7. Click the *Play* button once more to see the changes you have made to the animation. Things still aren't perfect, and you should now adjust the forward motion of the *BouncingBall* object, which means using the *X Position* attribute. Select the *BouncingBall* object (if it isn't already selected) and display only the *X Position* animation curve by clicking on it in the *Controller* section (left side) of the *Curve Editor*.

8. You don't need that keyframe at frame 50, so grab it in the *Curve Editor* and press the *Delete* key. You now have an S-type curve for the *X Position* attribute, which gives you a slow-in and slow-out movement.

9. You want the forward motion of the *BouncingBall* to stay at a constant speed, so to ensure this, select both keyframes (at frame 0 and frame 100) and click the *Set Tangents to Linear* button, which is highlighted in Figure 16.19.

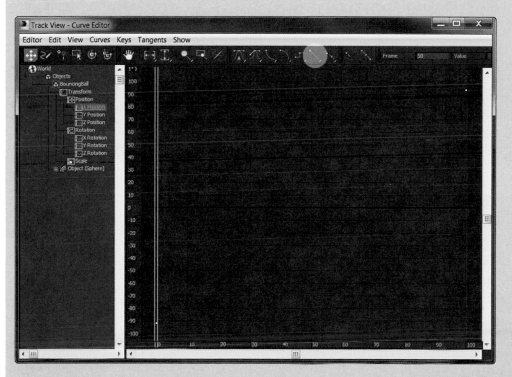

FIGURE 16.19
Use the *Set Tangents to Linear* button to change the animation curve from an S shape (which gives slow-in and slow-out movement) to a straight line. This gives the animation a constant speed.

10. Exit the *Curve Editor* and click the *Play* button to take a look at the animation once more. By changing the *Z Position* animation curve, you affected the bounce of the ball. By editing the *X Position* animation curve, you changed the forward motion (speed) of the ball. This is of course a basic example of animation curve editing, but you now have a foundation that should allow you to create and edit more advanced animations in the future.

By doing some minor adjustments to the animation curves and tangent handles of an animation, you can drastically improve, enhance, or even break an existing animation. Check out the file *SAMS_Hour16_BouncingBallCurves.max* to see my changes to the animation curves.

Stage 3: Bouncing-Ball Animation Final Touches

If you click the *Play* button in your bouncing-ball animation now, you will notice that the animation is kind of slow. There is nothing to stop you from grabbing the animation keyframes and sliding them around to different frames to speed it up. I'm keeping mine as they are for this demo, but you can feel free to go crazy!

Now that the main animation and curve editing are out of the way, you can add the final touches to this animation. One principle that this bouncing-ball animation example is missing is, of course, squash and stretch.

Often a good rig has all the controls and attributes needed to allow you, as the animator, to create all the animations and motions you want. However, when a rig is not provided, or when you are creating things from scratch, it is up to you to come up with solutions to these problems. Yikes! The following Try It Yourself will help you find your way.

▼ TRY IT YOURSELF

Using Modifiers to Simulate Squash and Stretch

There many ways you could address the squash and stretch principle in your bouncing-ball animation. In the following steps, you will use the built-in *FFD* (free-form deformation) *3x3x3* modifier to simulate the squash and stretch of the bouncing ball:

1. Open the file *SAMS_Hour16_BouncingBallCurves.max* or your own bouncing-ball file.

2. Select the *BouncingBall* object and add the *FFD 3x3x3* modifier to it from the *Modify* tab. This modifier surrounds the *BouncingBall* geometry with a lattice that you can manipulate by adjusting its control points.

3. In the *Modify* tab, click the plus (+) button next to the *FFD 3x3x3* modifier to show the drop-down menu. Click *Control Points* and then click and drag around all the control points in the viewport so that they are selected, as shown in Figure 16.20.

4. Click the *Filters* button, and in the new window, enable the *Modifiers* option so that you can keyframe the control points of the *FFD 3x3x3* lattice. With the control points selected, turn on *Auto Key* and use the *Key* button to add keyframes to the control points at frames 0, 50, and 100 (or wherever your *BouncingBall* object starts, bounces, and ends).

5. Edit the control points of the *FFD 3x3x3* modifier lattice. This affects the *BouncingBall* geometry and allows you to simulate squash and stretch. Scrub the time slider along to frame 50.

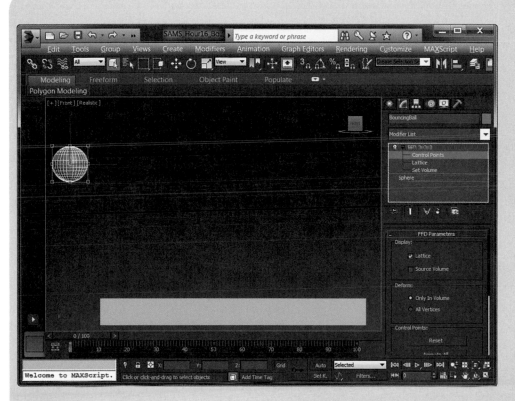

FIGURE 16.20
The *FFD 3x3x3 modifier* allows you to select and manipulate the control points of the lattice to affect the geometry it is attached to.

6. Using the *Move*, *Rotate*, and *Scale* tools, edit the control points so that the *BouncingBall* object is in a squashed position at frame 50. Figure 16.21 shows my squashed *BouncingBall* object.

7. When you're happy with the squishy-squashed look of your *BouncingBall* object, turn off *Auto Key* and click the *FFD 3x3x3* modifier so that you are no longer controlling the control points of the lattice.

8. Click the *Play* button and check out how the *FFD 3x3x3* modifier has changed your animation.

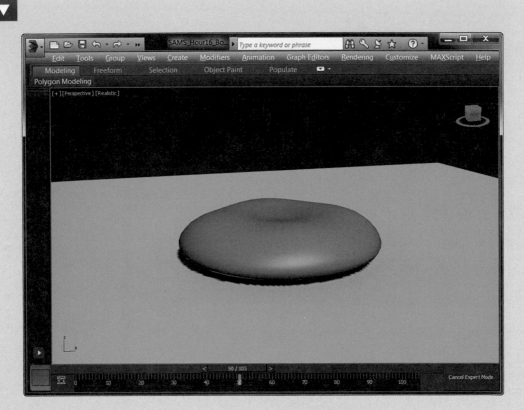

FIGURE 16.21
A *BouncingBall* object squashed by using the *FFD 3x3x3 modifier*.

As you can see, you are far from finished implementing the squash and stretch into the bouncing-ball animation, but no doubt you can see how incredibly powerful the *FFD 3x3x3* modifier is for manipulating and deforming geometry. Feel free to take a look at the file *SAMS_Hour16_ BouncingBallExample.max* to see how I completed this bouncing-ball animation example.

By spending time working with keyframes, animation curves, and modifiers, you can turn a basic animation into an animation with character.

Summary

In this hour you have learned about giving character to movement. You have also learned that anyone can create motion, but not everyone can actually animate. The bouncing-ball exercise is a great place to start, and working with it can teach you a lot about adding character to even an inanimate object. You can now take the skills and expertise you have learned during this hour and start applying them to more advanced objects and characters. There is a lot more to learn, and you'll face plenty more cliché animation tasks. 3ds Max still has a lot more areas you need to learn about.

Q&A

Q. Is character animation different from other animation?

A. Yes! Character animation focuses on animating characters, or giving character to objects. Animation is simply movement without that kind of thought.

Q. Where exactly do the 12 animation principles come from, and who created them?

A. Disney animators Ollie Johnston and Frank Thomas introduced the 12 principles of animation in their 1981 book *The Illusion of Life: Disney Animation.* Animators throughout the world have adopted these principles.

Q. Why does this hour cover only a bouncing-ball animation rather than a full character animation?

A. Well, you see, a bouncing ball is usually the first thing that animators learn how to animate—and for good reason! The bouncing-ball animation involves all 12 principles of animation, so it shows you everything you need to know without confusing you with many body parts. A ball is relatively simple and solidifies the principles and techniques needed for successful character animation. Of course, you have only just scratched the surface, and this hour serves only as an introduction to the possibilities of character animation.

Workshop

Animation is difficult—there's no doubt about it. This workshop will test your current knowledge and help push your character animation skills even further.

Quiz

1. What are the 12 principles of animation? List them.

2. What is probably the most important principle out of the 12 principles of animation?

3. Name a 3ds Max modifier you could use to simulate squash and stretch on an object.

Answers

1. These are the 12 principles:

    1. Squash and stretch

    2. Anticipation

    3. Staging

    4. Straight ahead and pose to pose

    5. Follow-through and overlapping action

    6. Slow in and slow out

    7. Arcs

    8. Secondary action

    9. Timing

    10. Exaggeration

    11. Solid drawing (or solid rigging, for us 3D folks!)

    12. Appeal

2. Squash and stretch is probably the most important principle of the 12 principles of animation.

3. You could use an *FFD 3x3x3* modifier to simulate squash and stretch on an object in 3ds Max.

Exercise

During the bouncing-ball animation, you looked into using the *FFD 3x3x3* modifier to simulate the squash of the ball as it hits the ground. But you didn't really look into the stretching of the ball as it flies through the air. Now is your chance to try adding stretch to your bouncing-ball animation. Take a look at the file *SAMS_Hour16_BouncingBallExample.max* for hints and tips. Oh, and if you master that easily enough, you should think about getting that ball to roll, too. Now that should keep you busy for a while, right?

If you're still hungry for more character animation, you can check out any of the many resources available. Simply browsing the Web and using your favorite search engine should get you access to loads of free content. Alternatively, you could pay for training from places like Digital Tutors or AnimationMentor.com (check it out; these guys are awesome!). If you would like to add some amazing books to your collection, give these two a try: *The Animator's Survival Kit* by Richard E. Williams and *The Illusion of Life: Disney Animation* by Frank Thomas and Ollie Johnston.

HOUR 17
Dynamic Simulations

What You'll Learn in This Hour:

▶ Introduction to *MassFX*
▶ Running simulations in 3ds Max
▶ Converting simulations to editable animation
▶ Simulating destruction

Dynamic simulations in 3ds Max are all about physics—in particular, forces and motion. These dynamic simulations automate the creation of complex, physics-based animation simulations using various forces. They create animations that are realistic, and they save you an incredible amount of time because you don't need to manually animate these situations on your own.

This hour specifically looks at the built-in physics tool called *MassFX*. *MassFX* is a complex physics simulation engine and toolset that comes built-in with 3ds Max. It includes a vast array of features that allow you to automatically generate complex physics-based dynamic simulations relatively quickly.

The MassFX Toolset

The *MassFX* tools are not enabled in the 3ds Max user interface by default. You need to enable access to them by right-clicking on any unused toolbar area and selecting the *MassFX* Toolbar option. Figure 17.1 shows you what I mean.

FIGURE 17.1
The *MassFX* toolbar is not shown by default, but opening it requires only a few clicks.

This small toolbar holds all the *MassFX* tools you need to access. You might notice that a few of the buttons have flyout menus (indicated by the small triangle on the bottom right of the button icon), and they contain additional options for you to work with. From left to right, these are the buttons on the *MassFX* toolbar:

▶ *World Parameters/Simulation Tools/Multi-Object Editor/Display Options* **(flyout menu)**—This section lets you control common aspects of a scene, gives you access to actions used during simulation development, lets you adjust multi-object parameters, and enables you to control display properties for an entire scene.

▶ *Set Selected as Dynamic/Kinematic/Static Rigid Body* **(flyout menu)**—This section of the toolbar allows you to set objects as dynamic, kinematic, or static rigid bodies for use within dynamic simulations.

▶ *Set Selected as mCloth Object/Remove mCloth from Selected* **(flyout menu)**—mCloth is a special version of the *Cloth* modifier that is designed to work with *MassFX* simulations.

▶ *Create Rigid Constraint/Slide Constraint/Hinge Constraint/Twist Constraint/Universal Constraint/Ball & Socket Constraint* (flyout menu)—These constraints restrict the movement of rigid bodies in *MassFX* simulations. All the constraints create the same type of helper object but have default values set to mimic the type of constraint selected to speed up the process of applying constraints.

▶ *Create Dynamic Ragdoll/Create Kinematic Ragdoll/Remove Ragdoll* (flyout menu)—*Ragdoll* allows animated characters to participate in simulations as either dynamic or kinematic rigid bodies.

▶ *Reset Simulation Entities to Their Original State*—This button resets a simulation by making any rigid bodies go back to their initial positions and transforms as well as setting the time slider to the first frame of the animation.

▶ *Start Simulation/Start Simulation Without Animation* (flyout menu)—You can start the simulation and have the time slider move along as expected, or you can start the simulation without the time slider moving.

▶ *Advance the Simulation by One Frame*—You can run the simulation one frame at a time.

Digging into each and every option of the *MassFX* tools wouldn't be any fun at all. Instead, I'm going to have you just jump right in and start using the tools so that you can figure out what they do as you go along.

TIP

MassFX from the Main Menu

You can gain access to all the *MassFX* tools from the main menu by selecting *Animation, MassFX* and then choosing from one of the multiple options.

VIDEO 17.1

Creating a Dynamic Bouncing Ball

This video takes a quick look at creating a dynamic bouncing ball by using *MassFX*.

Simulating a Dynamic Bouncing Ball

Remember doing those bouncing-ball animations last hour? Here you'll create a bouncing ball using physics instead:

1. Create a sphere that will be the ball for this demo.

2. Move the sphere up in the *Z* axis so that it is not on the *Ground* plane (grid) and can fall when you apply the simulation.

3. Enable the *MassFX* toolbar if you haven't already done so.

4. Select the sphere and click the *Set Selected as Dynamic Rigid Body* button, as shown in Figure 17.2. You now have a *MassFX Rigid Body* modifier applied to the ball. You know what that means, right? Well, it means that instead of using the *MassFX* toolbar, you could have just added that modifier from the *Modify* tab. I know, totally crazy! With just about everything in 3ds Max, you have a kaziblion (not an actual unit of measure!) ways to do the same thing.

FIGURE 17.2
You set the sphere as a dynamic rigid body by clicking the highlighted menu option.

5. Click the *Start Simulation* button, and you have a simulated bouncing ball. It's not super bouncy, but it does bounce a little!

The file *SAMS_Hour17_DynamicBouncingBall.max* contains my final dynamic bouncing ball. It's looking pretty good, but you might notice that you have no keyframes for this animation, so that's the next step.

Creating Keyframed Animation from Dynamic Simulations

The thing with dynamic simulations is that the motion and movement are calculated by the computer in as close to real time as possible. Therefore, no keyframes are created or needed in order for the simulation to run. This totally works, and it means that you can reset the simulation at any point, change some attributes and parameters, and then re-simulate and see the updated results.

Once you are happy with the simulation, though, you don't want to keep using processing power to simulate the dynamics. Actually, you might even want to be able to directly edit the motion and movement yourself. To do this, you need to bake the simulation to keyframes, and you can do that by using the *MassFX* tools.

VIDEO 17.2

Baking Simulations to Animation Keyframes

This video shows the steps you take to convert dynamic simulations to editable animation keyframes.

TRY IT YOURSELF

Converting Dynamic Simulations to Editable Animation Keyframes

When you are happy with your dynamic simulations, you can convert them to editable animation keyframes by using the *bake* tool in the *MassFX* tools. It's incredibly simple to do, and we should totally try it out:

1. Open the file *SAMS_Hour17_DynamicBouncingBall.max.*

2. Select the sphere and open the *MassFX* toolbar, if it isn't already open, by right-clicking on an unused section of a toolbar and clicking the *MassFX Toolbar* option.

3. Then click *Simulation Tools*, as shown in Figure 17.3, to open the *Simulation* window.

FIGURE 17.3
You can open the *Simulation* window from the *MassFX* toolbar.

4. It's pretty easy from here: Just click either the *Bake All* or *Bake Selected* button in the *Simulation* window, and the sphere should now have keyframes available for editing.

As you have just seen, baking simulations using the *MassFX* tools is super easy. There are even *Unbake* options, which, as you might guess, you use to unbake and remove the animation keyframes.

TIP

Baking from the MassFX Modifier

Don't want to open up the *Simulation* window? Simply click the sphere and in the *Modify* tab, click the *MassFX Rigid Body* modifier and then the *Bake* button. Yeah, you guessed it: It bakes the simulation down to animation keyframes as well.

You can open the file *SAMS_Hour17_DynamicBouncingBallBaked.max* to see my baked animation.

Causing Destruction with MassFX

Whenever I think of dynamic simulations, I imagine damage and destruction. This could be an issue I should address with a therapist, but I wouldn't want to spend my time that way and miss out on all the simulated destruction fun that is available with *MassFX* and 3ds Max.

To see what I'm talking about, you should totally destroy something right now! Next, you are going to take a wall and a demolition device, rig them up with *MassFX*, and watch the destruction unfold, live, in your viewport. What is this destruction going to look like? Well, probably something like what is shown in Figure 17.4.

VIDEO 17.3

 Causing Destruction with MassFX
This video shows you the steps needed to create a wrecking ball and have it dynamically smash through a brick wall.

Disclaimer: No real walls were destroyed in the making of this hour!

Creating a Demolition Device

Take a look at *SAMS_Hour17_DemolitionStart.max,* and you will see that it has both a demolition device (wrecking ball) and a wall available to use as a starting point for your demolition experiment. I think you probably just want to get on with things, so I will stop jabbering and get to it.

FIGURE 17.4
CRASH! BANG! BOOM! DESTRUCTION! All caused by *MassFX* and 3ds Max.

▼ TRY IT YOURSELF

Creating a Wrecking Ball

A wrecking ball attached to a linked chain seems like a good destruction device, and you already have the model created for you, so all you have to do is set up the *MassFX* side of things and test a suitable simulation for it. Follow these steps:

1. Open the file *SAMS_Hour17_DemolitionStart.max* and make sure you have the *MassFX* toolbar enabled.

2. Select the lvargest torus (colored in blue) and use the *MassFX* toolbar to select *Set Selected as Static Rigid Body*. This option keeps this object completely still, and it also affects the other objects that contact with it during the simulation.

3. With the larger torus (colored in blue) still selected, go to the *Physical Material* rollout in the *Modify* tab and change the *Preset* option to *Steel*, as shown in Figure 17.5.

4. Open the *Physical Shapes* rollout and change the *Shape Type* option from *Convex* to *Concave*. This changes the options available in the *Physical Mesh Parameters* rollout, so jump to that section and click the *Generate* button.

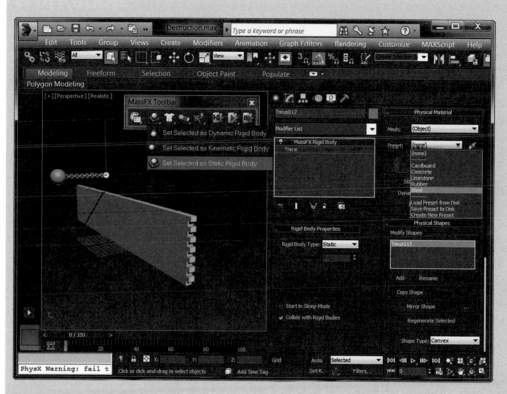

FIGURE 17.5
You set the larger torus as a static rigid body and change the *Preset* to *Steel* in the *Physical Material* rollout.

5. Next, work on the chain. All the torus objects in the chain, colored in gray, are instances of one another, and you can share attributes and settings with instanced objects. This means you can apply settings to one of the chain links, and the rest of the links update in the same way. To see this in action, select a torus (one of the gray ones) from the chain link and use the *MassFX* toolbar to set it as a dynamic rigid body.

6. Once again find the *Physical Material* rollout and change the *Preset* option to *Steel*.

7. Back in the *Physical Shapes* rollout, change *Shape Type* to *Concave* and then click the *Generate* button in the *Physical Mesh Parameters* rollout, as shown in Figure 17.6.

8. Select the wrecking ball (a sphere) and make it a dynamic rigid body and once again change the *Preset* option to *Steel* but this time leave the rest of the options as they are—no more clicking!

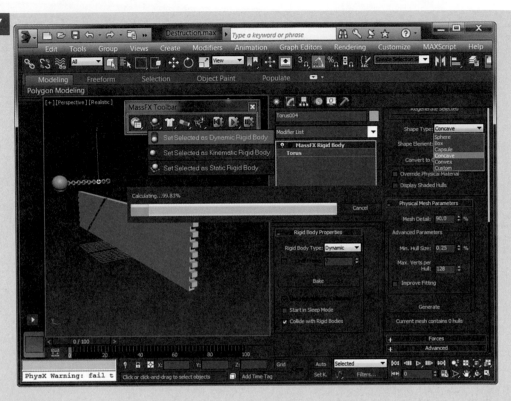

FIGURE 17.6
You set the chain links to dynamic rigid body objects, set their *Preset* to *Steel* in the *Physical Material* rollout, and generate their physical mesh parameters.

9. With the wrecking ball still selected, create a rigid constraint from the *MassFX* toolbar. A green box appears to represent the constraint limits. Resize it by moving the mouse until the green box fits inside of the wrecking ball. Click anywhere in the viewport when you're done.

10. With the constraint (green box) still selected, find the *General* rollout in the *Modify* tab and under the *Connection*, *Parent* area, click the *Undefined* button and select the chain link at the end that attaches the wrecking ball.

11. Try testing the simulation right now by clicking the *Start Simulation* button. The chain links actually break. Bummer! You need to fix this, but first you need to reset the simulation entities by clicking *Reset*.

12. Click the *World Parameters* button to open a new window.

13. In the *Scene Settings* rollout, change *Rigid Bodies, Substeps* to *50* and the *Rigid Bodies, Solver Iter.* to *25*, as shown in Figure 17.7.

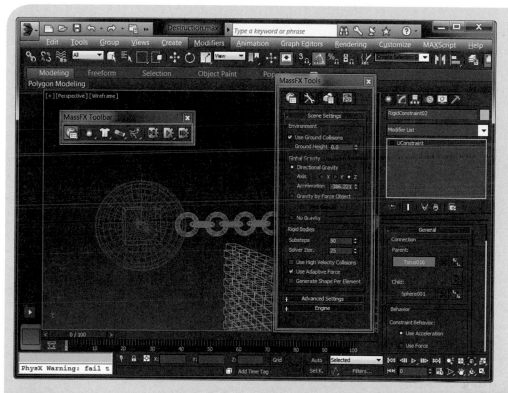

FIGURE 17.7
The constraint created needs to be smaller than the wrecking ball, and the constraint's parent needs to be *Torus16*.

14. Click the *Start Simulation* button to run the simulation once more. Everything should be working as you would expect it to at this point. Nice going!

Take a look at the file *SAMS_Hour17_DemolitionMiddle.max* to see how my wrecking ball behaves now.

Now that you have the wrecking ball and we've checked that it can be simulated, you need to focus on what to destroy: an awesome brick wall.

NOTE

Wrecking Ball Settings: Substeps and Solver Iter.

In step 13 of the wrecking ball example, you used some pretty specific numbers for both the *Substep* and *Solver Iter.* parameters. These weren't just good guesses; rather, I simply spent some time using trial and error to test and tune the settings until the simulation behaved correctly.

Wall Crash!

You're going to create a brick wall made from boxes that have been shaped and placed together to form the wall structure. You won't use any cement as that would be overkill for this situation.

▼ TRY IT YOURSELF

Setting Up a Wall of Destruction

Setting up the wall of destruction is pretty simple compared to creating the wrecking ball. Here's how you do it:

1. Open the file *SAMS_Hour17_DemolitionMiddle.max* or your own wrecking ball file.

2. Select a brick and use the *MassFX* toolbar to set it to a dynamic rigid body. All the bricks in the wall are instances of one another, so you can apply settings to one, and the rest of the bricks get the same settings. This makes the wall setup quick and painless.

3. For the bricks, change the *Physical Material*, *Preset* setting to *Concrete*.

4. Click the *Start Simulation* button and watch all the destructive work come to life!

Woo! You just used *MassFX* to create a wrecking ball and a wall that you totally destroyed! Check out the file *SAMS_Hour17_DemolitionEnd.max* to see what I ended up with here.

You might notice that some of the bricks take some time to settle when you start the simulation. This is obviously not realistic, but the example still gives you a good taste for what is possible by using *MassFX*. You've learned a lot in a relatively short amount of time.

As a final stage, I baked this simulation down to animation keyframes so that it is quicker and easier to play back in the viewports. You can take a look at it by opening the file *SAMS_Hour17_DemolitionBaked.max*.

Summary

That was some crazy destruction you just created, and it didn't take much effort. Imagine what it would have been like if you'd had to animate the wrecking ball swing and then the destruction of the wall. That would be quite some task, and not one that I think many folks would volunteer for.

This hour has given you some good information so that you can start creating your own dynamic physics-based simulations.

Q&A

Q. Why are you using *MassFX* specifically?

A. *MassFX* is a powerful simulation engine, and it is built directly into 3ds Max, which means you do not have to invest in plugins or additional software to create your simulations. This is a great solution, but there are obviously more powerful solutions available. But again, you don't have them for free like you do *MassFX*!

Q. Do you need a good computer system to be able to create dynamic simulations?

A. Yes, kind of. Creating simulations requires computations from your computer. The faster and better the computer is, the quicker the simulations will be and the less chance of the computer crashing. Also, having a better system allows for more complex simulations. However, you can use a slower and less powerful system; you will just have to make simpler simulations and/or wait longer.

Workshop

Ready to try some things on your own and step a little further into a dynamically simulated world? Use this workshop section to drive your learning even further.

Quiz

1. How can you easily access the *MassFX* toolbar?

2. Which item on the main menu gives you access to the *MassFX* tools?

3. How can you stop rigid bodies from breaking during a simulation?

Answers

1. You can easily access the *MassFX* toolbar by right-clicking any unused toolbar area and selecting the *MassFX Toolbar* option.

2. The *Animation* menu gives you access to the *MassFX* tools.

3. You can increase the *Substeps* and *Solver Iter.* parameters to stop rigid bodies from breaking during a simulation.

Exercise

Using the file *SAMS_Hour17_DemolitionEnd.max* as a starting point, change the parameters of the wrecking ball and wall to create an entirely new simulation. Go crazy and really destroy that wall, or take it easy and have the wrecking ball bounce off that wall like it's impenetrable.

When you're happy with your new simulation, bake it into keyframes so that it will play faster in the viewports. This could take some time, so be patient. Remember to save often and iteratively to avoid losing any of your work.

You have used a lot of the *MassFX* tools already, but you have not had a chance to explore either the *mCloth* or *Ragdoll MassFX* simulation options. Take some time right now to explore those options and learn how to utilize those tools on your own.

HOUR 18
Particles and Effects

What You'll Learn in This Hour:

▶ An introduction to particles and effects

▶ An overview of space warps

▶ Non-event-driven particle systems

▶ Event-driven particle systems (*Particle Flow*)

▶ A practical example of particles

You use *particles* when you want to simulate a visual effect that would be impractical, or even impossible, to do on your own. Particle systems procedurally create (spawn), destroy, and animate a large number of small objects to simulate various effects such as snow, water, fire, rain, or explosions.

3ds Max gives you access to two different types of particle systems: event-driven systems, which test various properties and send them to different events based on their results, and non-event-driven systems, which have consistent properties that do not change.

Due to the large number of small objects (with often complex calculations) that are involved with particle systems, it's important to note that your computer system needs to be very fast and have as much memory as possible. You can optimize particle systems, but the better the computer, the easier it is to simulate particles.

Space Warps

Although not exactly particles, space warps are kind of like modifiers that allow you to deform other objects to create various visual effects, such as waves and ripples, as shown in Figure 18.1.

Creating a space warp is just like creating any other object in 3ds Max. The main difference is that you have to use the *Bind to Space Warp* tool on the main toolbar to allow the space warp to affect an object.

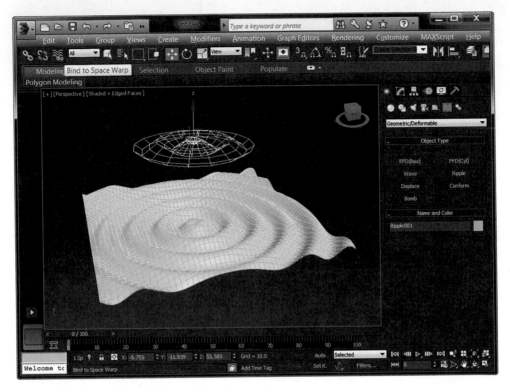

FIGURE 18.1
Space warps allow you to deform other objects so are not really particles, but you can use them in conjunction with particles to get great visual effects. Oh, and they are super fun to play with, too!

VIDEO 18.1
_____

Creating and Binding Space Warps

In this video you'll learn how to create space warps and how to bind them to other objects.
_____

▼ TRY IT YOURSELF

Creating a Ripple Effect Using Space Warps

Space warps can create various effects. In the following steps, you will get a *Ripple* space warp to affect a geometric plane:

1. In a new scene, create a plane with *Length* and *Width Segs* set to *50*.

2. To create a *Ripple* space warp, open the *Create* tab and select the *Space Warps* category and then the *Geometric/Deformable* subcategory. Then click the *Ripple* button in the *Object Type* rollout. Figure 18.2 shows where to find the *Geometric/Deformable* space warps subcategory.

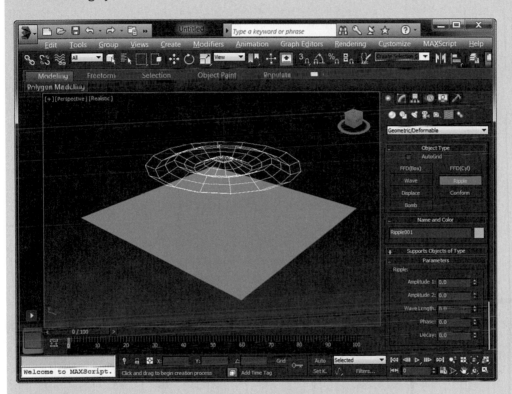

FIGURE 18.2
Space warps have their own category and multiple subcategories in the *Create* tab.

3. Click and drag in the viewport to create the base of the *Ripple* space warp and then let go and slide the cursor over to define the height of the ripple. Click once again to finish the ripple creation. Right-click to exit the creation process.

4. Select the space warp and open the *Modify* tab. Like most other objects, the *Ripple* space warp has parameters that you can set, tweak, and edit in this tab. Experiment with these now and notice that the *Ripple* space warp visually updates in the viewport as you change the various parameters. At this point, the space warp has not been bound to anything, so nothing else in the scene updates. You need to sort that out next!

5. On the main toolbar, right next to the *Unlink Selection* button, click the *Bind to Space Warp* button. Then click and drag from the ripple to the plane. When you let go, the space warp connects to that geometry.

6. Edit the position of the ripple to see how it affects the geometry and try out the parameters in the *Modify* tab to see what happens there. Figure 18.3 shows what happened to my plane object when I bound the space warp to it.

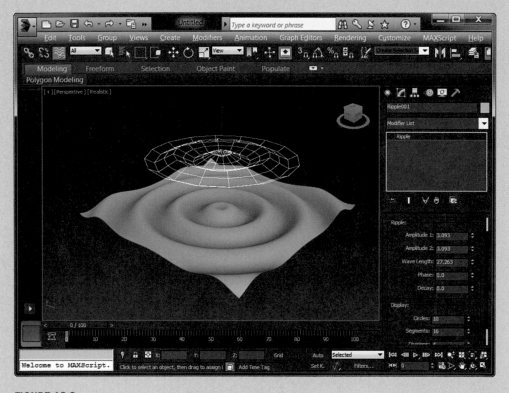

FIGURE 18.3
Binding a space warp to an object is incredibly simple. Just use the *Bind to Space Warp* button found on the main toolbar.

Feel free to check out my finished space warp test by opening the file *SAMS_Hour18_ RippleSpaceWarp.max.*

As you can see from the *Create* tab, there are a lot of space warps. They all do kind of awesome stuff. The thing is, there are just way too many of them to cover in this book. So, this is as far as we will go with space warps because we have way too many other cool things to cover in this hour. As always, feel free to experiment with them to see what they all do.

Onward, troops!

Non-Event-Driven Particle Systems

Non-event-driven particle systems provide a simple method for generating various particle effects. 3ds Max gives you access to six built-in non-event-driven particle systems:

▶ **Spray**—Just like the name says, *Spray* can simulate water drops like a garden hose or fountain.

▶ **Snow**—Yep, you guessed it! *Snow* allows you to simulate falling snow or even dust particles. It is similar to the *Spray* system but has some additional options and properties that can be handy for particles like snow and dust.

▶ **Super Spray**—This system is similar to *Spray* but has additional (advanced) particle options.

▶ **Blizzard**—This system is similar to *Snow* but has additional (advanced) particle options.

▶ **PArray**—You use this system to distribute particles on a geometric object or in sophisticated explosions.

▶ **PCloud**—This system is useful when you need a "cloud" of particles to fill a specific volume area.

You can find all these particle systems on the *Create* tab, in the *Particle Systems* category, as shown in Figure 18.4.

NOTE

What About PF Source?

Notice that the *PF Source* button is not highlighted in Figure 18.4. This is because that option does not relate to a non-event-driven particle system. Don't worry, though: You will learn about that button really soon!

FIGURE 18.4
You can find these six non-event-driven particle systems in the *Create* tab.

These non-event-driven particle systems are the easiest particle systems to create and use in 3ds Max. They are quick and easy to set up, with relatively few parameters for you to edit, and using them requires little prior knowledge. They are perfect for quick particle simulations or less complex particle routines.

VIDEO 18.2

Non-Event-Driven Particle Systems

This video takes a look at some of the available non-event-driven particle systems in 3ds Max.

▼ TRY IT YOURSELF

Creating Non-Event-Driven Particles

Creating a non-event-driven particle system is easy. Just follow these steps to get on your way:

1. Open the *Create* tab, select the *Geometry* category, and choose the *Particle Systems* subcategory. In this section you can choose from the non-event-driven particle systems that are highlighted in Figure 18.4.

2. Test out the *Snow* particle system by clicking the *Snow* button and then clicking and dragging in the scene.

3. Click the *Play* button to simulate snow, as shown in Figure 18.5.

FIGURE 18.5
Let it snow by using the *Snow* non-event driven particle system.

Now that you know how easy it is to create a non-event-driven particle system, be sure to explore the other five systems. You'll see that they are just as easy to set up and use as *Snow*.

Event-Driven Particle Systems: Particle Flow

Event-driven particle systems are a little more complicated than non-event-driven particle systems. *Particle Flow* is an advanced particle system that uses an event-driven model that we access using the *Particle View* dialog. To get to this dialog, you need to create a *PF Source* object, open the *Modify* tab for that object, and click the *Particle View* button (or use the keyboard shortcut *6*).

NOTE

PF Source

PF Source is short for *Particle Flow Source*. Using a *PF Source* object gives you access to *Particle Flow* and the *Particle View* dialog.

▼ TRY IT YOURSELF

Accessing the Particle View

Finding the *Particle View* dialog can be a little confusing, but follow these steps, and you'll soon be able to do it on your own:

1. Open the *Create* tab and select the *Geometry* category and then the *Particle Systems* sub-category.

2. Click the *PF Source* button and click and drag in your viewport to create a *PF Source* object.

3. With the *PF Source* object selected, open the *Modify* tab and click the *Particle View* button. The *Particle View* dialog appears, as shown in Figure 18.6.

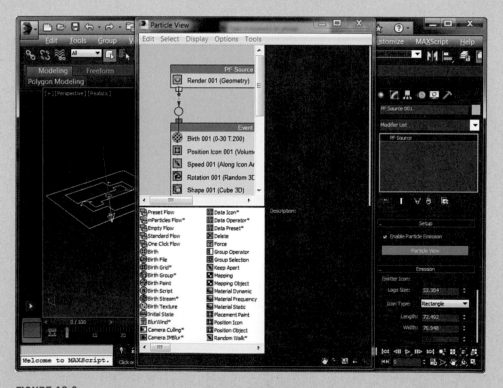

FIGURE 18.6
Finding the *Particle View* dialog can be confusing at first. Just remember that you can always find it by clicking the *PF Source* object you need to edit and then opening the *Modify* tab.

TIP

More Ways to Access the Particle View Dialog

You can also open the *Particle View* dialog quickly by pressing the shortcut key 6. Alternatively, you can go to the main menu and click *Particle View* under *Graph Editors*.

In the *Particle View* dialog, you use operators to set particle properties such as shapes, speed, direction, and rotation over a specific time period; then you group them together, and the group-ings are called *events*. You can wire together events to create a flow of various particle events, as shown in Figure 18.7.

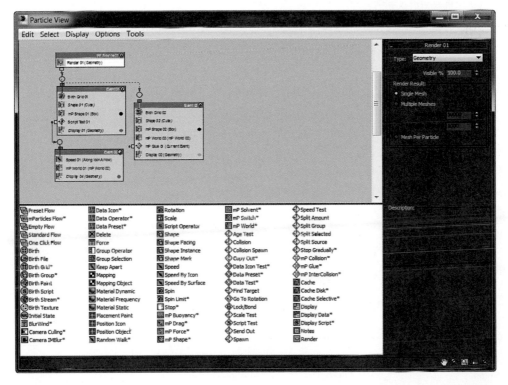

FIGURE 18.7
The *Particle View* dialog is where most of the action takes place when you're using the event-driven particle flow tools.

Yikes! This is getting pretty intense, huh? Stick with me on this. You will get through it and work all this stuff out.

Figure 18.7 shows the main interface that you need to get used to when working with *Particle Flow* as it is where you will spend most of your time. The light-gray section at the top is the particle diagram, where you create a flow by dragging items from the depot, just underneath it. By clicking various elements in the particle diagram, you open up the parameters and attributes that each element has; it's very much like what happens when you open an object in the viewport and then open the *Modify* tab.

Are you ready to create something using *Particle Flow*? Yeah, me too. I'm starting to bore myself!

VIDEO 18.3

Using Particle Flow

This video shows the basics of how to use *Particle Flow* and how you can build complex particle systems with it.

▼ TRY IT YOURSELF

Creating Event-Driven Particles Using Particle Flow

Particle Flow is a big topic, and mastering it can take a long time. You are going to use *Particle Flow* right now, but in a simple and straightforward example. In the following steps you'll use *Particle Flow* to create some rain:

1. Open a new scene that has nothing in it.

2. Open the *Particle View* dialog by either heading to the main menu and clicking *Graph Editors*, *Particle View* or by using the shortcut key, 6.

3. In the *Particle View* dialog, click the *Empty Flow* option in the depot (the white section at the bottom of the screen) and drag it up into the particle diagram area (the light-gray section). Check out Figure 18.8 to see what I'm talking about.

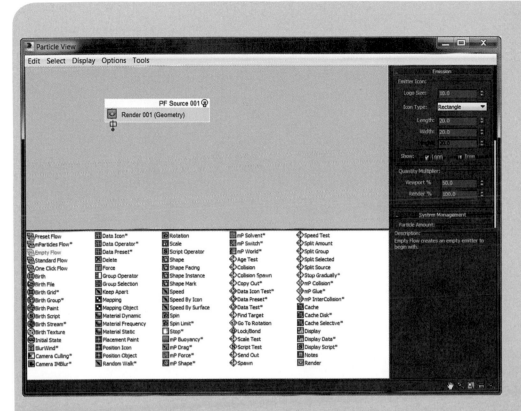

FIGURE 18.8
You can click and drag nodes from the depot (white area) to the particle diagram (light-gray area). By doing this, you actually create them in the scene.

4. In the particle diagram area, click the *PF Source 001* node. The properties and attributes of that object appear in the right-side column. In the *Emission* rollout find the *Quantity Multiplier* options and set the *Viewport %* to *100.0* so that the viewport displays the true number of particles (rather than half of them, which you get when the setting is *50.0*). Also increase the *Length* and *Width* parameters to *150.0* to make the *PF Source* object a little bigger. Figure 18.9 shows all this.

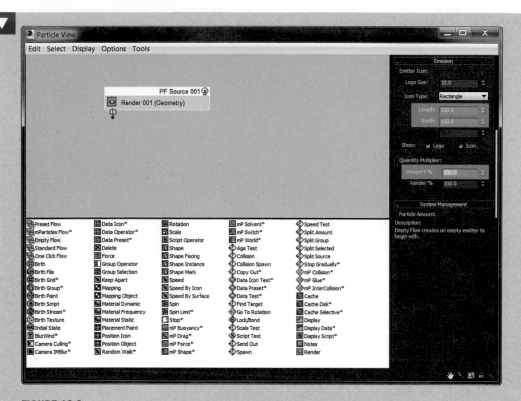

FIGURE 18.9
You can see all parameters and attributes for each node and each element of a node in the right-side window by simply clicking on the nodes and elements in the particle diagram area.

5. In the *Particle View* diagram, click and drag the *Birth* node into the particle diagram area. Now you have both the *PF Source 001* and *Event 001* nodes in there. Connect them by clicking and dragging from the blue dot (under the *PF Source 001* node) to the circle or hoop (at the top of the *Event 001* node), as shown in Figure 18.10.

6. Click *Position Icon* in the depot and drag it to the particle diagram to create a node for it, placed between the *Birth 001* and *Display 001* nodes on *Event 001*.

7. Select the *Birth 001* node and change its *Emit Stop* attribute to *100*.

8. Select the *Display 001* node and change the *Type* from *Ticks* to *Lines*.

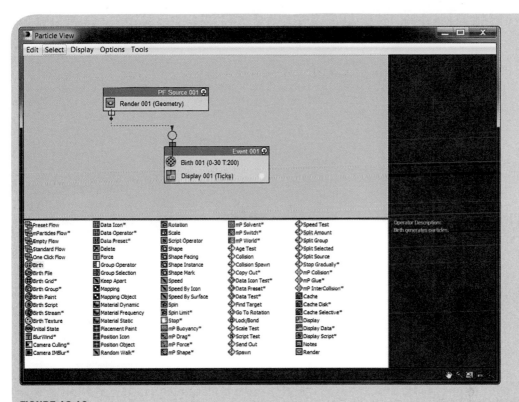

FIGURE 18.10
Connecting nodes is as simple as clicking and dragging between them.

9. Scrub the timeline, and you see particles being formed on the *PF Source 001* object. You want these particles (which will be rain) to fall. Go back to the *Create* tab, and in the *Space Warps* category, make sure you are in the *Forces* subcategory and click the *Gravity* button. Click and drag in the viewport to create it.

10. Switch back to the *Particle View* dialog and insert a *Force* node between the *Position Icon* and *Display* nodes in the *Event 001* node, as shown in Figure 18.11.

11. Click the *Force 001* node and click the *Add* button to select and include the *Gravity001* object from the scene. Figure 18.11 shows this.

FIGURE 18.11
You need to add forces to the main scene and then also add them to the *Particle Flow* diagram so that it can be properly evaluated.

You can probably tell that there is a lot more to *Particle Flow* than what you have seen here. However, even with just this quick example, you should now feel a little more confident using the *Particle View* dialog, and you may even feel inspired enough to try things out in there. In fact, I suggest you do that.

Take a look at the file *SAMS_Hour18_ParticleFlowExample.max*. It contains a super-basic scene, with some rain that reacts and bounces off the objects. Figure 18.12 shows what it looks like.

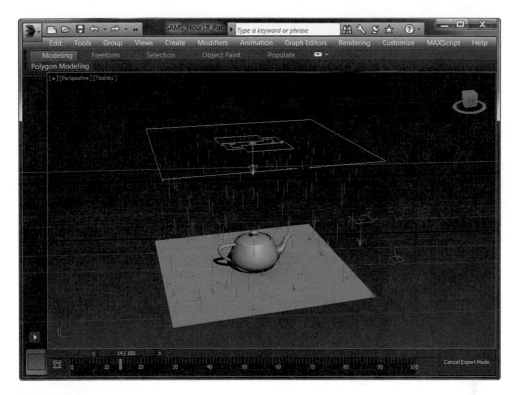

FIGURE 18.12
By combining space warps and *Particle Flow*, you can create an unlimited number of effects. In this hour you learned how to create rain. You can experiment with various effects, like including splashes as it hits and reacts to objects in a scene.

Summary

This hour has taken you through some of the basics and foundations for using both event-driven and non-event-driven particle systems in 3ds Max. You have access to six simple particle systems to get up and running quickly, and you can also use *Particle Flow*, which is a more advanced system that allows you to create some stunning event-driven particles.

It's exciting to think that these kinds of procedural systems, commonly used for visual effects such as smoke, rain, and snow, can also be used for a colony of ants or even a crowd of people once you get enough experience and skills working with them. Sadly, things like that are beyond the scope of this book, but with a lot of practice, you'll get there.

Q&A

Q. It seems like particles are complex simulations. Does this mean you need a powerful computer system to be able to create them?

A. I would definitely advise that you have at least a moderately powerful computer system before attempting complex particle simulations. Any simulation you create requires computations from your computer system, and the faster the system, the faster the simulation will run and the lower the chance that your system will freeze or crash.

Q. Is *Particle Flow* the most advanced particle system in 3ds Max?

A. Without using plug-ins, or a third-party system, *Particle Flow* is the most advanced and complex particle system that 3ds Max has to offer.

Q. Is there anything else I can do with these particle systems?

A. Yes! By using a node-based methodology, *Particle Flow* allows you to create various particle diagrams that flow and react to forces and other parameters. This opens up possibilities for basic AI (artificial intelligence) patterns, which you can use for crowd simulations, among other things. These simulations are somewhat more complicated than what you've seen so far, but there is definitely a lot of potential!

Workshop

Creating amazing particle effects requires disciplines in various areas of 3D production and creation, from knowledge of lighting, to materials, to modeling and even animation. What you have learned in this hour should put you on the right path for increasing your particle creation knowledge and allow you to complete this workshop relatively easily.

Quiz

1. What are particles?

2. What are the differences between non-event-driven and event-driven particle systems?

3. When using *Particle Flow*, what can you add to a scene to simulate various forces?

Answers

1. *Particles* simulate visual effects that would be impractical to re-create in real life. In fact, even when real-world special effects are used, 3D and 2D particle effects are often used to enhance the look of the real-world effects.

2. Non-event-driven particle systems allow you to quickly create particles that require no events to impact them. Event-driven particle systems are more complex simulations that require events to drive the particles.

3. You can add space warps to your scenes and link them into your *Particle Flow* diagrams to simulate various forces.

Exercise

Open the file *SAMS_Hour18_ParticleFlowExample.max*. Explore and experiment with the scene to see what has changed in it since the last Try It Yourself section in this hour. Then, using the same file as an example, create your own scene that includes rain that bounces off the objects you create.

If you're feeling adventurous, spend some time using non-event-driven particle systems to create a water hose that is spraying out water. You will have to model the water hose yourself and then render the final scene without any help. It will be difficult but certainly achievable.

HOUR 19

Cloth, Hair, and Fur Creation

What You'll Learn in This Hour:

- ▶ Simulating cloth
- ▶ Simulating hair and fur
- ▶ Using the *Cloth* modifier
- ▶ Using the *Hair and Fur* (WSM) modifier
- ▶ Loading and saving presets

Cloth, clothing, hair, fur. You can simulate all these types of materials by using 3ds Max.

Mastering cloth simulations as well as hair and fur simulations requires a lot of time, skill, and dedication—just like many other aspects of 3D production. 3ds Max includes a few excellent tools and features for working with both of these types of simulations, and this hour you're going to take a quick look into what's available.

Simulating Cloth

The advanced cloth simulation engine in 3ds Max allows you to create realistic garments for characters or other creations. Cloth has been designed to work with the modeling tools, and you can turn just about any 3D object into cloth. Alternatively, you can build garments from scratch, although that is a time-consuming and complex process.

NOTE

Experimenting with mCloth

You might remember from Hour 17, "Dynamic Simulations," that *MassFX* has its own cloth system called *mCloth*. *mCloth* is designed to work with *MassFX* physics simulations. Due to the complexity of working with both cloth and physics simulations, this book doesn't cover *mCloth*. However, I thought it would be good to at least acknowledge that it is there for you to experiment with if you want to!

Cloth provides an approximation of how real fabrics react under certain circumstances. You need to be aware of the system's limitations. Like particles, a cloth simulation can require vast computational resources. The density of the geometry and the level of realism you are trying to achieve affect the time it takes to run a cloth simulation. There is a trade-off between realism and simulation time, but this does not mean that a simulation will be unrealistic; it just means you have to be mindful of a scene's complexities.

Accessing and applying cloth in 3ds Max is as easy as creating a geometric object and then adding the *Cloth* modifier to it. Then you can access the cloth simulation properties of the object and create a cloth simulation for pretty much any kind of fabric you can think of. In fact, the *Cloth* modifier even includes some super-helpful presets for various kinds of fabrics that you can apply to objects quickly and easily.

VIDEO 19.1

Creating Cloth

This video takes a look at creating basic 3D cloth simulations, using the built-in *Cloth* modifier.

▼ TRY IT YOURSELF

Creating 3D Cloth Simulations

Cloth simulation sounds complicated, and the journey to cloth perfection can indeed be complicated. However, 3ds Max provides some pretty neat tools that can get you up and running quickly and easily. Follow these steps, and you'll be on your way to becoming a pro:

1. Open the file *SAMS_Hour19_ClothSimStart.max*. In this file you should see *TableCloth* and *Table* objects that you can work with.

2. Select the *TableCloth* object, and in the modifier list find and add the *Cloth* modifier to it.

3. In the *Object* rollout click the *Object Properties* button to open the *Object Properties* dialog. The *Object Properties* dialog, as shown in Figure 19.1, is where you can access, edit, and change the various properties for any object that will be used in the cloth simulation.

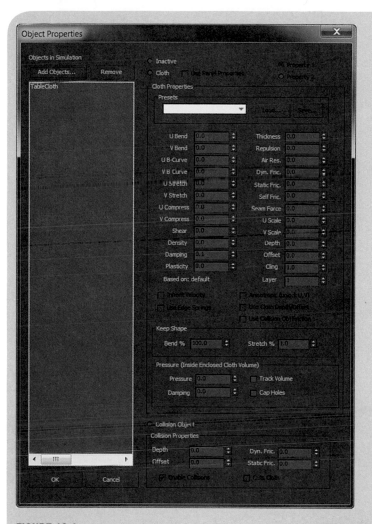

FIGURE 19.1
The *Object Properties* dialog gives you access to the various settings and parameters for any object that is part of the cloth simulation.

4. In the *Object Properties* dialog, click the *Add Objects* button and select the *Table* object to add it to the cloth simulation.

5. In the *Object Properties* dialog, select the *Table* object and select the *Collision Object* radio button, as shown in Figure 19.2. Leave all the *Collision Properties* settings just as they are for the moment, as they should work just fine for what you need right now.

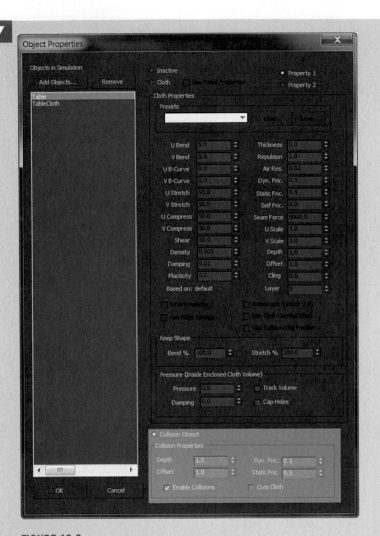

FIGURE 19.2
You can select the *Table* object and then *Collision Object* so that *Table* collides with any other objects that are in the cloth simulation.

6. Select the *TableCloth* object and set it to *Cloth* instead of *Inactive*. The *Cloth Properties* area of the *Object Properties* dialog gives you direct access to a lot of parameters. With parameters that affect the repulsion, air resistance, dynamic and static friction, and so on, you might be a little overwhelmed. The presets can help you out here.

7. From the *Presets* drop-down menu, choose the *Cotton* option, as shown in Figure 19.3. All the parameters now update with settings that simulate a cotton material.

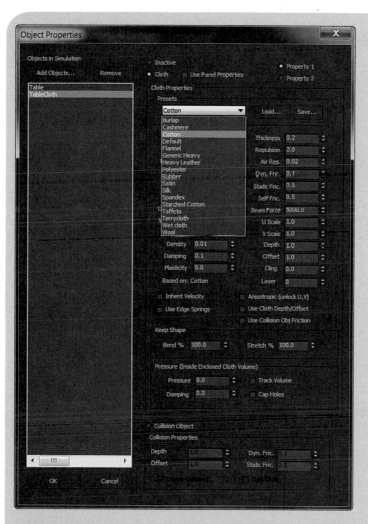

FIGURE 19.3
The *Cloth Properties* section contains a lot of parameters that can be somewhat overwhelming. Luckily, you can use the *Presets* drop-down menu to create specific types of cloth material simulations quickly and easily.

8. Now that everything is set correctly, click the *OK* button to save the settings and exit the *Object Properties* dialog.

9. In the *Modify* tab, scroll down and click the *Simulate Local* button to simulate this cloth experiment. When you are happy with how your cloth simulation looks, click the button again to end the simulation. You should have something that looks a little like Figure 19.4.

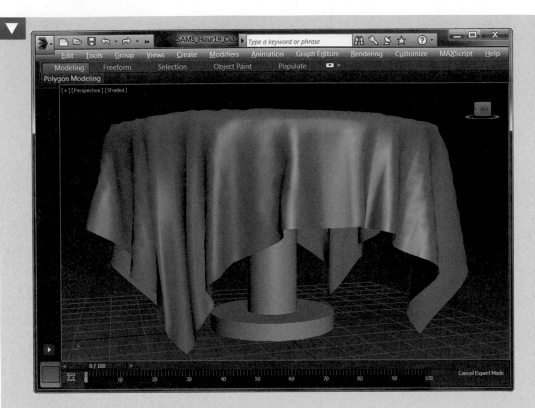

FIGURE 19.4
You've simulated a cotton tablecloth.

TIP

Using Garment Maker

The *Garment Maker* modifier allows you to create garments that replicate real-world clothing mechanics, such as seams and panels. By using this modifier in conjunction with the *Cloth* modifier, you can get an even more believable (and more complex/advanced) cloth simulation result.

Simulating Hair and Fur

The *World-Space Modifiers* section of the *Modify* tab includes the *Hair and Fur (WSM)* modifier, which allows you to apply hair and fur to any geometric or spline-based object.

When applying this modifier to an object, the viewport shows hair guides that represent the final output but are not selectable. By no means do they actually show what the final hair and fur will look like once it has been rendered. Figure 19.5 shows the differences between the viewport hair guides and the rendered hair.

FIGURE 19.5
The in-viewport (left) hair guides do not represent the true look of the rendered (right) hair and fur.

The *Hair and Fur (WSM)* modifier allows you to style the hair by using actions that are somewhat familiar, such as combing and cutting. Styling hair in 3D is kind of clunky, but with some practice and perseverance, you can get kind of good at it.

VIDEO 19.2

Creating and Styling Hair

This video shows you how to create and style hair using the *Hair and Fur (WSM)* modifier. The video ends with a look into the existing presets and how you can create our own.

▼ TRY IT YOURSELF

Creating and Styling Hair

It's not difficult to create hair and fur in 3ds Max, but getting it to look and behave as you want it to takes incredible skill. Follow these steps to try a basic example of creating and styling hair:

1. Open the file *SAMS_Hour19_Melmin.max.* In it you find Melmin, a cartoony head, made from four spheres. He is not exactly a complicated model, but he gives you something fun to work with.

2. Select Melmin's head and apply the *Hair and Fur (WSM)* modifier from the modifier list, under the *World-Space Modifiers* section, as shown in Figure 19.6.

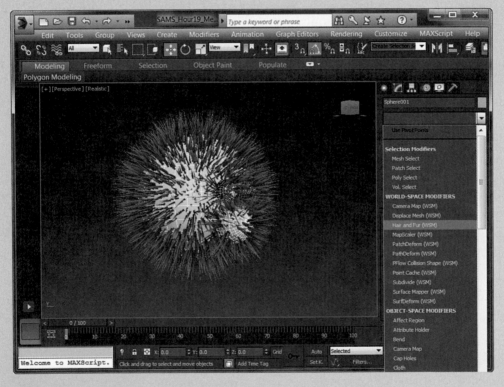

FIGURE 19.6
You apply the *Hair and Fur (WSM)* modifier to Melmin to start making this little guy a little bit hairy.

3. In the *Selection* rollout, choose *Polygon* and select only the upper-half of the head sphere. Then click the *Update Selection* button to change where the hair and fur grow from, as shown in Figure 19.7.

FIGURE 19.7
The *Selection* rollout allows you to specify where you want hair and fur to grow from.

4. Click the *Polygon* button once more to end the selection process. You have just applied hair and fur to an object and updated where the hair and fur grows from. It was pretty simple, right?

5. Check out what Melmin looks like right now by doing a quick render (using the shortcut *F9*). This could take some time, depending on how powerful your computer is, but stick with it to see the end result. You may see something similar to Figure 19.8.

FIGURE 19.8
Rendered hair often looks very different from what you see in the viewport. It's a good idea to do render tests as you edit and work on creating and styling hair in 3ds Max.

6. To style the hair, scroll down to the *Styling* rollout and click the *Style Hair* button. Some additional hair guides appear in the viewport, and your viewport cursor has a brush guide attached to it.

7. Click and drag over the orange guides to comb and update the hair style. By experimenting with styling and the styling tools, you should be able to create some wacky hair.

Creating and styling hair is a lot of fun—at least I think it is. Figure 19.9 shows my final hair styling for Melmin, and you can take a look at the finished styling in 3ds Max by opening the file *SAMS_Hour19_MelminHair.max*.

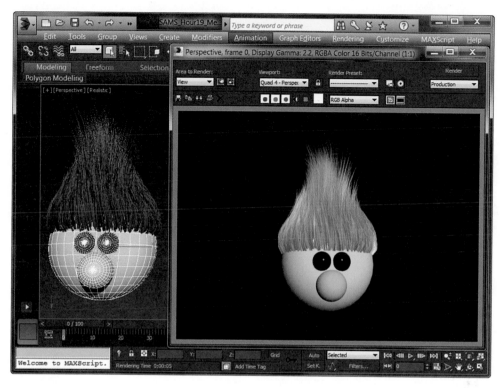

FIGURE 19.9
I hope Melmin likes his new hair style! The left side of this figure shows the viewport view, and the right side shows the rendered view.

CAUTION

Rendering Hair Error

You can render hair and fur only from the *Perspective* and *Camera* viewports. Attempting to render hair in an *Orthographic* viewport causes an error message.

Just like when you're simulating cloth, when you're simulating hair, you can load and save presets. The hair and fur presets give you a chance to load a preset as a starting point for your own creations or save your own hair properties for later loading.

▼ TRY IT YOURSELF

Loading and Saving Hair Presets

Now that you can make and style hair, you need to know how to quickly save and load preset hair styles. Follow these steps:

1. In a new scene, create a sphere and apply the *Hair and Fur (WSM)* modifier to it.

2. Find and expand (if it is closed) the *Tools* rollout. Find the *Presets* section and click the *Load* button. A new window appears. It should be similar to the one shown in Figure 19.10.

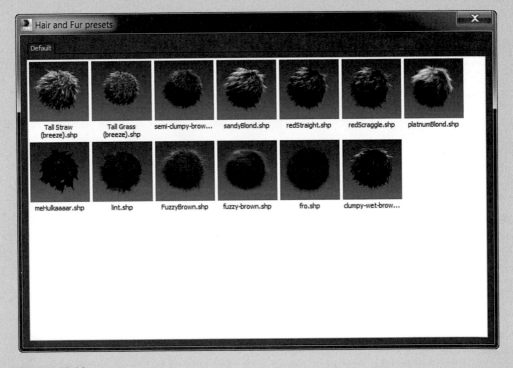

FIGURE 19.10
The presets give you hair and fur style options to get you started.

3. Double-click one of the presets to apply it to your hair and fur. The preset is a good starting point that gets you closer to the hair and fur style that you want.

4. Edit this style by changing the colors and reshaping it; then, to save your preset style, click the *Save* button in the *Presets* section and give it a name. Yep, that's all there is to it!

Summary

You've only started to pick at the seams of cloth, hair, and fur in 3ds Max. (I know, that pun is incredibly lame, but it sounded amazing in my head!) There are many more options, parameters, and settings you need to look into to start creating super-realistic simulations. This hour has given you a good starting point. As you now know, creating these simulations is easy enough, and with some time and perseverance, you could become a cloth, hair, and fur master!

Q&A

Q. **Do you need specific hardware for simulating cloth, hair, and fur?**

A. You don't need specific hardware, but you should have a very good computer system. In particular, rendering and simulating hair and fur can take a lot of processing power, and even with the best systems, it can take a long time to render correctly.

Q. **This hour mentions the *Garment Maker* modifier. Where is it?**

A. 3ds Max uses a lot of contextual menus and/or options (where things appear only if you're in the right place at the right time). The *Garment Maker* modifier is not available for geometry objects. However, if you create a spline, this modifier is added to the modifier list, and you should be able to add it to your spline objects.

Workshop

To see what you have picked up from this hour, answer a few quiz questions and then attempt to add cloth, hair, and fur to a character you have already built.

Quiz

1. Why should you use presets when creating hair and fur?

2. What does *WSM* stand for in the name of the *Hair and Fur (WSM)* modifier?

3. Is using the *Cloth* modifier the only way to create cloth in 3ds Max?

Answers

1. You don't have to use presets, but doing so is quicker than starting from scratch. It is also incredibly handy to be able to save your own created styles so that you do not have to re-create them later.

2. *WSM* stands for *World-Space Modifier*, and can be found under the *Modify* tab in the *Command Panel*.

3. Nope! You could also use the *MassFX mCloth* solution for creating cloth in 3ds Max.

Exercise

Now that you know how to create cloth, hair, and fur, it's time to start applying these tools and techniques to objects and characters that you have previously built.

Open the file *SAMS_Hour15_GreenMan.max* and add hair and fur to the character in this file. Remember to be selective about where the hair and fur should be applied and then style and edit as needed. Of course, feel free to use presets to get started.

Once you're happy with your hair and fur setup on the character, think about what you could add as a cloth object. Perhaps a cape would be a good starting point? If you're feeling adventurous, you could look at using the *Garment Maker* modifier to create a t-shirt or something like that, but it's worth keeping in mind that this is a far more advanced method than you have used to this point, and you'll need to do some research and development on your own to get it working.

Mental Ray Rendering

What You'll Learn in This Hour:

▶ An introduction to *Mental Ray*

▶ Using rendering presets

▶ Common rendering settings

▶ The *Mental Ray* daylight system

▶ How to render scenes with *Mental Ray*

Way back in Hour 12, "Rendering for Production," you took a look at the basics of rendering using 3ds Max's *Default Scanline* rendering engine. With it, you got some pretty nice results without putting in too much effort.

The output of the *Default Scanline* renderer is not completely realistic, though, but 3ds Max also offers the *Mental Ray* rendering engine, which is more complicated to use but yields better results. *Mental Ray* rendering is a lot more accurate and realistic, and in this hour you'll take a look at the vastly superior rendering engine. The main advantage of the *Mental Ray* rendering engine is that it can produce physically correct lighting simulations; this makes your final renders, and indeed your work in general, way more appealing and believable.

Mental Ray Introduction

In my opinion, the *Mental Ray* rendering engine is a little more difficult to use than the *Default Scanline* rendering engine. However, while the *Default Scanline* renderer is a versatile rendering tool, its results do not compare to what you can achieve when using *Mental Ray*. Because *Mental Ray* is not the default renderer in 3ds Max, you have to manually enable *Mental Ray* rendering before you have access to it and its materials and tools. As with just about everything else in 3ds Max, there are a number of ways to enable the *Mental Ray* rendering engine, and one of the easiest ways is to just use *Rendering Presets*.

During the rest of this hour you are going to be using *Mental Ray* rendering in a very specific way. This hour does not walk you through a full solution to rendering with *Mental Ray*, but it will increase the visual appeal of your renders greatly and put you on the right path for your own rendering experiments.

Rendering Presets

Preset rendering options are available from three areas of the 3ds Max interface: the *Render Setup* dialog, the *Rendered Frame* window, and the *Render Shortcuts* toolbar.

3ds Max has presets already created—some for quick preview renderings and others for slower but higher-quality renderings. Once again, you can set up your own rendering options and save them as a custom preset that you can use later. In addition, the default presets that ship with 3ds Max are good for many situations, including the following Try It Yourself. In this case, you'll use the *mental.ray.daylighting* preset.

▼ TRY IT YOURSELF

Switching Rendering Presets

Switching between the various preset rendering options is quick, painless, and easy. Follow these steps to see for yourself:

1. Open the *Render Setup* dialog either through the main menu or main toolbar or by pressing the keyboard shortcut *F10*.

2. At the bottom of the *Render Setup* dialog, click the *Presets* drop-down menu and choose *mental.ray.daylighting* (see Figure 20.1).

3. In the *Select Preset Categories* dialog that appears, make sure everything is selected and click *Load*. You have now loaded the *Mental Ray* rendering engine.

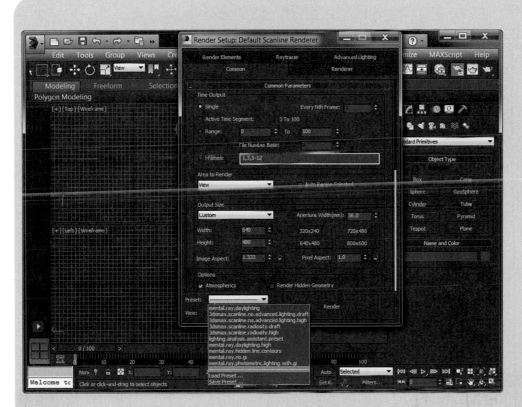

FIGURE 20.1
You select the *mental.ray.daylighting* option from the rendering presets area.

4. Do a quick render (by pressing *F9*) and notice that the background is no longer black but a deep blue. Also note that *Mental Ray* does not render from top to bottom but in sections known as *buckets*. Figure 20.2 shows the deep-blue background. *Mental Ray* rendering also gives you the default *Select Preset Categories* options that should be selected and loaded.

5. Add some standard primitives to your scene and do another quick render (by pressing *F9*). Notice that all the objects appear fully black because there are no lights in the scene; you can rectify this by adding lights to the scene and adjusting their parameters as needed.

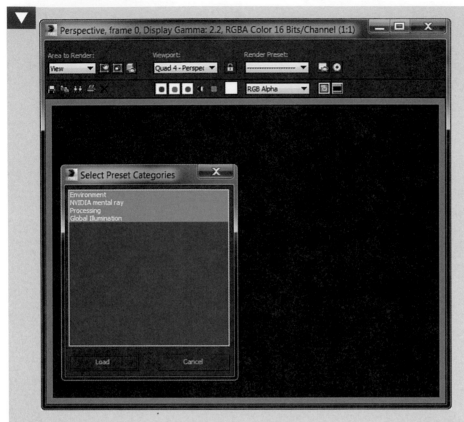

FIGURE 20.2
You need to load the correct preset categories to enable correct *Mental Ray* rendering for this hour. Simply make sure all the options are selected and click the *Load* button to load them.

Common Render Settings

There are a lot of rendering settings, no matter which rendering engine you decide to use, and when I say *a lot*, I really mean *A LOT*. There are too many options and settings to cover them all this hour, but you'll learn about some of the settings you'll use the most, such as those in the *Common* tab and the *Renderer* tab of the *Render Setup* dialog (see Figure 20.3). The following sections discuss these two tabs as well as the *Mental Ray*–specific tabs.

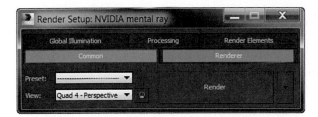

FIGURE 20.3
The *Common* tab and *Renderer* tab of the *Render Setup* dialog are always available, no matter which rendering engine you use.

The Common Tab of the Render Setup Dialog

This *Common* tab of the *Render Setup* dialog contains controls that apply to any rendering, regardless of which rendering engine you use. It is also where you can choose which renderer you want to use.

The *Common* tab is split into four main rollouts:

▶ **Common Parameters**—The *Common Parameters* rollout sets parameters common to all renders. You have options to affect the time output of the render, which area of the scene to render, the actual output size of the render, the location where the render will be saved, and a number of more advanced options that are less commonly used.

▶ **Email Notifications**—This rollout allows you to set email notifications about renders. Notifications can be handy if you launch a lengthy render and don't want to sit at the computer while 3ds Max and your computer system are rendering.

▶ **Scripts**—This rollout allows you to specify scripts that can run before and after rendering. This is a rather advanced option that this hour doesn't cover. However, you will learn some very basic scripting in Hour 23, "Scripting in 3ds Max Using MAXScript."

▶ **Assign Renderer**—The *Assign Renderer* rollout displays which renderer is currently assigned and allows you to change the assigned renderer.

The Renderer Tab of the Render Setup Dialog

The *Renderer* tab of the *Render Setup* dialog contains the main controls for the active renderer. Because each renderer is different, the rollouts in this tab change to facilitate the unique capabilities of the assigned renderer that you have chosen.

Mental Ray–Specific Tabs in the Render Setup Dialog

When you enable the *Mental Ray* rendering engine, you get access to three panels that specifically work with *Mental Ray*. These are more advanced *Mental Ray* options, and you don't really need to poke around in them until you have a little more experience with *Mental Ray* rendering. However, here's a brief explanation of the three tabs to get you thinking about what's available:

▶ *Global Illumination*—The *Global Illumination* tab provides various methods for the renderer to bounce light within an environment, such as by using final gathering, caustics, and photons. You can use these options to increase the realism and visual appeal of scenes, but it's a rather advanced rendering topic.

▶ *Processing*—This tab offers controls to manage how the *Mental Ray* renderer operates. You can override scene materials and even cache geometry to speed up the rendering process.

▶ *Render Elements*—The *Render Elements* tab allows you to specify exactly what object the renderer outputs. This can be incredibly useful for separating scene elements (such as foreground, characters, backgrounds, and effects) so that they can be combined and composited later.

All these panels affect the rendering and the rendering process. Changes to just one setting can drastically change the look of a render. For your purposes right now, you do not need to edit any of the settings as you are going to use the presets in 3ds Max, which do a pretty good job of getting you most, if not all, of the way to a great render.

The Mental Ray Daylight System

By using the *mental.ray.daylighting* preset, you have loaded the *Mental Ray* daylight system into the rendering engine, replacing the *Default Scanline* renderer. This allows you to use a daylight system that follows a geographically correct angle of movement of the sun over the earth at a specific location, as shown in Figure 20.4.

Adding daylight to a scene in 3ds Max is relatively simple, but the complexity increases as you start digging into all the available options and parameters.

VIDEO 20.1

Mental Ray Rendering Using Daylight Settings

This video includes great coverage of *Mental Ray* rendering using daylight settings in 3ds Max. Be sure to check it out for a quick reference guide to all this stuff!

FIGURE 20.4
A daylight system has been set up in this scene, and you can see how the different hours of the day affect the lighting in a realistic manner.

TRY IT YOURSELF ▼

Creating Daylight

The daylight system in *Mental Ray* offers lots of options, and it can all be a little overwhelming when you take your first look. In the following steps, you are going to create a daylight system and adjust only two parameters so that you get a great-looking render quickly and easily:

1. Open the file *SAMS_Hour20_DaylightStart.max*. You should recognize this city scene from Hour 11, "Adding and Editing 3D Cameras."

2. Open the *Render Setup* dialog and apply the *mental.ray.daylighting* preset, loading all of the preset categories.

3. Do a quick render (by pressing *F9*), and you should see something similar to Figure 20.5. Yikes!

4. You need some lights in this scene so that you can see the objects. As mentioned earlier, you are going to create some daylight, so open the *Create* tab and select *Systems*, *Standard* and click the *Daylight* button (see Figure 20.6).

FIGURE 20.5
This scene looks a little too dark to me!

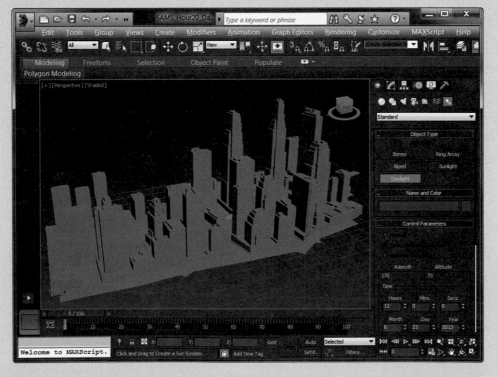

FIGURE 20.6
You can access 3ds Max daylight settings in the *Create* tab, under the *Systems* category and the *Standard* sub-category.

5. Click and drag in the viewport to create the compass for the daylight system. Let go and then slide the cursor to drag out the actual daylight "light."

6. Create another quick render of the scene (by pressing *F9*), and you should now be able to see the objects better, as shown in Figure 20.7. This already looks good, but you can quickly make it even better!

FIGURE 20.7
Now that you have some lighting, you can actually see what you have in the scene.

7. Select *Daylight* (the light, not the compass) and open the *Modify* tab.

8. In the *Daylight Parameters* rollout, ensure that the *Sunlight* and *Skylight* options are enabled. Change the drop-down menu options from *Standard* to *mr Sun* and *Skylight* to *mr Sky*.

9. Once again do a quick render (by pressing *F9*) and check out how a few changes have vastly improved the look of the render (see Figure 20.8).

FIGURE 20.8
Changing just a few settings has already made the scene look a lot better.

Now that you have a daylight system in place, and your renders are starting to look pretty amazing, you can affect the time of day for the scene.

In the *Daylight Parameters* rollout, you can use the *Position* section to manually place the sun; affect it by date, time, and location; or include a weather data file to accurately and specifically place the sun.

To manually place the sun, you use the *Move* tool to determine the sun's position. By choosing the *Date*, *Time*, or *Location* option, you can get into the *Setup* area and affect the sun's position using those specific parameters; this is one of the best ways I've found for getting accurate lighting simulations for my scenes. Finally, the *Weather Data File* option allows you to load a file that places the sun directly and accurately. This option is the most accurate but of course the most complicated as well.

Daylight and Additional Lights

With a daylight system in place, you can affect the time of day quickly and easily. You can get some very impressive rendering results, but obviously the sun is not the only source of lighting in the real world.

You can use either standard or photometric lights in a daylight scene to simulate lighting from various sources. In addition, you can use the *Environment and Effects* window (which you open by pressing the keyboard shortcut 8) to change the look and feel of the entire scene. It's worth digging into these extra options because you can use them to change things dramatically without affecting the lights that are already set in the scene. Figure 20.9 shows the *Environment and Effects* window.

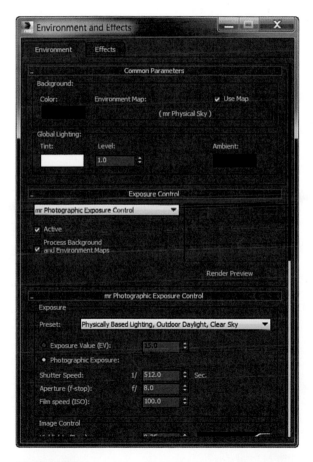

FIGURE 20.9
The *Environment and Effects* window lets you dramatically change the look of the rendered scene.

Summary

Now that you have an understanding of some of the 3ds Max rendering methods and systems, you can start experimenting with various options and parameters to get the best out of your renders. Like other advanced renderers, *Mental Ray* ships with a number of tools, settings, and parameters—and even its own materials. All these things can drastically enhance your final rendered images. You just need to invest time into practicing with the tools to get great renders.

You have now started digging deeper into more advanced rendering techniques, and although there is still a lot more to learn, you are on your way to becoming a rendering know-it-all. Congratulations!

Q&A

Q. **What is *Mental Ray*, and why should you care about it?**

A. *Mental Ray* is an advanced general-purpose rendering engine that you can use to create physically correct lighting simulations. It is more advanced than the *Default Scanline* renderer and is built into 3ds Max as standard, so it makes sense for you to use it.

Q. **Why should you render with *Mental Ray*? Are there other options?**

A. By rendering with *Mental Ray*, you can create more realistic and more appealing images than you can with a less advanced rendering engine. You also have the option of using the *Default Scanline* renderer, but the results you get with this tool will not be nearly as good as what you can get with *Mental Ray*. You can also purchase additional rendering engines and plug them into 3ds Max at an extra cost; many of these solutions are comparable to or even better than *Mental Ray*.

Workshop

Using *Mental Ray* to render your scenes is a relatively straightforward process. However, there are additional and more advanced options that you have not looked into yet. This workshop covers a few of those more advanced areas, and you may have to do some detective work of your own to be able to work through this section.

Quiz

1. What is global illumination?

2. What does the *Processing* tab give you access to?

3. Do standard materials render correctly with *Mental Ray*?

Answers

1. Global illumination is a method for rendering bounced light within an environment; it includes final gathering, caustics, and photons.

2. The Processing tab of the *Render Setup* dialog allows you to control and manage how the *Mental Ray* renderer operates.

3. Yes! Standard materials work when you render something with *Mental Ray*. We have access to *Mental Ray*–specific materials also, and they can give you advanced (though optional) effects to use with *Mental Ray* rendering.

Exercise

Are you ready to light and render a full scene using *Mental Ray*? Of course you are!

Using the file *SAMS_Hour20_Exercise.max*, get everything ready for *Mental Ray* rendering. You need to set the *Mental Ray* renderer yourself, and you should light the scene using either standard or photometric lights. Be sure to use the supplied camera for the scene framing. Also note that you need to light only what is being shown through that camera view. After all, if you can't see it, it's not worth spending the time making it look pretty.

HOUR 21
3ds Max Project Management Techniques

What You'll Learn in This Hour:

▶ Scene workflow

▶ Naming conventions

▶ Projects and folders

▶ Project management techniques for production

▶ Working with multiple team members

If you work on small scenes, and in particular on small scenes on your own—you don't really have to worry about scene or project management at all. However, when your 3D scenes start getting bigger, and especially when you start working with a team in an actual production environment, scene and project management are really important (as is creating great work, of course).

During this hour you're going to look at the tools and techniques that help you organize and navigate larger scenes, multiple scenes, and collaborative scenes.

Scene Workflow

You can think of a *workflow* as a set of steps or a sequence of operations in a process.

When working in a production environment, there may be certain steps (workflows) that you have to correctly follow, or your 3D assets won't work with the project. When you're working on your own, it might not seem too important to have a solid workflow in place, so why do you need one?

Well, the thing is, you don't! You can quite happily forget this hour completely and go about your business as you usually would. However, by creating, developing, and following your own workflow, you have an opportunity to speed up the development of your own projects and creations. In addition, if you follow some guidelines for each scene you create, it will be easier to come back to a scene you worked on a long time ago and instantly, or at least very quickly, be able to fathom what is going on without having to stress out about it too much.

The previous hours have neglected workflows, but that was purely so you could quickly move along and start creating things. It's time to take a break from creation, though, and look at the management aspect of creation.

Workspaces

Workspaces allow you to quickly jump between different interface layouts. Figure 21.1 shows where you find the drop-down menu for workspaces—at the top of the 3ds Max user interface. This drop-down lists four default workspaces you can choose from, along with an option to manage workspaces (that is, create your own).

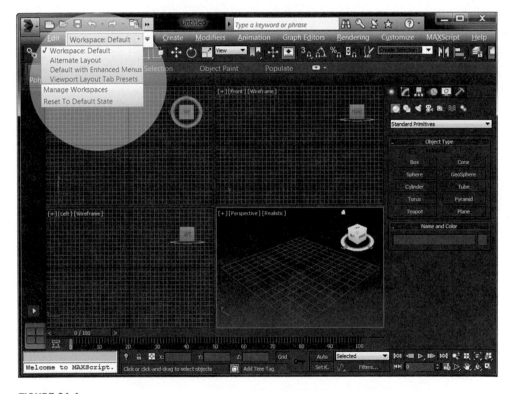

FIGURE 21.1
You select workspaces at the top of the interface. You can create and save your own workspaces for use with specific tasks.

You can tailor workspaces to specific tasks to make working on those specific tasks easier. Creating your own workspaces will likely speed up your workflow. You use the *Manage Workspaces* option from the drop-down menu to add, edit, and delete workspaces.

VIDEO 21.1

Creating and Managing Custom Workspaces

This video looks at creating and managing custom workspaces, which can make it easier to work with 3ds Max.

TRY IT YOURSELF ▼

Switching and Creating Workspaces

You can create workspaces that make it easy to access all the tools you use the most—and this can really speed up your workflow. You can always get back to the default workspace if you need to. Follow these steps to learn about switching and creating workspaces:

1. Customize your current workspace, based on your experience to this point in 3ds Max. Change it up and make it work for you by changing the viewport configuration, opening new toolbars, and adding toolbars to the interface. Make it your own.

2. You're going to be creating your own workspace, so click the *Manage Workspaces* option, as shown in Figure 21.2. The *Manage Workspaces* dialog appears. The left side of this dialog lists all the current workspaces that have been created already and that you can choose. Notice that you can click a red X to delete a workspace but that you can't delete *Workspace: Default* because you need at least one workspace in the list. On the right side of the dialog you can save your current viewport layout by clicking the *Save as New Workspace* button, you can set a default workspace state by clicking the *Save Default State* button, and you can even restore the state to the default by clicking the *Restore to Default State* button. Under those three buttons you can set some parameters for a new workspace. You can give it a name, specify what to load, and even run a *MAXScript* when the workspace loads.

FIGURE 21.2
Click the *Manage Workspaces* option to create your own workspace.

> **3.** Using the *Manage Workspaces* dialog, edit the options and save your new workspace.
> Pretty simple, right?

Figure 21.3 shows the *Manage Workspaces* window in its default state.

Layers

Here's a handy feature I use a lot: You can store objects on different layers, which gives you a chance to organize your scenes more effectively. Using layers makes it easier to manage the objects that you have in your scene. They are primarily used to control the visibility of objects in your scene, but they can be used to control the color of multiple objects and whether or not they are selectable.

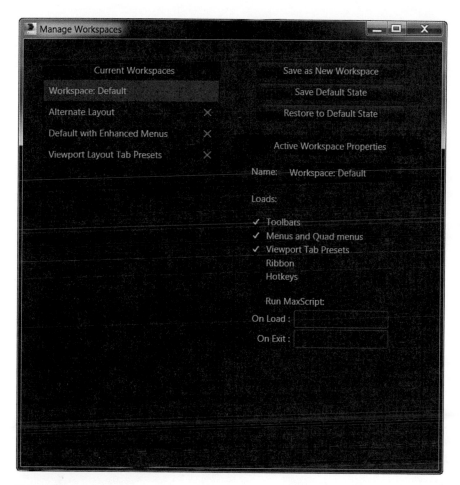

FIGURE 21.3
By using the *Manage Workspaces* dialog, you can add, edit, and delete workspaces to make working in 3ds Max quicker and easier.

All objects are assigned to the 0 (default) layer when they are created. You can create more layers and add objects to whichever layer is most appropriate for your own workflows. Each layer has its own set of properties, and you can do things like hide or unhide or freeze or unfreeze layers to make working in larger 3D scenes much easier.

VIDEO 21.2

Working with Display Layers

Using display layers is an incredibly handy way to control various display attributes for the objects in a scene. This video takes a look at how easy and helpful layers are.

Figure 21.4 shows a few ways you can access the *Layer* window. In this window, the checkmark shows which layer you are currently working on. You can expand layers to see what is contained within a layer, and you have control of the *Hide, Freeze, Render, Color,* and *Radiosity* options for each layer and each object. I suggest you spend some time working with it and with layers as doing so could improve your workflow phenomenally.

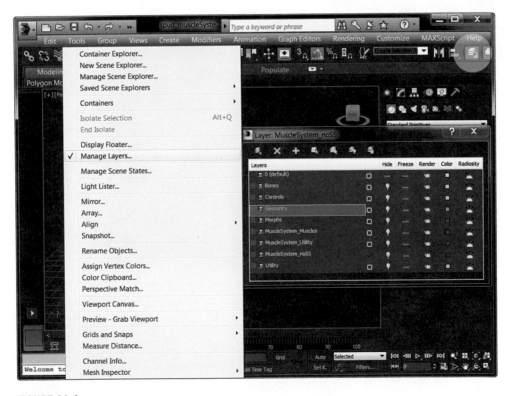

FIGURE 21.4
Using layers can really help you navigate a complex scene and just generally help you keep things organized.

Managing Display Layers

Display layers allow you to control what is visible, hidden, frozen, unfrozen, and even renderable in a scene. They also help you keep your scenes tidy. The best part is that they are very simple to use. Follow these steps to give them a go:

1. On the main toolbar click the *Manage Layers* button. The *Layer* window appears, as shown in Figure 21.5. As you create objects in a scene, they are added to the 0 (default) layer. Across the top of the *Layer* window are buttons you can click to create new layers, delete layers, add selected objects to layers, and select, hide, and freeze specific layers.

FIGURE 21.5
The *Layer* window is easiest to access by clicking the *Manage Layers* button on the main toolbar.

2. Try creating a few objects in a scene right now as well as creating a few layers and adding objects to those layers. Working with layers and objects in layers is relatively easy, so spend some time right now experimenting.

The Schematic View

In Hour 14, "Rigging Objects for Easier Animation," you took a look at the node-based *Schematic* view, so I won't say much about it here. I just want to mention that I find using the *Schematic* view one of the best ways to organize and find things in a scene, along with using the *Layer* window, of course.

The Scene Explorer

The *Scene Explorer* is a pretty neat tool to know about. It provides another way to view, sort, filter, and select objects in 3ds Max scenes; using it is similar to using the *Schematic* view. In addition, you can rename, delete, hide, and freeze objects; edit properties; and create/modify hierarchies of an object or multiple objects all at the same time. You access the *Scene Explorer* on the main menu, in the *Tools* menu. Figure 21.6 shows an example of the *Scene Explorer* in use on a moderately complex character rig.

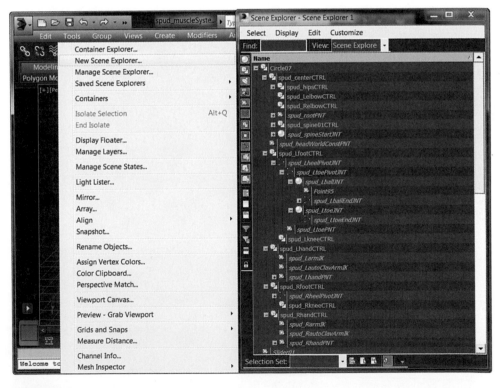

FIGURE 21.6
The *Scene Explorer* is a very handy tool to have at your disposal and can dramatically speed up your workflows.

Groups, Containers, and Other Tools

Many other tools that are available straight out of the 3ds Max box can help you manage your projects and scene workflows. It's up to you to find the tools, techniques, and methods that work best for you and your projects. Workspaces, layers, the *Schematic* view, and the *Scene Explorer* should put you on your way to good scene management practices. You should also take a look at using groups and containers to see how they could also help you out.

TRY IT YOURSELF ▼

Grouping Objects

Grouping objects is super easy. Check out how to do it right here:

1. Make sure you have a few objects in your scene and select the objects you would like to group together.

2. With your objects selected, in the main menu, click the *Group* menu and then select the first option, *Group*.

3. When the *Group* window appears, prompting you to name your group, name it something that you will remember. Your items are now grouped, and you can see the connection by looking in the *Schematic* view.

4. Try to select any of the grouped objects. You actually select all of them and the group node itself. Pretty neat, huh?!

Naming Conventions

Naming conventions are guidelines for how to name things; I know, you're not exactly surprised by that at all! Anyway, having a dedicated naming convention is useful for helping you and even others navigate the objects in a scene. It makes life a lot easier for everyone and helps give even the biggest scenes a little more clarity.

In a production environment, the naming convention may already be chosen, and you might have to follow along with whatever that convention is. If you're working on your own, as you have been doing throughout this book, you can come up with your own naming conventions.

So far you have been creating objects and not worrying too much about what they are named within a scene. I have deliberately not mentioned naming objects correctly as it can get a little tedious listening to someone tell you over and over to name things. However, naming things correctly by following a naming convention is a very important thing that you definitely should be doing. It is especially important if others are working on your scenes.

A naming convention can be anything that you want it to be; it just needs to be clear, concise, and consistent—the three Cs, if you will. (I just came up with "the three Cs" right now. It is not a real thing; I just thought it sounded cool!) I have my own naming convention, many productions have—and should have—their own conventions, and I urge you to come up with a naming convention for yourself. It's good practice, and sooner or later you're probably going to need one.

I don't want to go into too much further detail right now, as this is something that can be (and often is) debated for hours. Why not check online and see if you can get some reference that you can adapt for your own purposes? Or better yet, check out Table 21.1 for a brief example of some generic naming conventions, which can be used as a prefix or suffix.

TABLE 21.1   An Example of Some Generic Naming Conventions

Element	Naming Convention
Animation	_ANIM
Morph target	_MT
Camera	_CAM
Code or script	_CODE
Controller item	_CTRL
Geometry or mesh	_MESH
Inverse kinematic chain	_IKC
Bone	_BN
Dummy or helper object	_DUM

Naming Conventions Outside 3ds Max

It's important to understand that a naming convention does not just live inside 3ds Max. Sure, the elements and objects that you create need to be named correctly, according to the naming convention. The thing is that the stuff that is outside 3ds Max also needs to follow a naming convention. Things like folders, texture files, saved scenes, and even text documents should follow a consistent naming convention. This may seem like overkill, but when you start getting into thousands of files, perhaps with hundreds of people working on the same project, using a naming convention that everyone can understand makes a lot of sense. Without one, well, you may have chaos and anarchy.

Project Setup and Folder Handling

When saving a file in 3ds Max, you may have noticed that the default location where that file will go seems to be pretty specific. Well, it is! You see, 3ds Max allows you to set a project folder, which provides a simple way of keeping all your files for a particular project organized.

3ds Max set a default project folder located somewhere like the following path for Windows 7 and later: *C:/users/<username>/My Documents/3dsMax/* (or *3dsmaxdesign* for 3ds Max Design). Figure 21.7 shows what this looks like.

FIGURE 21.7
This is the default project folder setup for 3ds Max.

To keep your projects organized, and to make things easier to find, you can set your own project path by clicking the *Application* button, *Manage, Set Project Folder*. From there you can name the project folder, and 3ds Max automatically creates a number of subfolders for you, which it then uses to find and keep all the data associated with the project you have set.

I have to admit that I work on many different projects, and I usually neglect to set up my project folder handling correctly. So I can tell you that managing your folders isn't required. But I do know that staying organized can help you avoid errors like losing files.

Project Management in Production

Managing projects or even just a few 3ds Max scenes in a full production environment is a complicated task that often functions correctly only because of technical specialists and production staff.

3ds Max provides few project management tools that can cope in bigger environments, but it does give you the ability to link external tools—ones that handle more complex project management tasks—directly into the 3ds Max interface. By clicking the *Application* button and then *References*, you can find the *Asset Tracking* options for 3ds Max, as shown in Figure 21.8.

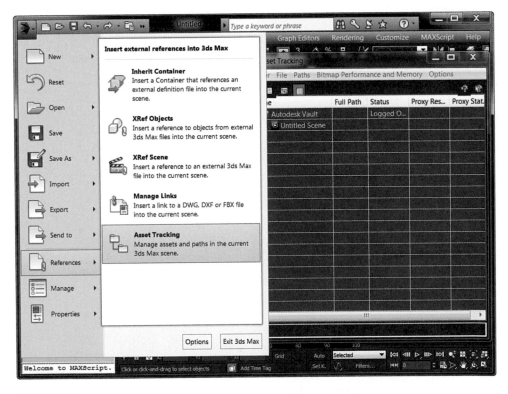

FIGURE 21.8
3ds Max includes its own *Asset Tracking* dialog that you can access from the *Application* button.

You probably don't want to be thinking about more tools and more programs just now. But it's worth making a mental note that if you're jumping into a 3ds Max production environment, you will probably be using a whole host of other programs and applications that supplement 3ds Max as the main 3D package.

Multiple-Team-Member Production Methods

When working with multiple team members, often on separate elements that form part of the same scene, you have to use specific tools and techniques in order to collaborate well as a group.

3ds Max provides *external references (XRefs)*, which allow you to reference either specific objects or other scenes into your own scenes. This means several users can work collaboratively on the same objects without having to wait around for the objects to be finalized.

XRefs come in two flavors:

▶ **XRef Objects**—*XRef Objects* allows you to reference specific objects from another scene. This is known as object referencing.

▶ **XRef Scenes**—*XRef Scenes* allows you to reference whole scenes in your current scene. This is known as scene referencing.

When changes are made to either referenced objects or scenes, those changes are automatically shown to you as you work in a scene that references those elements.

To externally reference either an object(s) or a scene(s), click the *Application* button, *References* and then choose either *XRef Objects* or *XRef Scene*, as shown in Figure 21.9. Notice that this menu also includes the options *Inherit Container* and *Manage Links*, which also relate directly to referencing and scene/project management.

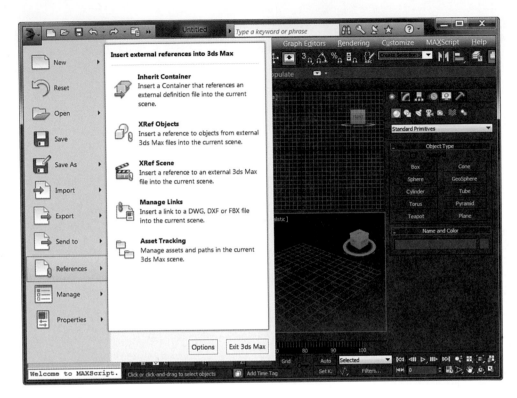

FIGURE 21.9
You can add an *XRef* to either an object or a scene in this menu.

Summary

Scene workspaces, layers, naming conventions, folder structures, *Schematic* view, hierarchies, groups, containers, and all other things covered in this hour are important for creating great 3D. By managing projects, scenes, folders, and everything else, you can increase your 3D output by speeding up your working processes, making it easier to collaborate on various elements, and taking advantage of a complete pipeline solution that anyone and everyone can navigate, create, edit, and manage.

Like pretty much everything else in 3D, project management is a big, complex task that requires dedication, conventions, and adherence to a predefined structure of sorts. This hour has shown you the importance of good project management for 3D productions and given you insight into some of the tools and tricks you have at your disposal.

Q&A

Q. **What is project management?**

A. Project management is a specific discipline that deals with planning, organizing, and controlling resources to achieve specific goals.

Q. **Does project management relate to 3ds Max?**

A. In relation to 3ds Max, project management refers to the planning of projects, the organization of scenes and files, and the control of the resources available for the current production.

Q. **Should you care about project management in 3ds Max when you can create scenes and files without any trouble right now?**

A. Yes and no! If you're always going to be working on small files that only you access, then working without any knowledge of project management is probably okay. However, if you start digging into bigger projects, and in particular any projects that require you to work with multiple 3ds Max users, then project management is going to become more important in the process. You should at least get familiar with everything discussed this hour and then pick and choose the elements of 3ds Max project management that work best for you.

Workshop

Project management may seem arbitrary, but the correct use of the tools available can dramatically help you when you're working alone and even more so when you're working in collaboration with others. This workshop will push your understanding of the project management tools and workflows even further than this hour has done so far.

Quiz

1. What are workspaces?

2. Where can you find the *Layer* window, and what does it do?

3. What kinds of referencing can you do in 3ds Max?

Answers

1. Workspaces allow you to save and switch between various user interface layouts.

2. You can find the *Layer* window on the main toolbar. It helps with various object display options within the viewports when you work with 3ds Max scenes.

3. There are two kinds of referencing in 3ds Max: object referencing and scene referencing. Each does what its name implies that it does!

Exercise

Set up a new project folder structure and create three separate files: one containing a cube, one containing a sphere, and one containing a few extended primitives. You should be able to find these newly saved scene files easily if you have saved them in the correct place in the new project structure.

Next, start a brand-new 3ds Max scene. Reference the scenes and/or objects you just created. (It's up to you which type(s) of *XRef* you use here.) Save this new scene and open a new 3ds Max window. Try editing one of the three referenced files and see how your changes affect the scene that contains the references.

Combining Advanced Techniques to Create a Showcase

What You'll Learn in This Hour:

▶ Creating a showcase project from scratch

▶ Combining all the elements from the past 21 hours

▶ How to use some more advanced techniques

I don't know about you, but I think it's kind of incredible that in just 21 hours, you have gone from the absolute basics of 3ds Max to talking about more advanced and complex tools, topics, and techniques in the same program. You should be proud of yourself for getting this far; it has been no easy journey, that's for sure.

This hour you are going to do something similar to what you did way back in Hour 13, "Combining Techniques to Create a Showcase." You are going to create another showcase, but this time you are going to include both the more simple topics covered in the earlier hours and the more complicated topics covered in recent hours.

Take a deep breath and jump on in!

Stage 1: Getting Started

The first thing you need to do as you create your showcase is to work out what you are doing. This is a time to be creative and take some time exploring what you would actually *like* to create as well as what you *can* create.

It's important to remember your strengths and weaknesses, as well as your limitations. This is not to say that you should keep your sights aimed low. Far from it, in fact. But you need to be aware of where your skills are and what you feel you can achieve. Then, once you have found that bar, you should aim just over it so that you are challenged enough to improve your skills but not challenged so much that you become demotivated while trying to achieve a goal that is unrealistic and unreasonable.

Now, as with the previous hours in this book, you can feel free to follow along directly with me or come up with something on your own and use these sections as a guide. I don't mind which path you take. Just have some fun with it.

So, you need something to showcase. All right, so what are you going to do?! Decisions, decisions....Okay, I've made up my mind. I'm going with creating and showcasing a bedroom. Why a bedroom? I could have chosen literally anything. A bedroom scene has multiple uses when you're working in 3D. It could be used for the scene/stage of an animation, or it could be used for architectural visualization purposes. Of course, you could use something else for these purposes as well, but a bedroom scene allows you to easily combine all the tips, tricks, and techniques covered over the previous 21 hours.

A bedroom scene has multiple objects, various textures and materials, and optional lighting solutions; it can be old or new, which can dramatically change the mood, effects, and feeling; and it can be as simple or as complicated as you want it to be. So, it's a perfect test for your final, more advanced showcase of work.

Stage 2: Preparation

All right! Now that you know what you're going to create for your showcase, you should start collecting some reference material; you can even create your own reference materials by creating some sketches (or scribbles, in my case) and diagrams of exactly what you are imagining for the final outcome of this showcase.

Really spend some time here, gathering and creating as much reference materials as possible; doing this should help you out a lot in the upcoming stages. Gathering and creating reference materials can take longer than you might expect it to, and it's an important step that you shouldn't brush aside.

Maybe ask yourself some questions about the bedroom you want to create. What kind of bedroom are you building? Is it for children or adults? Boys or girls? What shape is the room? Is this a shared room? With queen or single or bunk beds? You need to answer these types of questions at this stage.

Stage 3: Project Management

You should now be ready to start your brand-new showcase project in 3ds Max. Your very first step here should be to create a project folder for this production. So click the *Application* button, select the *Manage* category, and click on the *Set Project Folder* option. You can then choose where to store your new project, as shown in Figure 22.1. Remember that your project location can be anywhere you want it to be.

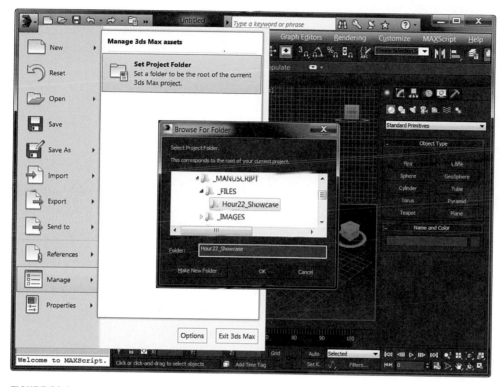

FIGURE 22.1
It's time to set up a new project folder for your final showcase.

3ds Max creates the appropriate folders for you, and this should help you keep your files organized.

You are going to create a scene with many elements, and you are going to break them down into separate files so that you can work on them individually and then bring them together later, using referencing, to create the final scene that you will render. So, using the reference materials as a guide, I have broken down the bedroom scene into 12 elements:

- The stage and/or set (walls, floor, ceiling, and so on)
- Rug
- Picture frame
- Shelf
- Bed
- Bedside table
- Bedside light
- Toy box
- Desk
- Laptop
- Chair
- Wardrobe

For each one of these separate elements, you need to create a new scene so that you can work and focus on each individual element on its own. For now, save an empty scene for each of the 12 individual elements so that you have a guide for each object that needs to be created. Name the files as follows:

- ▶ *SAMS_Hour22_Bed.max*

- ▶ *SAMS_Hour22_BedsideLight.max*

- ▶ *SAMS_Hour22_BedsideTable.max*

- ▶ *SAMS_Hour22_Chair.max*

- ▶ *SAMS_Hour22_Desk.max*

- ▶ *SAMS_Hour22_Laptop.max*

- ▶ *SAMS_Hour22_PictureFrame.max*

- ▶ *SAMS_Hour22_Rug.max*

- ▶ *SAMS_Hour22_Shelf.max*

- ▶ *SAMS_Hour22_Stage.max*

- ▶ *SAMS_Hour22_ToyBox.max*

- ▶ *SAMS_Hour22_Wardrobe.max*

Figure 22.2 shows what the saved empty scenes should look like, in their correct place inside the new project folder structure you just set up.

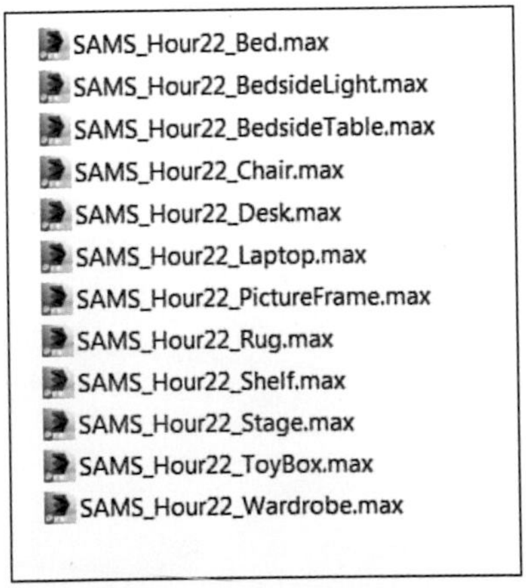

FIGURE 22.2
You now have 12 empty scenes saved in the correct location, ready for you to start working on them.

Stage 4: Creation

Now you're ready to dig into the fun stuff. You already have the skills you need to create each and every object and item needed for this showcase. The elements themselves are relatively simple, and you can create them from standard primitives. It may take you some time, but you know everything you need to know to go through each of the 12 individual files and create each of the objects. Figures 22.3 to 22.5 show all the individual elements that I have created for the bedroom scene. These aren't particularly complex objects at all, but they work well for the bedroom scene. You can make yours look just like mine or let your own style shine here.

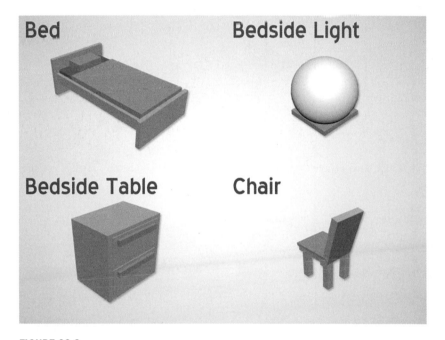

FIGURE 22.3
Here are my interpretations of four of the main elements for the bedroom scene: the bed, bedside light, bedside table, and chair.

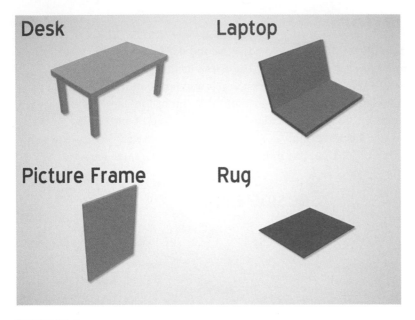

FIGURE 22.4
Here are my interpretations of four other elements for the bedroom scene: the desk, laptop computer, picture frame, and rug.

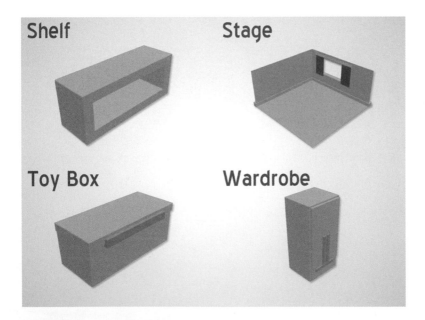

FIGURE 22.5
Here are my interpretations of the last four elements for the bedroom scene: the shelf, main stage (room), toy box, and wardrobe.

As I created the objects for the bedroom scene, I opted to make them very basic and only color each of the objects rather than use materials and texture maps. Of course, you can feel free to add textures and go crazy with materials if you'd like to experiment more with those techniques and end up with a fancier showcase. Remember, too, that you can create basic elements for now—boxy and with no materials/textures—and come back to each element/object a bit later and change or update things for the final composition.

Stage 5: Layout

Now that you have all the objects created in separate files, you need to start bringing each of the elements together and into the same scene file that you will use for the rendering of the final showcase.

Referencing

In this project, you're going to be using both scene and object referencing, but first you need a brand-new empty scene to start working with. So you need to save an empty scene as a starting point. Name it *SAMS_Hour22_000_MAIN.max*. This scene is going to be the main scene that you work with, and you are going to reference all the other objects into this one place.

With your main scene file open, you need to reference the main stage file. Click the *Application* button, select the *References* category, and click on the *XRef Scenes* option. The *XRef Scenes* dialog appears, as shown in Figure 22.6.

To reference the stage file into your scene, click the *Add* button and choose the *SAMS_Hour22_Stage.max* file. Before you close the *XRef Scenes* dialog, click the *Automatic* check box in the *Update File* section so that any changes you make in the stage file will automatically be shown in the referenced scene. Awesome!

TIP

Selection in Scene and Object Referencing

Now that you have the stage file referenced into your new scene, you might notice that you cannot select any object or element of the referenced file. This is one of the main differences between scene and object referencing. When you use the *XRef Scenes* option, you cannot select the reference; when you use the *XRef Objects* option, you can select what you have referenced.

You now need to start bringing in the elements to this scene because this empty room is looking pretty boring right now. Again click the *Application* button, select the *References* menu, and click the *XRef Objects* option.

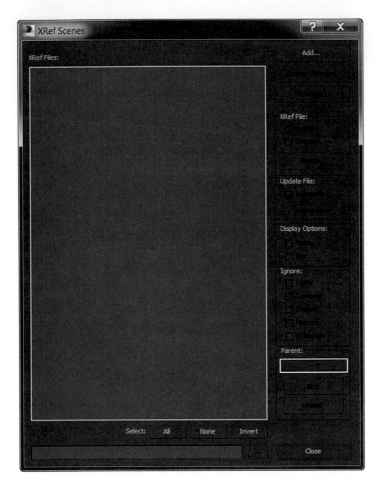

FIGURE 22.6
The *XRef Scenes* dialog is easy to use when you get the hang of it.

In the *XRef Objects* dialog, use the top-left button to create an *XRef* record by choosing the file you want to reference (maybe the bed) and then select all the objects associated with it. Figure 22.7 shows a brief example of this procedure.

When you're finished, you should see the object referenced in your scene. Notice that you can select it and manipulate it to some extent. However, geometric modifications are not directly available in the *Modify* tab, although you can use modifiers if you want to change something with the objects in this scene directly.

Be sure to click the *Automatic Update* button in the *XRef Objects* dialog. As in the *XFRef Scenes* dialog, this allows you to change your referenced files and have the scene automatically update.

FIGURE 22.7
Using *XRef Objects* is a little different from using *XRef Scenes* as it allows you to choose exactly what objects you want to bring into the reference.

Continue bringing in all the other objects so that they are all available in the scene. When you're all finished, remember to save the scene. Figure 22.8 shows my scene with all the references included. Next you need to start playing interior designer to get all these objects into a realistic, pleasing layout.

Scene Layout

Using the *Move* tool, select the various objects and position them however you like to form a bedroom scene. Take a look at Figure 22.9 to see how I've easily transformed a jumbled mess into a realistically laid-out bedroom.

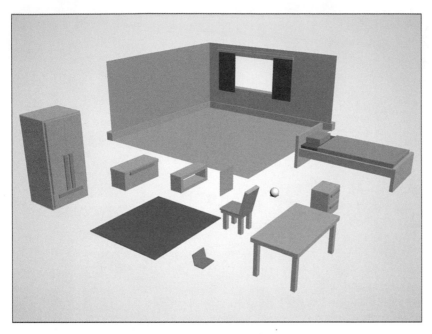

FIGURE 22.8
It's a little bit messy right now, but all the objects have now been referenced into the scene.

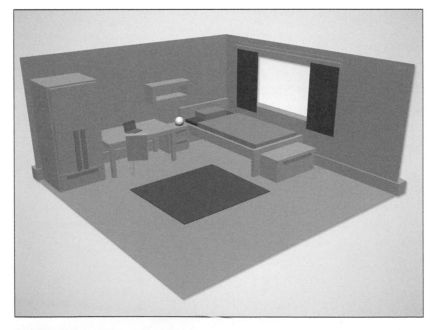

FIGURE 22.9
A mess is transformed into a bedroom space.

CAUTION

Fit for Purpose

As I created the various objects in the scene, I used a box to help me with the scale of the objects. So, if you're working with my files, you should be able to reference and position them without having to worry about any scale issues. However, if you're working with your own files, you may have to go back into the references and edit them to get them to the correct scale. Think about changing the grid size and keeping a constant unit setup for your scenes to ensure a consistent scale throughout your various files. Remember that you need to check that your references *automatically update* when you make changes to the original files!

The scene is already starting to look great. Spend a little time perfecting the layout and try a few quick render tests (by pressing *F9*). Next, you need to start thinking about where you're going to place your camera.

Stage 6: Camera and Lensing

Setting up the camera and sorting out the lens choice seems like it would be pretty easy, but it can take a little time to get just the shot you want. There's no point in my chatting again about everything that you already know, so get in there and set up a camera that works for your scene. Remember that the *Cameras Safe Frame* is affected by the render setup, so get in there and sort that out, too!

My final camera uses an 8 mm lens, positioned in such a way that each element that has been created for this bedroom is in view, with an output image size of *1280x720* (HDTV). Figure 22.10 shows the camera settings and view that I've decided to go with.

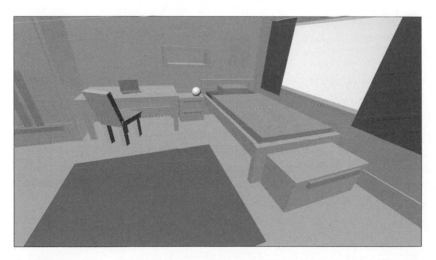

FIGURE 22.10
You need to choose a camera angle that shows off the hard work you've put into creating the bedroom scene.

Stage 7: Animation and Visual Effects

Things are really starting to come together in the bedroom scene. By doing a quick render (by pressing *F9*), as I did for Figure 22.10, you can get a better idea of what the final showcase will look like.

Now that all the core elements of the scene are in place, in this stage, you are going to work on the animation and visual effects (VFX) for the scene.

Animation

Animation for this scene is a bit tricky. You have a bedroom with no characters and nothing that appears to need any kind of animation. In fact, if you take a look at the way the objects in this scene have been modeled, you will notice that you don't really have the ability to even open the doors to the wardrobe. So what exactly are you going to animate?

Well, you could add a character. He could be hiding under the bed or sitting in the chair. You could add a bouncing ball that bounds in from offscreen and settles next to the desk. You could create a pencil and use dynamics to simulate the pencil falling from the desk. The possibilities are there; you just need to use your imagination.

Because you are already doing so much in this showcase, how about keeping the animation side of things as simple as possible. You can simply animate a very simple camera move. I know, it's not as imaginative or exciting as some of the other possibilities, but for the purpose of this section, it will work perfectly. This camera animation contains only position and rotation movements over 840 frames, or roughly 35 seconds of animation at 24 fps.

Visual Effects (VFX)

With the animation, you can start thinking about using visual effects (VFX) to make this scene look a little more interesting.

One effect you can add to make the scene more realistic is some dust particles floating in the air. There are a number of ways to do this, but to keep things simple, you can simply add a *PCloud* particle system, which you access in the *Create* tab, under the *Geometry* category and *Particle Systems* subcategory. You want *PCloud* to cover the full room, and you'll need to make adjustments to it to get this behaving and working correctly. There are a lot of settings and options available with any kind of particle system, and this is a great time for you to experiment and explore the *PCloud* parameters. Just try things out and see where it gets you! Figure 22.11 shows some of the changes I have made to the *PCloud* parameters.

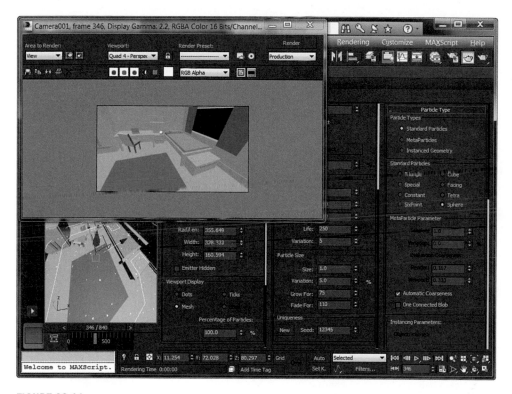

FIGURE 22.11
You can use *PCloud* to simulate dust particles in the air for the bedroom scene.

You can take a look at the file *SAMS_Hour22_001_MAIN.max* for some practical help and to see what my version of the bedroom scene looks like at this point.

NOTE

Where Are the References?

It's worth noting that I do not have any references in that file because you and I are working on different systems with different folder structures, and references would not likely work. Your scene should be referenced, though!

What other VFX can you add here? Well, you could add things like bloom and lens effects, but those are lighting issues, which you will tackle in the next stage.

Stage 8: Lighting

Lighting is a key element of any scene, and it is incredibly important to this scene in particular because it will drastically affect the look and feel of the final rendered showcase.

In keeping with the theme of this hour or using more advanced tools, you will be using *Mental Ray* as the renderer for this scene. So, in the *Render Setup* dialog, you need to change *Preset* to *mental.ray.daylighting*. As discussed in Hour 20, "Mental Ray Rendering," you need to create a *Daylight* system and change the *Sunlight* setting to *mr Sun* and the *Skylight* setting to *mr Sky*. Doing a quick render (by pressing *F9*) at this point should give you some pretty good results already, as you can see in Figure 22.12, but there is still more work to be done.

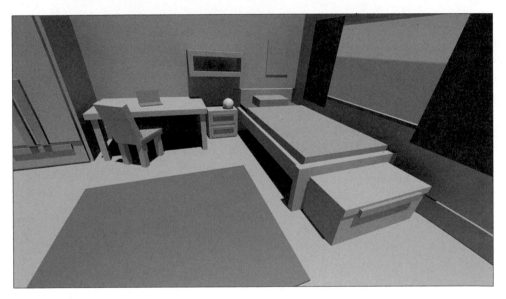

FIGURE 22.12
Simply switching to *Mental Ray* rendering and adding in a *Daylight* system can drastically improve the render of your scene, but you can do more to make it a little bit special.

One change you can make is the position of the sunlight so that you can simulate the time of day you want. I'm going for around 9:00 in the morning so that the environment is nice and bright and has long shadows for some great contrast.

In addition, because there is a window in this scene, you can use the *mr Sky Portal* setting (find it in the *Create* tab, under the *Lights* category and the *Photometric* subcategory) to simulate light coming in from the outside. You can make this visible to the renderer, too, so that you can make the window appear fully white if you want to. It's worth noting that the *Multiply* parameter for *mr Sky Portal* can make a big difference in how the scene is affected by outside lighting.

Alternatively, you could add a plane with a texture image if you wanted to show a picture of the world outside this bedroom scene.

You can also add extra lighting from an imaginary ceiling light, or even the strange spherical-looking bedside table light. Of course, these are not necessary for a super-bright 9:00 morning scene, but it's something to consider as you try some time-of-day experiments.

Figure 22.13 shows what I have come up with for lighting. Feel free to experiment and see what works for you!

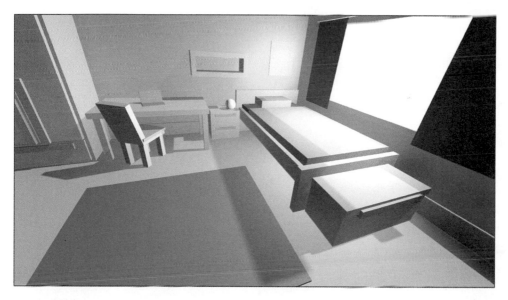

FIGURE 22.13
In this super-bright 9:00 a.m. bedroom lighting scene, notice that the *mr Sky Portal* setting adds some nice lighting from "outside" that wouldn't otherwise be possible.

Stage 9: Final Changes

This stage is all on you; you should tweak, edit, change, and adapt the scene and the references until you are happy with them. I really don't want to give you any direction here; you know what you're doing well enough already. Make your final showcase look as amazing as you can, and when you're ready, move on to the last stage, where you will focus on rendering and finally showing this thing to the whole wide world.

Stage 10: Rendering and Output

You have done all the hard work, and you're up to the final stage for your advanced showcase. To complete this project, you need to output both a single still-frame image and the 840 frames of animation.

Be sure to work on the single still-frame image first, as it is not only quicker to render but also allows you to check that everything is looking really good. If you notice a problem, simply jump back to stage 9 and fix it up! When you're ready to render the single still-frame image for real, be sure to select the best frame of your animation and press *F9* to render. Check out my final image in Figure 22.14.

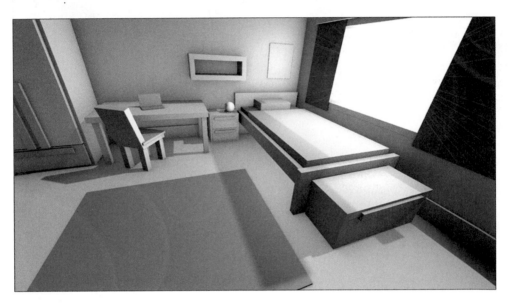

FIGURE 22.14
My final bedroom scene image is finished and rendered with *Mental Ray*.

Finally, you need to render all 840 frames of animation. Refer to Hour 12, "Rendering for Production," if you get stuck with the rendering and be sure that you don't need to access your computer during the rendering process. Remember, this is a rather advanced and complicated scene, so it may take your computer system a while to render it. Good luck!

VIDEO 22.1

Assembling an Advanced Showcase

This video takes a look at the assembly of this advanced showcase and discusses some of the challenges in creating content for more complex scenes.

You can examine my final scene by opening the file *SAMS_Hour22_ShowcaseComplete.max.* Oh, and I did an alternative 9 p.m. scene, too, which is shown in Figure 22.15, and you can take a look at in the file *SAMS_Hour22_ShowcaseAlternative.max.*

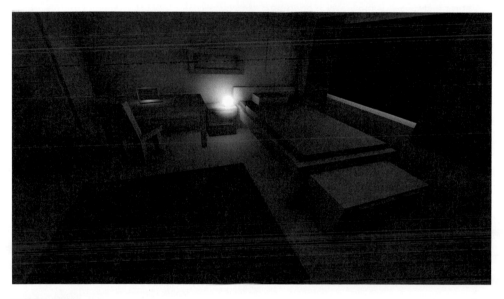

FIGURE 22.15
The final alternative bedroom scene is exactly the same shot, but the lighting represents a 9 p.m. scene in winter.

Summary

By combining all the skills, tricks, tips, and techniques you have learned in the past 21 hours, you have now taken your skills to the next level. This hour, you combined some pretty advanced techniques to create both a rendered still-frame image and a full 840-frame animation that will be going straight into your portfolio. Congratulations! I know it hasn't been easy to get this far, but your commitment is certainly paying off.

Q&A

Q. Why learn each skill and/or discipline separately before combining them into a project?

A. Each skill and/or discipline is challenging to learn and incredibly difficult to master. By keeping them separate, you can focus on one specific area at a time and learn the skills and techniques needed to excel in that area. You can then combine various skills into a project, just as you did this hour, so that you understand how the different disciplines fit together and affect one another. Learning them all at the same time would be incredibly confusing, to say the least!

Q. Is creating a showcase/show reel a good next step?

A. Absolutely! A show reel can help open a door into the industry, and the more projects and show reels you create for yourself, the better you will become at working with 3D. It's also a great idea to ask for feedback from friends and peers as you work on your own projects, as they will often be able to help and guide you, which will enable you to create bigger and better things.

Workshop

This hour you've created a more advanced showcase for your portfolio. Although you haven't learned any new techniques during this hour, you have learned a lot, as you have combined tricks, tips, and techniques into one (or multiple) file. This workshop should help you solidify some of this combined knowledge.

Quiz

1. What is the main difference between *XRef Scenes* and *XRef Objects*?

2. What can you not do with any referenced geometry?

3. Why use *Mental Ray* instead of the *Default Scanline* renderer for this showcase?

Answers

1. The main difference between the *XRef Scenes* and *XRef Objects* tools is that *XRef Scenes* allows referencing of whole scenes, but the scenes are not selectable. *XRef Objects*, on the other hand, allows referencing of specific objects, and once an object is referenced, you can manipulate it somewhat.

2. When you reference geometry, you are not able to directly manipulate the geometric shape of it without using some kind of modifier.

3. *Mental Ray* has greater realistic rendering capabilities than *Default Scanline*. Although they are more complicated, the final renders with *Mental Ray* are often more appealing than those from the *Default Scanline* rendering engine.

Exercise

You have worked incredibly hard this hour, and the results have definitely been worth it. For this exercise, take a look at the files *SAMS_Hour22_ShowcaseComplete.max* and *SAMS_Hour22_ ShowcaseAlternative.max.* Both of the scenes contain some additional lighting effects. Using the appropriate tools, analyze the scenes and figure out which effects have been used.

When you're confident that you know exactly what is going on with these scenes, open the file *SAMS_Hour22_ShowcaseComplete.max* once again. The geometry in this scene is rather basic, and it's time for it to be updated. So jump right in and start editing the geometry to make the scene more realistic, more appealing, and far more complicated. This is going to take a while. However, when you finish this exercise, you should have something that looks way better than the renders you created earlier in this hour. Oh, and don't forget to think about using cloth or some other more advanced method, too. Just go crazy with it!

HOUR 23
Scripting in 3ds Max Using MAXScript

What You'll Learn in This Hour:

▶ An introduction to scripting and programming basics
▶ An overview of *MAXScript* and its tools
▶ Creating a simple script with *MAXScript*
▶ Creating a simple interface with *MAXScript*

Programming is a specialized skill and not something that this book has talked about yet—even though 3ds Max is what it is today because of the work of talented programmers. Someone had to spend time programming every single element, from the creation of a sphere to the interface itself.

Users, like you and me, can extend the capabilities of 3ds Max by using a number of programming methods. Of course, to do this, you need to have some programming skills, and that leaves a lot of us out of the loop. However, 3ds Max has its own built-in scripting language called *MAXScript*. Think of a scripting language as an easier-to-use/easier-to-understand version of programming. This scripting language makes it possible for nonprogrammers to dig a little "under the hood" and affect 3ds Max in some ways that would not be possible otherwise.

This hour you'll get more familiar with programming and scripting basics, and you'll even make some of your own scripts. Oh, and don't worry. Nothing this hour is too complicated!

Programming and Scripting Basics

Learning to program or script is a time-consuming process—just like learning any other language that is not native to you. The great thing about learning a programming or scripting language is that once you master a language, other languages are easier to decipher. There are differences between programming and scripting languages, of course, but all of them are relatively similar.

This hour focuses purely on *MAXScript*, which is 3ds Max's version of a scripting language and is available only inside 3ds Max.

MAXScript works in mysterious ways. Okay, not really mysterious, but it does have specific quirks that you need to consider. Actually, think about the English language. Only one of the following two sentences is grammatically correct:

> I like to eat salad.
>
> To eat I salad like.

The first sentence is the correct one, the one you understand. The second does not make sense, but you can work it out if you have to. *MAXScript* and 3ds Max are not as clever as you. If you put things in the wrong order, *MAXScript* will spit out an error, telling you it has no idea what you want. Therefore, you need to know the right *syntax* to make sure 3ds Max understands you. (Every programming and scripting language has its own syntax.)

Okay, what else do you need to know about *MAXScript*'s quirks? Well, just like you are doing with this book, *MAXScript* reads from the top to the bottom of a page/script. So whatever you script at the top will be done first, and the final line will be done, or *evaluated*, last.

Theory is all good, but it's a little boring. So let's not spend any more time on it but move on to the tools available to you while you're working with *MAXScript*.

The MAXScript Tools

There are three main *MAXScript* tools for you to work with while creating scripts:

▶ **Command line (*Mini Listener*)**—In the bottom-left corner of the 3ds Max interface is the command line, or *Mini Listener*, as shown in Figure 23.1. The pink area is the macro recorder section, and if it is enabled, it shows in *MAXScript* what you are doing in the viewport. The white area is the scripter window; this is where 3ds Max prints any errors, and it's also where you can type in very short scripts and evaluate/execute them.

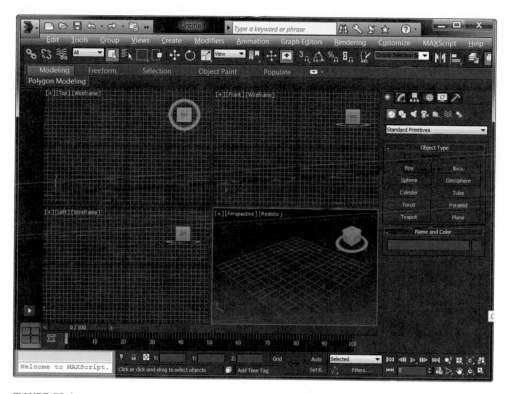

FIGURE 23.1
The *Mini Listener* is in the bottom-left corner of the 3ds Max UI.

▶ **Listener**—The *Listener* is the daddy of the *Mini Listener*. It includes the same sections as the *Mini Listener* but in its own window. It also includes additional options, and it is where you can access the macro recorder if you want to record (in *MAXScript*) what you are doing in a scene.

You can access the *Listener* by pressing the keyboard shortcut *F11*, or from the main menu you can select *MAXScript* and then *MAXScript Listener*. Figure 23.2 shows the *MAXScript Listener* window that appears.

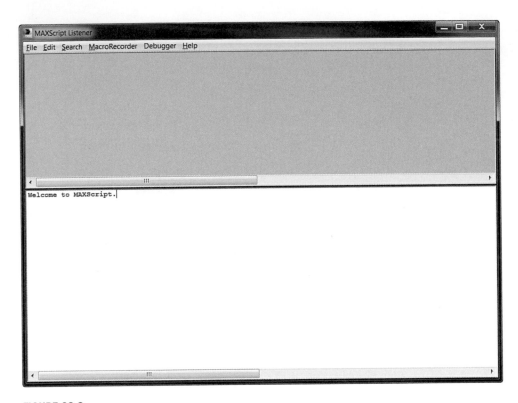

FIGURE 23.2
The *MAXScript Listener* looks like this. If you're missing the pink section, check just under the menu area for a place where you can drag down to show it.

> ▶ **MAXScript window**—The *MAXScript* window is the main place where you create scripts. This window contains a number of options and features, such as syntax highlighting and line numbering. In fact, this is where you will spend most of your *MAXScript* time as it allows you to test scripts without any feedback from 3ds Max getting in the way of the view. Figure 23.3 shows a standard *MAXScript* window, which you can access from the main menu by selecting *MAXScript, New Script*. Or you can get there from the *MAXScript Listener* by clicking *File, New Script*.

So these are the main *MAXScript* tools. It's time you put them to use and actually create something!

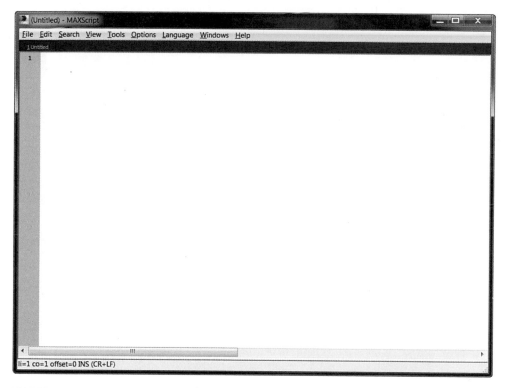

FIGURE 23.3
The *MAXScript* window is the place where you can write some pretty big scripts and where you will spend most of your time with *MAXScript*.

Basic MAXScript Scripting

It may be a little bit of a cliché, but the "Hello World" example is usually the very first thing that most people learn when they start out with a programming or scripting language. We might as well start there, too. Creating this script is so simple that it really doesn't require a Try It Yourself. All you have to do is open the *Mini Listener* and type the following in the pink section:

```
print "Hello World"
```

Press the *Enter* key to evaluate/execute the command. You can expand the *Mini Listener* by pulling on the right-hand side of it if it is too small to show all the text. You should end up with something that looks similar to Figure 23.4.

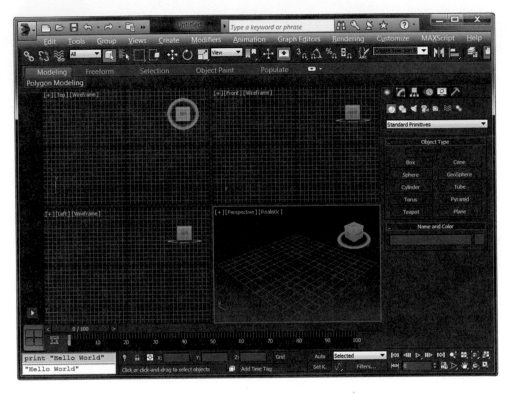

FIGURE 23.4
If things went according to plan, you should have something similar to what you see here. I have expanded the size of the *Mini Listener* here just a little to make it easier to see the text.

This really is the most basic scripting example ever! The *print* command tells 3ds Max to print exactly what you type between the quotation marks, and that's all there is to it! You can type pretty much whatever you want between the quotation marks, and 3ds Max will repeat, or print, it back to you. You can try this yourself by printing some words of your choosing. Oh, and try to keep things clean, okay? This is a family-friendly book!

Scripting and a lot of other stuff you do inside 3ds Max is based on mathematics. This book doesn't include any math lessons, but I do want to point out that you can use *MAXScript* as a sort of calculator. It actually does the hard part of math for you!

Making MAXScript Do the Math

Instead of working out any basic math for yourself, you can be totally lazy and let *MAXScript* do all the hard work for you. Follow these steps to see how:

1. Open the *MAXScript Listener* (by pressing *F11*) and clear any text from the pink and white sections.

2. In the white section type in a math problem and then press *Enter*. *MAXScript* figures out the answer for you and displays it in the white section of the *MAXScript Listener*. It feels a little like cheating, but it's really a great way to take advantage of the tools you have at your disposal. And it's kind of fun to let someone or something else do the hard work. Figure 23.5 shows some basic math equations done in the *MAXScript Listener*.

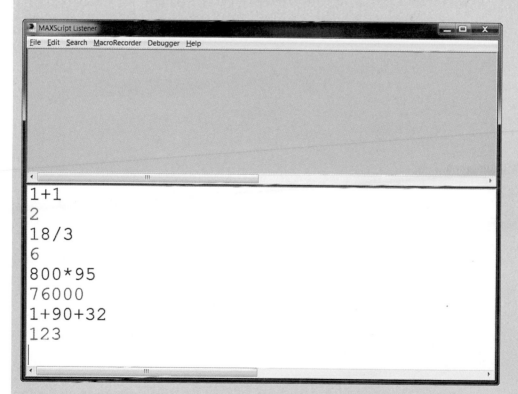

FIGURE 23.5
You can let *MAXScript* work out your math problems as though it's a calculator.

So far *MAXScript* has been amusing and sort of handy, but can you really do anything with it? Yes, and it's actually pretty easy! For instance, to create a sphere, we simply type *Sphere()* into the pink or white section of the *MAXScript Listener*. No, I'm not joking; by typing *Sphere()* into the *MAXScript Listener*, you actually create a sphere in the viewport. Go on, check it out for yourself!

▼ TRY IT YOURSELF

Using MAXScript to Create Objects

As long as you know the correct command, getting *MAXScript* to create things for you is really super easy. Try these steps to see for yourself:

1. Open the *MAXScript Listener* (by pressing *F11*) and clear any text from the pink and white sections.

2. In either the pink or white section of the *MAXScript Listener*, type *Sphere()* and then press *Enter*. Figure 23.6 shows an example of what you should now see in your *MAXScript Listener* and viewport.

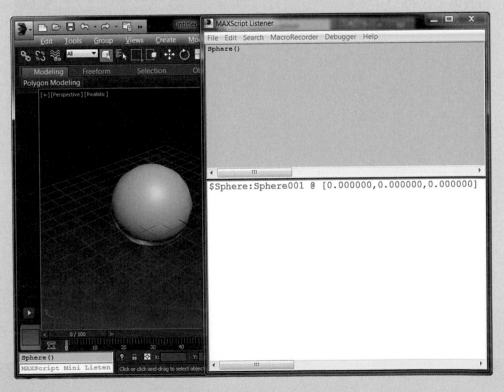

FIGURE 23.6
You just created a sphere by using *MAXScript* instead of the *Create* tab.

Notice that along with creating a sphere in the viewport, 3ds Max has printed some information to you in the *MAXScript Listener*. Don't worry about this stuff for now; it pretty much just lets you know that it recognizes the command and has executed it and created a sphere that it has called *Sphere001*. How nice of 3ds Max to do that for you!

Congratulations! You have officially started scripting in 3ds Max, using the *MAXScript* language. Of course, you haven't even scratched the surface of the possibilities available using a scripting language, but you are on the right path. This isn't a scripting book but a basic introduction to scripting, so it's time for you to move on and start creating your very own user interfaces.

Using MAXScript to Create User Interfaces

You can use *MAXScript* to create impressive and complex user interfaces that you can deploy using *MAXScript*'s own floating window or even directly in the 3ds Max user interface. These user interfaces obviously include access to tools that you have built or that are already available, but the interface itself is where users will directly interact with what you have created. Therefore, you have to make sure that interfaces are functional, easy to use, and not convoluted or annoying (even though they might be complex).

You're just starting out on your scripting journey, so creating something amazingly complex and snazzy is probably a little out of your reach right now. However, you can at least start to get an idea of how to go about creating user interfaces.

You already know how to create a sphere using *MAXScript*, and you will now create an interface with a button that you can click to create more spheres. This will be a lot easier than having to type *Sphere()* into *MAXScript* every time you want to create a sphere via scripting. Figure 23.7 shows the interface you're going to create via *MAXScript* scripting.

So how do you get to this point? Well, you need to type in the script. Listing 23.1 shows the full and final script you use to create the user interface shown in Figure 23.7.

LISTING 23.1   The MAXScript Sphere-Maker User Interface

```
 1:   /*---------------------------------------------------------------
 2:   ///
 3:   /// Filename: SphereMaker.ms
 4:   /// Author: Stewart Jones
 5:   /// Version: 1.0.0a
 6:   ///
 7:   /// DESCRIPTION \\\
 8:   /// Press the button to create a Sphere!
 9:   ///
10:   ----------------------------------------------------------------*/
11:
12:   rollout sphereMaker "Create"
```

```
13:  (
14:      button makeSphere "Make A Sphere"
15:      on makeSphere pressed do
16:      (
17:          Sphere()
18:      )
19:  )
20:  createDialog sphereMaker
```

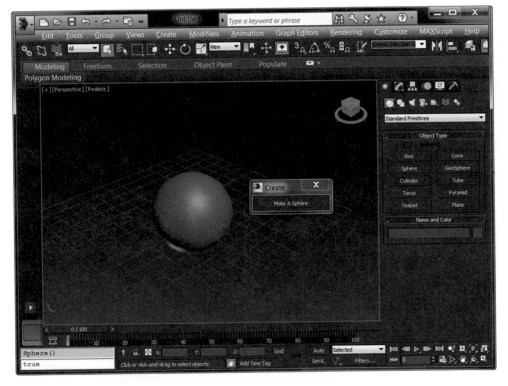

FIGURE 23.7
This is what your *MAXScript*-created user interface will look like.

With 20 lines of script, you can see that this is starting to get way more complicated than the single-line scripts you've been writing so far. But if you look at it line by line, you see that it's actually pretty easy to understand.

Lines 1 to 10 are the *header*. The header contains information about the script such as the file-name, author, version number, and basic description. This section doesn't actually affect the script at all, and it is there just as a guide for humans. The various symbols (/* and *\) included in this section simply tell 3ds Max not to evaluate anything between them, as they are just meant for us to read and not the computer!

Lines 12 to 20 are the script that *MAXScript* actually evaluates. You create a rollout with the name *sphereMaker* on line 12. Then you make a button on line 14. In lines 15 to 18, you tell *MAXScript* what to do if the button is clicked.

You show the floating window interface to the user in line 20, and that's all there is to it!

The following Try It Yourself shows you exactly how to create this script.

Using MAXScript to Create and Run Scripts

You can create the sphere-maker user interface yourself, or we can simply run the *MAXScript* that is provided. It's up to you how far you want to dive into the world of scripting. If you want to try it yourself, follow these steps:

1. In a fresh scene, go to the main menu and click *MAXScript, New Script*. The *New Script* window appears.

2. Either type the script shown in Listing 23.1 into the *New Script* window or simply open the file named *SphereMaker.ms*. Either way, your window should now look as shown in Figure 23.8.

3. From the *Tools* menu, select *Script Window* and then the *Evaluate All* option. *MAXScript* evaluates (that is, runs) the script.

4. In the *Create* window that appears, click the *Make a Sphere* button. A new sphere magically appears in the viewport. Success!

That teeny little window you just created is probably not the most exciting thing you've seen on your 3ds Max adventures so far, but the super-cool thing about it is that *you* created it. It didn't come from the team at Autodesk that makes the 3ds Max software. It is your creation, and you did all the work and can take the credit.

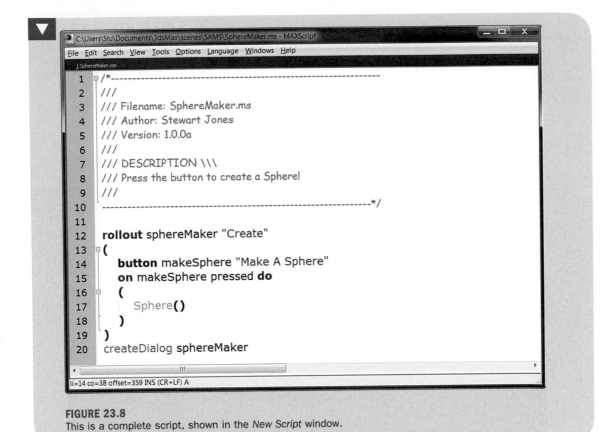

```
C:\Users\Stu\Documents\3dsMax\scenes\SAMS\SphereMaker.ms - MAXScript     _ □ X
File  Edit  Search  View  Tools  Options  Language  Windows  Help
1 SphereMaker.ms
 1   /*---------------------------------------------------------
 2   ///
 3   /// Filename: SphereMaker.ms
 4   /// Author: Stewart Jones
 5   /// Version: 1.0.0a
 6   ///
 7   /// DESCRIPTION \\\
 8   /// Press the button to create a Sphere!
 9   ///
10   ----------------------------------------------------*/
11
12   rollout sphereMaker "Create"
13   (
14       button makeSphere "Make A Sphere"
15       on makeSphere pressed do
16       (
17           Sphere()
18       )
19   )
20   createDialog sphereMaker
li=14 co=38 offset=359 INS (CR+LF) A
```

FIGURE 23.8
This is a complete script, shown in the *New Script* window.

VIDEO 23.1
_____

Creating an Interface with MAXScript

MAXScript is a complicated topic and can be a little daunting, especially if you're new to scripting and programming. This video covers the creation of *SphereMaker.ms* from beginning to end to show how easy it is.

_____

Summary

In this somewhat technical hour, you got an introduction to programming and scripting languages, created a few of your own *MAXScript* scripts, and even started to look into what it takes to create a user interface. You have taken just a few small steps toward becoming a *MAXScript* master. To get the rest of the way there, you just need to put in more time, effort, energy, and perseverance—just like with almost any other skill! A big congratulations to you. You have officially started to dig under the hood a little and gotten to know the inner workings of 3ds Max.

Q&A

Q. What exactly is *MAXScript*, and how do you find out more?

A. *MAXScript* is the built-in scripting language in Autodesk 3ds Max. To find out more about *MAXScript*, open the *MAXScript Listener* and use the *Help* menu, which is really rather handy!

Q. Is there anything specific that *MAXScript* allows you to do?

A. Many things! *MAXScript* enables you to use scripts to do almost anything you can also do with the 3ds Max UI, such as modeling, animation, rendering, and so on. You can create new tools, create interfaces, and even automate time-consuming and/or boring tasks that you often do.

Workshop

MAXScript is a rather advanced topic, even for folks who have been using 3ds Max for a long time. Creating tools and scripts for 3ds Max is usually left to programmers or technical artists who are able to bridge the artistic and programming sides of 3D. Having said that, with the knowledge gained from this hour, you can create some basic scripts of your own, and this workshop should help you think about other uses for these new-found skills.

Quiz

1. What is syntax?

2. List the three places you can use *MAXScript*.

3. Do you have to include a header in each *MAXScript* file that you create?

Answers

1. *Syntax* is the arrangement of words to create a correctly formed sentence in a language. It refers to the specific ways that *MAXScript* needs to be told things because it is not clever enough to figure it out for itself.

2. You can use *MAXScript* in three different places: the command line (also called the *Mini Listener*), the *Listener*, and the *MAXScript* window.

3. Nope! You do not need a header in a *MAXScript* file. However, a header is a handy place to make notes, keep track of changes, and note bugs and work-in-progress comments and such. So, it's not required, but it's a nice addition that you can include with very little effort.

Exercise

Instead of starting something brand new, in this exercise you will add to and enhance the already created *SphereMaker.ms* script by adding a button that creates boxes.

The first thing you need to do is to work with *MAXScript* and figure out how to create a box, in the same way that you worked out how to create a sphere earlier this hour. Once you have an understanding and have figured out what code you need to create a box, extend the *SphereMaker.ms* interface with that additional button. Your final outcome should be a user interface that includes two buttons: one to create spheres and one to create boxes.

HOUR 24
Conclusion

What You'll Learn in This Hour:

▶ An overview of the past 23 hours

▶ Further developing your skills

▶ How to choose a 3D discipline

▶ A great piece of advice that could help you further

▶ Where to find additional help and guidance

Wow, you've made it to the last hour! You have covered an incredible amount of 3ds Max–related stuff during the past 23 hours of this book, and you are still only just starting to scratch the surface of the amazing 3D possibilities that you could achieve.

3ds Max is a complex and rather difficult program to learn and master. As you start to move into creating your own projects and productions, don't worry if you're left scratching your head or getting frustrated that things aren't going your way. This happens to all of us at times, and it's just part of the learning experience.

The tricks, tips, and tools you've learned in this book will definitely make your adventures into 3D easier. There is still much to learn and accomplish, but sadly there are not enough pages in this book for me to go much further on the journey with you.

For this last hour, you can put away 3ds Max. I'm going to talk to you a little bit about what you have achieved already and what you need to do next to continue on your journey.

Hour 24: The Final Hour

After writing the heading for this section and then reading it back to myself, it actually sounds a little more sinister than I thought it would. "The final hour"—creepy!

But this really is the final hour of this book, and it's the last hour of the journey we have been on together. It's been some journey, huh? Let's take a quick look at what you've learned over the past 23 hours.

You quickly jumped from an introduction to this book and some of its structure straight into the 3ds Max interface and the viewports. From there you took a look at primitive objects and started modeling with them, using various sub-objects. With your new skills in modeling, you then looked at adding colors, materials, and textures to your creations, and then you figured out how to animate things in 3D scenes. Next, you jumped into illuminating scenes by using lights, worked out how to add cameras, and then checked out some basic rendering techniques in order to bring together everything in your very own showcase project.

After showing off what you have been up to, things got a little more technical, and you took a look at rigging and skinning, which then led back into animation, but this time you looked into animating characters. With character-based stuff out of the way, you destroyed a wall using physics and dynamics, learned how to add particles and effects to scenes, created some clothing, and even had a Vidal Sassoon moment styling hair and fur. Exhausted, you pushed forward and took a look at more advanced rendering by using *Mental Ray*, and you considered some stuff related to managing projects. Then you showed off your new skills in yet another, way-more-advanced showcase, and then you began to dabble in scripting using *MAXScript*. And now you're here: the final hour.

Phew! It certainly has been a roller-coaster of a 23-hour ride so far!

Developing Your Skills

Each hour of this book has introduced you to new topics, new tools, new tricks, and new techniques for working with various disciplines in 3ds Max. Put all these together, and things can become a little overwhelming, but you've taken the time to get a better understanding of each of them, and you should now be able to comfortably and confidently use 3ds Max.

Of course, there is still a long way to go. You've only just tasted some of the tools and techniques needed to become an expert in any of the many different areas and topics included in this 3D application. But you have gotten a broad overview and understanding of what 3ds Max has to offer.

To develop your skills further, I recommend that you go back through this book once more. Quickly skip through the hours and sections that you can complete easily and take additional time to study the areas that you found more difficult or confusing. This will solidify the information that you have been absorbing over the past 23 hours, and you may have a few "eureka" moments as you go back through the text and supplementary materials.

Spending 24 hours studying a program will definitely make you more comfortable with its uses, but you should expect to spend many years to really appreciate and learn all the various nuances of 3D and 3ds Max. Even then, after spending all kinds of time learning and developing your skills, you will still be amazed at the new things and new techniques that you will continue to learn. It really is a continuously evolving 3D world!

Picking and Choosing a Discipline

You may have enjoyed some hours of this book more than others. Notice what excited you: It could be a clue about which 3D discipline(s) you prefer.

This book covers pretty much all the disciplines available. From lighting to rendering, from animation to rigging, each and every one of these disciplines has its own workflows, methodologies, and tools for you to come to grips with. Some of them you will find easier than others, and some will interest you more than others.

When you're just starting out, working on your own projects, you need to become familiar with each and every discipline. However, if you decide to make 3D your career, one of the main choices you will have to make is whether to specialize in one or a few areas of 3D or whether you would like to be a generalist with good knowledge of all areas. The 3D industry needs both specialist skills and generalist skills.

Why not try thinking about this right now? Did you enjoy each and every hour in this book? Did you have a great interest in a few sections but not so much in others? Your gut feeling could already be telling you which areas you want to start specializing in, if any at all.

Of course, having generalist skills in all areas of 3D production is important even if you decide to specialize in just a few. After all, you will be working with other people and other departments, and without knowledge of what they are doing, you could end up holding up the production!

In addition, you may find that you prefer the more artistic side of things over the technical or vice versa. This is something else to think about as art and tech have different roles in the 3D production pipeline. Although even the art-based disciplines have to be rather technical these days, and the tech-based disciplines have to be artistic, both disciplines have to be creative. After all, it's a creative industry!

Preparing for Life in the 3D Industry

One of the most amazing things about the 3D industry and the job roles within it is that each and every discipline is constantly evolving. You have to continually learn, develop, and update your skills.

New tools, tips, tricks, and technology help push forward the advances in the 3D world extremely quickly. Just as you learn one solution to a problem, a brand-new tool or solution appears, and you have to learn that one, too. This makes 3D jobs incredibly exciting but also incredibly pressured.

You are already taking the right steps in your preparation for the 3D industry. By learning and continuing your education, pushing and enhancing your abilities, you are on the right track. It's a competitive industry out there, especially when you're trying to land your first job and the odds are really stacked against you. However, practice, time, effort, and perseverance will get you there. All the same qualities that make you a great 3D artist will make you a great candidate for roles in the industry.

One Piece of Advice

This is the best advice I can give you at this point: Keep a notebook and write in it.

If you've worked with me before or know of me and we've chatted about work, then you will probably know that I preach about keeping a notebook close at hand. It may seem like a basic and silly idea, but keeping a notebook and writing down tips, tricks, and useful notes can really help you on your learning journey!

When I write something in my notebooks, it helps me solidify the information that I have just found. This can be anything from something mentioned that I thought was pretty awesome, or something I've read, or even something I managed to figure out. Keeping this information in a notebook also gives me a really handy, pocket-sized reference guide that I can check through any time I need it. I mean, I don't know about you, but I certainly can't remember everything all the time!

Figure 24.1 shows a few of my trusty personal notebooks, some old and some new.

FIGURE 24.1
My own personal notebooks. Keep out...they're all secret and stuff!

Additional Help and Guidance

Now that you are ready to venture into the 3D world on your own, you probably want to know where you can go to get help, guidance, and advice for more complex 3ds Max topics.

The first and certainly one of the best places to look is in the help files that ship with 3ds Max. Often these helpful documents are overlooked, but they contain an amazing amount of information directly from 3ds Max. Simply press the *F1* key, and 3ds Max opens its help files (see Figure 24.2). You can find pretty much everything and anything relating to 3D in 3ds Max here. I urge you to check it out. I do!

FIGURE 24.2
The 3ds Max help files are actually very helpful. Be sure to check them out.

And, of course, the Internet is a great resource. If you have a problem with something, you can probably imagine that someone else has been in your shoes with exactly the same problem. And that person has probably already asked online for the solution you're looking for. This means that it's very likely that somewhere out there on the World Wide Web, you can find the solution to your problem—so be sure to check for it.

Finally, probably the most valuable resource that any of us have available is other people! Most folks who are involved with 3D are happy to help, give advice, or help you solve a particular problem. All you have to do is ask!

Oh, and I almost forgot! You may find that one or two of those helpful 3D people may be willing to give you a little more help than most. These sorts of people can really help you learn and develop. I, like so many others, like to call these good people *mentors*. Mentors can be invaluable in helping you, and they can push your skills further and faster in your quest for 3D greatness than what you even thought possible.

VIDEO 24.1

Thank You and Goodbye!

The final video is simply a thank you and goodbye from me!

Summary

Congratulations! You're at the very end of your 24-hour journey into the world of 3D and 3ds Max. It has been a sometimes difficult and confusing journey, but you have managed to cover just about every single area of 3ds Max in a relatively short amount of time. You have been truly amazing, and I am proud of you. You made it!

Thank you for spending your first foray into the 3D world with me. I hope you got a lot out of this and possibly much more than you had hoped for.

That's all, folks!

Q&A

Q. Is this really the end?

A. Yes, it is.

Q. Where are those mentors who can help you learn more about 3D and 3ds Max?

A. Good question! Sadly, there is no place that I'm aware of where they are advertised! I suggest being an active member of the 3D community, either online or in person (at events). I'm sure there will be a few people out there you can start to rely on for great and honest feedback and help on your work.

Q. Is this the very last Q&A question for this book?

A. Yup!

Workshop

You've finished the book, but there is still learning to be done! This final workshop includes a number of questions repeated from the previous hours of this book. If you can answer them on your own, that's great. If not, some of the information may not have sunk in just yet, and you may need to reference some of the previous hours to be able to answer the questions successfully.

Quiz

Here are 24 questions, most of which are taken from previous hours in this book. Try to answer them yourself, but you can reference earlier hours if you need to.

1. Which version of 3ds Max does this book cover?

2. Where will you spend most of your time while using 3ds Max?

3. Where can you toggle the *ViewCube* and *SteeringWheels* on and off?

4. What two kinds of primitives does Hour 4 cover?

5. How can you check the local/object space of an object?

6. Which keyboard key allows you to duplicate objects and/or sub-objects?

7. What are the differences between an editable poly object and the *Edit Poly* modifier?

8. What does *UVW* represent?

9. What does *fps* stand for in relation to animation?

10. When is the 3ds Max default lighting available?

11. This book uses a number of acronyms and abbreviations. What do *FOV* and *DOF* stand for in the world of cameras?

12. What is the quickest way to render a single frame, image, or picture in 3ds Max?

13. What should you do often while you work in 3D to protect your work?

14. What are the names of the four IK solvers that are available in 3ds Max?

15. Which technique gives you better results for skinning: enveloping or manual weighting?

16. What are the 12 principles of animation? List them.

17. How can you easily access the *MassFX* toolbar?

18. What are particles?

19. Why should you use presets when creating hair and fur?

20. What is global illumination?

21. Where can you find the *Layer* window, and what does it do?

22. What is the main difference between *XRef Scenes* and *XRef Objects*?

23. What is syntax?

24. What is your (yes, *your*!) favorite discipline related to working in 3D and 3ds Max?

Answers

1. This book covers Autodesk 3ds Max 2014.

2. You will spend most of your 3ds Max time in the viewports.

3. You can toggle the *ViewCube* and *SteeringWheels* on and off either in the main menu or by pressing the plus (+) icon in any viewport to bring up that viewport's options.

4. Hour 4 covers standard primitives and extended primitives.

5. By changing *Reference Coordinate System* to *Local*, you can check the local/object space of a selected object.

6. The *Shift* key allows you to duplicate objects and sub-objects in 3ds Max. This is a little bit different from most other programs, in which the *Shift* key allows you to add to a selection.

7. An editable poly object and the *Edit Poly* modifier give you access to the same tools, but an editable poly object removes the object's base level, so you can no longer edit those parameters. When you use the *Edit Poly* modifier, you get to keep the object's base level; you can simply edit, turn off, or remove the modifier from the scene.

8. *UVW* refers to horizontal (*U*), vertical (*V*), and depth (*W*) dimensions.

9. FPS stands for frames per second.

10. The default lighting is available in 3ds Max when the program starts or when no other lights are in the scene.

11. *FOV* stands for *field of view*, and *DOF* stands for *depth of field*.

12. The quickest way to render a single frame, image, or picture in 3ds Max is to use the quick rendering technique: pressing the *F9* key.

13. You should save often while working in 3D. It's a useful habit to get into, and frequent saving can prevent a lot of frustration that would result from something going wrong, like the program or your computer crashing. Losing hours of work is possibly one of the most annoying things in the world—ever!

14. The four IK solvers in 3ds Max are *HI* (History-Independent) *Solver*, *HD* (History-Dependent) *Solver*, *IK Limb Solver*, and *Spline IK Solver*.

15. Manual weighting gives you more fidelity and better control over each and every vertex weight on a skinned object, which means you can tweak and edit to perfection...or at least close to perfection.

16. These are the 12 principles:

    1. Squash and stretch

    2. Anticipation

    3. Staging

    4. Straight ahead and pose to pose

    5. Follow-through and overlapping action

    6. Slow in and slow out

    7. Arcs

    8. Secondary action

    9. Timing

    10. Exaggeration

    11. Solid drawing (or solid rigging, for us 3D folks!)

    12. Appeal

17. You can easily access the *MassFX* toolbar by right-clicking any unused toolbar area and selecting the *MassFX Toolbar* option.

18. *Particles* simulate visual effects that would be impractical to re-create in real life. In fact, even when real-world special effects are used, 3D and 2D particle effects are often used to enhance the look of the real-world effects.

19. You don't have to use presets, but doing so is quicker than starting from scratch. It is also incredibly handy to be able to save your own created styles so that you do not have to re-create them later.

20. Global illumination is a method for rendering bounced light within an environment; it includes final gathering, caustics, and photons.

21. You can find the *Layer* window on the main toolbar. It helps with various object display options within the viewports when you work with 3ds Max scenes.

22. The main difference between the *XRef Scenes* and *XRef Objects* tools is that *XRef Scenes* allows referencing of whole scenes, but the scenes are not selectable. *XRef Objects*, on the other hand, allows referencing of specific objects, and once an object is referenced, you can manipulate it somewhat.

23. *Syntax* is the arrangement of words to create a correctly formed sentence in a language. It refers to the specific ways that *MAXScript* needs to be told things because it is not clever enough to figure it out for itself.

24. Umm, this is a question that only you can answer! Spend some time really thinking about it because it could have quite an impact on your work in 3ds Max.

Exercise

Go back through the first 23 hours of this book and redo all the Try It Yourself sections. Even though you should have already completed these the first time, this second round will help you solidify your learning, and you may also find some things easier. Oh, and be sure to time yourself for each hour. See how long those sections actually take you to complete now, and I'm sure you will be pleasantly surprised!

Congratulations on completing all the workshops and exercises in this book. I think you are more than ready to work on your own now, and your final task should be to chill out for a while. You have earned it!

Index

E

Edged Faces, 72, 86

edges, 73

Edge sub-object mode, 74

editable animation
keyframes, 259-260

editable poly objects, 73

editable poly sub-object
rollouts, 76

Edit Envelopes button, 220

Edit Geometry rollout, 80

editing
cameras, 157
envelopes, 221-222
geometry, 75
keyframes, 138-141
Material Editor, 109-114
objects, 47
parameters, objects, 44
spheres, 75
sub-objects, 73
views, 33
workspaces, 319

Edit UVWs window, 126

effects, 269
event-driven particles,
274-278
lenses, 195
non-event-driven particles,
273-274
ripples, 270-272
space warps, 269-270
texture maps, 125
VFX (visual effects), 342-343

elements, 12-27, 74
Command Panels, 23-26
lower toolbars, 25-27
main menus, 19
main toolbars, 20-21
quad menus, 27
title bars, 19
viewports, 22-23

Element sub-object mode, 74

Email Notifications rollout, 305

enabling
Auto Key, 137
Edged Faces, 72
MassFX tools, 255
SteeringWheels, 34-35

engines
Mental Ray rendering. See
Mental Ray rendering
rendering, 170

envelopes
editing, 221-222
skinning techniques, 218

Environment and Effects window,
146, 311

event-driven particles, 274-299

extended primitives, 48-49.
See also primitives

external references. See XRefs

extra lighting, adding, 345

Extrude tool, 87

F

fabrics, 288. See also cloth

faces (cartoon), formatting, 85-93

field of view, 157

files
AVI, 180
showcases, 186. See also
showcases
stage, referencing, 338

final changes
advanced showcase
techniques, 345
showcases, 196-197

FKs (forward kinematics), 201,
206-210

flashlight beams, 151-154.
See also lighting

flipping normals, 82

flow, particle, 274-278

flyout menus, 21

folder setup, 325
Set Project Folder option, 332

formatting
advanced showcase
techniques, 331-332,
335-337
animation, 135-141, 258-261
bones, 206-207
boxes, 47
cameras, 159
cartoon faces, 85-93
cloth, 288-291

G

H

I

icons, Home, 23

IDs, materials, **117**

IKs (inverse kinematics), **142, 201, 206-210**

illuminating scenes, **145**

  adding, 151

  overview of, 145-148

  photometric lights, 150

  standard lights, 147-150

images

  animation, 131. *See also* animation

  saving, 178

  still, rendering, 178

influence areas, skinning techniques, **218**

InfoCenter toolbar, **19**

Inset tool, **93**

installation, **7**

interfaces

  elements, 12-27

  MAXScript, formatting, 359-361

  navigating, 11

  quad menus, 27

  workspaces, 316

inverse kinematics, **142, 201, 206-210**

Iterative Render mode, **177**

J-K

keyframes, **131**

  animation, formatting, 258-261

  editing, 138-141

keys

  Auto Key, 165

    disabling, 138

    enabling, 137

  controls, animation, 27

L

languages, **351**. *See also* programming

layers, **317-319**

layouts

  advanced showcase techniques, 337-341

  scenes, 339-341

  Viewport Layout tab, 37-38

lenses, **158**. *See also* cameras

  advanced techniques showcases, 341

  effects, 195

l-ext primitives, **50**

lighting, **145**

  adding, 151, 345

  advanced showcase techniques, 344-345

  ambient, 146-148

  materials, 113

  overview of, 145-148

  photometric lights, 150

  shadows, 146

  showcases, 194-195

  standard lights, 147-150

Limb solver (IK), **210**

linking

  Bone tools, 204

  rigging objects, 201-205

Link tool, **202**

Listener (MAXScript), **353**

loading

  hair presets, 298

  Mental Ray rendering presets, 304

  predefined rigs, 213

Loop button, **77-78**

lower toolbars, **25-27**

M

main menus, **19**

main toolbar, **20-21**

Make Unique button, **65**

Manage Workspaces window, **317**

managing projects, **315**

  advanced showcase techniques, 332-334

  containers, 323

  groups, 323

  layers, 317-319

  naming conventions, 323-324

  in production, 326-327

skeletons, 204-206. *See also* skinning techniques

skill development, 366-368

Skin modifier, 217, 219-222

skinning techniques, 217
- characters, animating, 225-231
- envelopes, 218
- influence areas, 218
- manual skin weighting, 223-228
- overview of, 217
- Skin modifier, 219-222

Skin Weight table, 224

skylight, 149

Sky Portal setting, 345

Slate Material Editor, 109, 111

sliders, time, 25, 133, 165

smoothing
- Auto Smooth, 197
- groups, 197

Snow, 273

snowmen, formatting, 57

Soft Selection tool, 78-79, 87

solvers, IKs (inverse kinematics), 210

spaces, switching, 67

spaceships, formatting, 93-100

space warps, 269-270

sphere primitives, 48

spheres
- bouncing balls, creating, 257-259
- editing, 75
- formatting, 42, 47
- MAXScript, 359-360

spindle primitives, 50

Spline IK solver, 210

splines, 105

Spray, 273

stacks
- modifiers, buttons under, 64-65
- Pin Stack button, 65

stage files, referencing, 338

stages, 185-186

standard lights, 146-154, 311. *See also* lighting

standard primitives, 47, 49, 73. *See also* primitives

starting advanced showcase techniques, 331-332

status bars, controls, 27

SteeringWheels, 34-35

still image rendering, 178

stock lenses, 158. *See also* cameras

Style Hair button, 296

styles, hair, 293. *See also* hair

subcategories of primitives, 51

sub-objects, 71
- applying, 73
- editable poly sub-object rollouts, 76
- geometry, editing, 75
- modifying, 74-76
- multiple, selecting, 76
- normals, 81-82
- overview of, 71-73
- rollouts, 80-81
- shortcuts, 81
- Soft Selection tool, 78-79
- spheres, editing, 75

sun, positioning, 307. *See also* daylight system (Mental Ray)

Super Spray, 273

support, 369-371

switching
- Mental Ray rendering, 344
- rendering presets, 302-304
- spaces, 67
- workspaces, 317-318

Symmetry modifier, 96

T

tab, Common, 304-305

tables, Skin Weight, 224

tabs
- Common, 175
- Create, 42
- Global Illumination, 306
- Hierarchy, 134
- Modify, 61-64
- Motion, 134
- Processing, 306
- Render Elements, 306
- Renderer, 175, 305
- Viewport Layout, 37-38

targets
- cameras, 159
- direct lighting, 149
- lights, 150
- spot lighting, 147

teapot primitives, 48

How can we make this index more useful? Email us at indexes@samspublishing.com

How can we make this index more useful? Email us at indexes@samspublishing.com

X-Y-Z

SAMS

REGISTER

THIS PRODUCT

informit.com/register

Register the Addison-Wesley, Exam Cram, Prentice Hall, Que, and Sams products you own to unlock great benefits.

To begin the registration process, simply go to **informit.com/register** to sign in or create an account. You will then be prompted to enter the 10- or 13-digit ISBN that appears on the back cover of your product.

Registering your products can unlock the following benefits:

- Access to supplemental content, including bonus chapters, source code, or project files.
- A coupon to be used on your next purchase.

Registration benefits vary by product. Benefits will be listed on your Account page under Registered Products.

About InformIT — THE TRUSTED TECHNOLOGY LEARNING SOURCE

INFORMIT IS HOME TO THE LEADING TECHNOLOGY PUBLISHING IMPRINTS Addison-Wesley Professional, Cisco Press, Exam Cram, IBM Press, Prentice Hall Professional, Que, and Sams. Here you will gain access to quality and trusted content and resources from the authors, creators, innovators, and leaders of technology. Whether you're looking for a book on a new technology, a helpful article, timely newsletters, or access to the Safari Books Online digital library, InformIT has a solution for you.

informIT.com
THE TRUSTED TECHNOLOGY LEARNING SOURCE

Addison-Wesley | Cisco Press | Exam Cram
IBM Press | Que | Prentice Hall | Sams

SAFARI BOOKS ONLINE

FREE
Online Edition

Your purchase of **Sams Teach Yourself 3ds Max in 24 Hours** includes access to a free online edition for 45 days through the **Safari Books Online** subscription service. Nearly every Sams book is available online through **Safari Books Online**, along with thousands of books and videos from publishers such as Addison-Wesley Professional, Cisco Press, Exam Cram, IBM Press, O'Reilly Media, Prentice Hall, Que, and VMware Press.

Safari Books Online is a digital library providing searchable, on-demand access to thousands of technology, digital media, and professional development books and videos from leading publishers. With one monthly or yearly subscription price, you get unlimited access to learning tools and information on topics including mobile app and software development, tips and tricks on using your favorite gadgets, networking, project management, graphic design, and much more.

Activate your FREE Online Edition at
informit.com/safarifree

STEP 1:   Enter the coupon code: PURXDDB.

STEP 2:   New Safari users, complete the brief registration form.
Safari subscribers, just log in.

If you have difficulty registering on Safari or accessing the online edition,
please e-mail customer-service@safaribooksonline.com